Anthropos and
the Material

Anthropos and the Material

Penny Harvey,
Christian Krohn-Hansen, and Knut G. Nustad, eds.

DUKE UNIVERSITY PRESS   DURHAM AND LONDON   2019

Printed in the United States of America on acid-free paper ∞
Designed by Courtney Leigh Baker and typeset in
Minion Pro and Helvetica by Westchester Publishing Services

Library of Congress Cataloging-in-Publication Data
Names: Harvey, Penelope, [date] editor. | Krohn-Hansen,
Christian, [date] editor. | Nustad, Knut G., [date] editor.
Title: Anthropos and the material / edited by Penny Harvey,
Christian Krohn-Hansen, and Knut G. Nustad.
Description: Durham : Duke University Press, 2019. |
Includes bibliographical references and index.
Identifiers: LCCN 2018040996 (print)
LCCN 2018055650 (ebook)
ISBN 9781478003311 (ebook)
ISBN 9781478001799 (hardcover : alk. paper)
ISBN 9781478002864 (pbk. : alk. paper)
Subjects: LCSH: Geology, Stratigraphic—Anthropocene. |
Nature—Effect of human beings on—Political aspects. |
Human ecology—Political aspects. | Environmentalism—Political
aspects. | Environmentalism—Social aspects. | Anthropology—
Environmental aspects. | Ethnology—Political aspects.
Classification: LCC GF75 (ebook) | LCC GF75 .A645 2019 (print) |
DDC 304.2—dc23
LC record available at https://lccn.loc.gov/2018040996

Cover art: Lauren Adams, *Mountain II*. Oil and acrylic
on canvas. 25" × 25". Courtesy of the artist.

CONTENTS

ACKNOWLEDGMENTS

The editors would like to acknowledge the generous funding of the Research Council of Norway for the research program on Anthropos and the Material (project no. 222828), granted to the Department of Social Anthropology at the University of Oslo. This wide-ranging research program ran three focused thematic projects on ritual, domestication, and labor. Knut Christian Myhre, Marianne Lien, and Christian Krohn-Hansen directed these themes, and many faculty members, postdoctoral researchers, and postgraduate students enriched our discussions over several years. Two heads of department, Ingjerd Hoëm and Knut G. Nustad, coordinated the more general project, together with Rune Flikke, and hosted workshops in which all the contributors to this volume were able to participate at least once. The participation of Penny Harvey, John Law, Marisol de la Cadena, and Anna Tsing was supported by this wider research program and by the University of Oslo. Our meetings were supported by the administrative staff at the department, and we are particularly grateful to Nina Rundgren and Mette Kristin Stenberg. We are also grateful to the editorial team at Duke University Press, particularly Gisela Fosado and Lydia Rose Rappoport-Hankins. The volume was much improved thanks to the productive feedback that we received from two anonymous reviewers, and the careful attention of our copyeditor, Kim Miller, and production editor, Christi Stanforth.

Introduction

Penny Harvey, Christian Krohn-Hansen, and Knut G. Nustad

Anthropos and Anthropology

The clearance of rain forests for soy and cattle production, the destruction of mountains to get at minerals, billions of microscopic plastic beads in the ocean, and a climate that is becoming increasingly warmer—we are daily reminded of the destructive effects of modern industrialized societies. These effects have profoundly shaped the planet and, according to recent claims, will leave a record in the geological strata. Some have proposed that they amount to a new geological epoch, the age of humans, or Anthropocene, set to replace the Holocene. The claim is contentious, and at the time of writing, the Submission on Quaternary Stratigraphy has yet to rule on whether such a change in nomenclature is justifiable. But whatever one thinks of the term, it points to a set of challenges and concerns that have huge implications for how we think the human (*anthropos*), approach the material, and imagine the possibilities for politics.

These challenges, rather than the term itself, are the key concerns of this present volume. Dipesh Chakrabarty (2009) argues that the environmental conditions that trigger discussion of the Anthropocene destabilize humanist intellectual projects in an overt challenge to the primacy of the human. This "decentering" of the human has roots in poststructuralism but also resonates with contemporary debates in feminism, queer theory, postcolonialism, multispecies approaches, new materialisms, science and technology studies, posthumanism, and the so-called ontological turn.[1] There are many important differences between these approaches, but they all both call into question universalist notions of human being and explore the limits of human agency. As anthropologists, we are similarly invested in a critique of liberal humanist assumptions. Our contribution in the present volume is to question how "problems" configured beyond the human scale inflect understandings of the human, and of human capacities to respond to the dramatic changes in the ecological matrices that constitute the possibilities for livelihoods and for the coexistence of life forms. In this respect the approach of this volume engages the recent turn to the nonhuman (Grusin 2015) in a specifically anthropological way. Acknowledging the force and creativity of those broadly philosophical genealogies that have generated the powerful critique of liberal humanist subjectivity, our focus is more squarely on the understandings of those who never were committed to such a position.

We propose that an ethnographic mode of attention to everyday practices offers a fruitful foundation for discussion of these issues. Ethnography allows us to articulate a politics that begins with the acknowledgment of human-material entanglement, that assumes the simultaneous importance of both planetary ecologies *and* local historical conditions, that approaches research as an attentiveness to process rather than to discrete "research objects," and that fosters an awareness of the constitutive presence of uncertainty. Ethnography, we argue, holds out the possibility for articulating new political perspectives on the rich and varied registers of lived experience. The Anthropocene is one such register. Amelia Moore (2016, 27) notes that the Anthropocene configures a "contemporary problem space" that anthropology is well placed to address. In particular, she suggests that ethnographic methods and orientations can be deployed to keep track of how the Anthropocene is framed as a problem and how new (authoritative and scientifically authorized) arguments about collectivity and responsibility are deployed in the urgent rush to respond to perceived threats to human interests. Bruno Latour (2014) goes so far as to argue that the naming of the Anthropocene is a gift to anthropology, as it marks a shift away from the modern paradigms that have dominated mainstream social and natural sciences, particularly those separations that constitute the key disciplinary divisions between natural and social worlds, science and politics, nature and culture.

These reconfigurations are intellectual challenges, but also deeply political ones. The problem space configured by the Anthropocene affects the lifeworlds that we notice and those that we do not notice. Marisol de la Cadena's neologism the "anthropo-not-seen" (this volume) refers to configurations of the human that focus on embodied immersion in material worlds rather than on species being or on human cognitive understandings of a material world from which we stand apart. A reflexive understanding of "anthropos" affects how we describe, conceptualize, and engage human and other-than-human sociality, the entanglements and interdependencies as well as the differences and ultimately the indifference that life-forms might have for each other.

While the idea of the Anthropocene provokes us to think through the challenges ahead, it also comes with clear limitations and problems. Robert Macfarlane, in a 2016 review of a range of recent publications, summarizes what he sees as the three main objections to the idea of the Anthropocene: namely, that it is arrogant, universalist, and capitalist-technocratic.[2] It is *arrogant* because it resolutely places humans as the central force of historical change and thereby continues the disregard for other-than-human life that has contributed so centrally to the current ecological crises, and *universalist* because it poses humanity as species, a homogeneous universalizing force, and thereby overlooks historically constituted processes of differentiation that produce entrenched social divisions (of race, class, gender, sexuality, age, and many more) and ignores the imperial histories that have produced the extremes of wealth and poverty that severely hamper efforts to confront our current environmental conditions. Humans are differently implicated in creating these problems, and the poor are disproportionally affected by them. Indeed, some argue that the Anthropocene might be more appropriately labeled the Capitalocene (J. Moore 2016). Last, it is *capitalist-technocratic* because too many arguments about the Anthropocene reduce global history to a set of technological inventions (the taming of fire, the combustion engine, nuclear power) that are presented as the real drivers of global history. This position, as critics points out, easily leads to a belief in the value of technocratic fixes and to the elaborate, all-consuming "solutions" of geoengineering.[3]

How, then, can we engage the challenges of the Anthropocene without embracing arrogance, universalism, and naive materialism? There is more at stake here than getting our nomenclature right. How we meet these challenges analytically has profound implications for how we meet them politically. The terms of engagement configure the possibilities for response. We have retained the core dichotomy of "anthropos" and "the material" in the title of this volume to signal the challenge and the politics implied by the collapse of this opposition. The gift to anthropology that Latour refers to is of course also a challenge, as theorists of the gift have long taught us to expect. Gifts create relationships and expectations of return (Mauss [1925] 1990). However, we contend that anthropology has much to contribute to wider debates, not least to the ways in which ethnographic research connects us to perspectives and possibilities that are often forgotten, sidelined, or ignored altogether. In what follows we address the three core challenges of anthropocentrism, universalism, and capitalist-technocratic determinism, highlighting some of the ways in which we might think beyond these strictures. In brief, the argument is as follows: First, we acknowledge the need to find ways of addressing structural effects that we refer to with terms such as "global capitalism" and "colonialism" without turning complex and heterogeneous forces into singularities or falling prey to naive materialism. Second, we respond to the limits of anthropocentrism (see, for example, Bennett 2010; Braun and Whatmore 2010; Masco 2014), following Chakrabarty's argument that the idea of the Anthropocene invalidates any distinction between natural and human history.[4] This raises the question, debated for decades now, of how we conceive of human and nonhuman agency. Here, we take seriously the call to think human history and natural history together and to build conceptual and analytic repertories that neither erase the human nor render humanity as an abstract category. Third, the process of thinking natural and social history together has implications for how we conceive of diversity. Collapsing boundaries between natural and human history undermines any notion of universal man. And yet the alternatives offered by the new theoretical paradigms of recent years (mentioned above) have all become somewhat mired in controversy as new dichotomies emerge and new relations between parts and wholes are configured. We cannot solve this problem, but we can look more closely, and more ethnographically, at how our descriptive and analytic practices conceive parts and wholes (or indeed collapse that distinction altogether), as a way of keeping open an unsettled space that allows us to remain attentive to a multiplicity that does not settle, and to uncertainties that are never simply resolved.

The Value of Ethnographic Methods

In what follows we look in more detail at the value of those ethnographic methods that pay as much attention to processes of formation as they do to particular cultural or social forms. Anthropology brings a disciplinary perspective founded on long-term fieldwork and participant observation.[5] Ethnographic work has long shown its capacity to establish a critical relationship to the modernity of which it is a part. In particular, we acknowledge the need to address the ways in which change is apprehended both within and beyond the modern telos. Thus, for example, the group of scholars who became known, in the 1950s and 1960s, as the Manchester school deployed ethnographic methods to make sense of the social transformations that they associated with the industrialization of southern Africa. Recognizing that ethnography as it had been developed until then, as a route to describing the interconnectedness of the social institutions of a particular society, was not up to the task, they argued for using case studies of ongoing social processes. They studied legal proceedings in the so-called native courts and followed land disputes, the opening of a bridge in Zululand, or industrial actions on the mining compounds, and, by so doing, they aimed to elicit and describe the structural forces that gave shape to these unfolding cases (for example, C. Mitchell 1956, 1969; Gluckman 1958; Gluckman and Southall 1961; Van Velsen 1967; Epstein 1992). By referring to these studies as "extended cases," they highlighted the temporal dimensions of these unfoldings. An ethnographic description had little analytic value until the case was reinserted into the historical process from which it was abstracted.

Ethnographic case studies also have another quality that is important for our task. Ethnographic descriptions, even those that Tim Ingold (2014) accuses of turning lived unfolding lines into objects, have always operated across the boundaries of modern classifications (of human and natural worlds, or humans and nonhuman beings). In many ways this boundary transgression has been the raison d'être of classic anthropology (in that it is a very modern, reflexive critique of the modern!).[6] E. E. Evans-Pritchard (1940), for example, in his study of the Nuer, described the ecology of the Sudan and the Nuers' conception of time and temporality as deeply intertwined and their relationship with their cattle as symbiotic. "It has been remarked," he wrote, "that the Nuer might be called parasites of the cow, but it might be said with equal force that the cow is a parasite of the Nuer, whose lives are spent in ensuring its welfare" (36).

This claim for the transformative potential of ethnography might seem surprising to those who think of the approach as resolutely small scale and thus an unlikely go-to method for addressing global problems. However, in recent years several anthropologists have stressed the importance of looking at ideologies of scale, and particularly at those assumptions of proportionality and extension that render the particular of little relevance to more general problems (Strathern 1991; Green 2005; Ong 2008; Corsín Jiménez 2010; Tsing 2015).

Anna Tsing has been a key voice calling for systematic ethnographic attention to the possibilities and the obfuscations of scale making as a social practice. Tsing suggests that we should look both at projects of scale making—that is, the specific practices that distinguish and enact (bring into being as lived realities) localities, nations, regions, and planetary entities—and at "ideologies of scale," by which she is referring to unquestioning assumptions about how we perceive the relative importance or relevance of particularity: how we perceive what is "big," "extensive," or "important." "If we want to imagine emergent forms of resistance, new possibilities, and the messiness through which the best laid plans may not yet destroy all hope, we need to attune ourselves to the heterogeneity and open-endedness of the world. This is not, however, an argument for 'local' diversity; if anything, it is an argument for 'global' diversity and the wrongheadedness of imagining diversity—from an unquestioning globalist perspective—as a territorially circumscribed, 'place-based,' and antiglobalist phenomenon" (2000, 352).

The issue is not about choosing which scale to endorse but rather about thinking through the particular holisms invoked by overarching concepts such as capitalism, neoliberalism, globalization, and of course the Anthropocene, as well as their effects. Such concepts are ill equipped to deal with the challenges of planetary environmental futures because they can never grasp the particular grounded historical specificity of actual circumstances. Instead, they offer a temporary means of drawing diverse situations into a comparative frame.

There is thus a politics at stake in our juxtaposition of anthropos and the material in the sense that we understand that ethnographic interventions, such as those included in this volume, have the capacity to disrupt established ways of thinking and the potential to exemplify alternative ways of configuring the very conditions of human existence from the perspective of their participation in complex, emergent material worlds. Classic political anthropology has looked at how relations of power are enacted and conceptualized, how particular social orderings are created and reproduced, asking what forms of politics (struggle), power (force), authority (legitimacy), and government (institutional arrangements) are operating in particular times and places (Krohn-Hansen 2015). However, we are not simply thinking of providing instances that might expand the horizons of those who think from the provincial heartlands of global policy making. We also want to address the problems of legibility that have sometimes impeded the take-up of ethnographic work. To this end, we have structured the volume around three sections, each displaying a particular way in which we might approach the entanglements of anthropos and the material. In the first section, "Materializing Structures," we draw attention to structuring forces to demonstrate how ethnographic exploration can open new perspectives on globalizing processes. The second section, "Material Potential," presents four analyses that emerge from an ethnographic focus on material relations and material vitality, emphasizing the interplay between material potentiality and human agency. The third and final section, "Material Uncertainties and Heterogeneous Knowledge Practices," presents three analyses that are especially preoccupied with the instability of things and the material conditions of contingency, uncertainty, and the production of knowledge.

Part I: Materializing Structures

There is much brilliant research to build on as we work to think beyond capitalist-technocratic determinism without denying the global force of the military-industrial complex, global energy politics, and the vested interests that shape global media circulations. Timothy Mitchell (2013) has provided one of the most celebrated accounts in recent years in his work *Carbon Democracy: Political Power in the Age of Oil*, which traces the complex historical connections among hydrocarbon energy systems, industrial expansion, contemporary democracy, and American forms of imperialism. The production and the use of nuclear energy are also embedded in the conditions of modern democracy and the forms of imperialism on which it depends. According to Philip Johnstone and Andrew Stirling (2016), for example, it is the United Kingdom's continued ability to maintain a level of independent national capabilities to construct and operate nuclear-propelled military submarines that drives the nation's *civil* nuclear politics. Scholars such as Mitchell, Johnstone, and Stirling critically examine the histories that track the emergence and reproduction of specific economic-military sectors (the political economy of coal and oil and of nuclear power). Their works make visible the global and transnationalized political contours in which contemporary lives, both human and nonhuman, are lived.

But there were anthropologists who well before Mitchell, Johnstone, and Stirling followed particular materials to build accounts of imperial formations or globally extended structures of power. In his pioneering *Sweetness and Power: The Place of Sugar in Modern History* (1985), Sidney Mintz wrote a history of sugar, a tropical substance. His study focused on two processes through which sugar became a commodity: colonial production and capitalist circulation and consumption. Specifically, Mintz was able to demonstrate how political, economic, and cultural life in an industrializing England, then the heart of empire, changed as a consequence of shifts in the West Indian colonies. The book narrates how the growing supply of sugar to Europe contributed to new forms of European consumption, including wholly new meanings attached to sugar as, over time, it went from being a luxury commodity consumed only by elites to becoming a taken-for-granted element in the everyday life and diet of the masses.

But little of this would have been possible had sugar not been readily available because of its suitability for plantation production and for long-distance trade. If we wish to investigate and understand how forms of life and politics are affected and shaped through engagements with, and uses of, specific materials, we first need to ask why and how (and sometimes where) the materials in question became available in the first place. It is thus essential to preserve a deep interest in forms of large-scale political and economic history and in contemporary global capitalism as a structuring force. As Mintz puts it, "Before the rich and powerful who first ate sugar in England could give it new meanings, they had to have it" (1985, 167). As in the case of global energy politics, the narratives of the emergence and the transformations of contemporary capitalism and global trade have enjoyed huge prominence, and the subdisciplines of economic anthropology and material anthropology have offered many examples and insights into structural forces that drive the production, distribution, and consumption of commodities and things (see, for example, Appadurai 1988; Miller 1987, 2005, 2008, 2010; Coronil 1997; Yanagisako 2002, 2013; Guyer 2004; Fisher and Downey 2006; Martínez 2007; Gregory 2014; and Ferguson 2015). The growing body of work on digital anthropology and social media also signals the importance of recognizing the many ways in which information and data are now integral to these circulations (see, for example, Boellstorff 2008; Miller 2012; Boellstorff and Maurer 2015; Matthews and Barnes 2016; and the discussion of bitcoin by Keir Martin in this volume—the list could proliferate in many directions). The key point is that if we want to grasp the histories and the futures of, for example, specific landscapes, geographies, roads, wastelands, or pollution, we need this Mintz-like preoccupation with how power is constituted in particular imperial histories and globally extended capitalist networks (Baca, Khan, and Palmié 2009; Tsing 2009, 2015; Stoler 2013; Masco 2014; Harvey and Knox 2014; Gordillo 2015; Harvey, this volume; Nustad, this volume).

Such networks, and their material effects, are also a key interest of Michael Taussig. Taussig's various works on human histories of resource extraction and commodity trade (1980, 2004, 2008) reveal an anthropologist who, in many ways, directs the same attention to the properties of specific materials and the vibrancy of matter as he does to the dynamics of world history and the forces of capitalism. His ideas are brilliantly illustrated in his essay "Redeeming Indigo" (2008), which seeks to reconfigure our awareness of what it took to bring the color blue into our everyday material world. Taussig is interested in the hidden and forgotten histories of materials and things, and the capacities of these histories to shock when they are revealed. The reason that the histories of mundane substances and things have this capacity to surprise, disturb, or provoke scandal is quite simply that they so often contain incredible, frightening, or vicious and cruel labor histories.

The story of the color blue tells of Bengali indigo workers in seventeenth- and eighteenth-century India. Taussig describes the routine violence or dehumanization that is associated with so many (colonial and postcolonial) labor relationships. These workers, he writes, wore "masks with only the eyes exposed on account of the smell, while those close to the work drank milk every hour, 'this being a preservative against the subtlety of the indigo.' The workers would spit blue for some time after work" (2008, 7). Such histories of capital and labor do not belong only to the past, a vanished time. Many, perhaps most, of our things and materials—from tea to paint to plastic to smartphones—have the capacity to shock because these things that are mundane in some places are directly connected to dramatic and violent social and material relations in other places.

Some global material-social histories appear to especially demand attention today. Many anthropologists today seek to chart and examine the networks or structures that have given shape to the contemporary world's various forms of energy politics (Masco 2006; Behrends, Reyna, and Schlee 2011; Boyer 2014; Howe and Boyer 2015, 2016; Campbell, Cloke, and Brown 2016), large-scale plantations and forms of agroindustry (Striffler and Moberg 2003; Tsing 2004; Hetherington 2013), open-pit mining activities (Rolston 2013; Kirsch 2014; Perreault 2015), vast infrastructure projects (von Schnitzler 2013; Fabricant and Postero 2015; Schwenkel 2015), shifts in warfare technologies and uses of political violence (along with their effects in terms of sufferings, ecological ruinations, inequalities, and national and international migration patterns; Finnström 2008; D. Pedersen 2013; Hinton and Hinton 2015; Lyons 2016), and the digital revolution with its new types of connectivity, social media, and political practices (Mazzarella 2010; Juris 2012; Poggiali 2016).

Global and transnational configurations are always in the making, constantly shifting. They should be viewed as power-laden fields and as continually emergent political formations and practices. They are the outcome of myriads of small and large negotiations and struggles. For example, Stuart

Kirsch (2014), in his book on the contemporary transnational mining industry, argues that what he describes as the dialectical relationship between large corporations and their critics (representatives of local communities, indigenous populations, social movements, global nongovernmental organizations, and so on) has become "a permanent structural feature" of today's capitalism. He goes on to note that the underlying dilemmas associated with mining and other kinds of capitalist production and consumption are rarely entirely resolved; instead, they can only be renegotiated in new forms (3), hence the always shifting relations, alliances, and battles.

One reason a set of ecologically destructive material-social practices, or dominant political projects, can be so hard to fight or change has to do with the force of sentiments and desire, or affect, among humans (Williams 1977; Masco 2014; Flikke, this volume). Historically constituted affective structures shape human motivations and provoke and sustain powerful feelings and needs. William Mazzarella (2009, 298–299), who sees affect as structurally integral to modernity, argues that therefore "any social[-material] project that is not imposed through force alone must be affective in order to be effective." Kath Weston (2012, 2017) has worked with this insight in her investigations of our contemporary world's political ecologies. She maintains that far too many engagements with climate change and potential ecological disaster "incorporate an affective stance that allows people to live with apparent contradictions, reassuring them that they can poison the world without limit even as they recognize that a limit must be out there somewhere and suturing them to ecological demise even as they work against it" (2012, 429). Her programmatic essay "Political Ecologies of the Precarious" examines the part played by Fordism's perhaps most iconic material object, the car, in fostering this affective stance "by bringing 'the masses' into an intimate, visceral engagement with the products of synthetic chemistry" (429).

While all the chapters in this volume connect their ethnographic studies to wider historical processes and transnational circulations and to the contingent forces through which such circulations affect and are, in turn, affected by the material fabrics of everyday life, three of our contributors, Marisol de la Cadena, Christian Krohn-Hansen, and Ingjerd Hoëm, focus particularly on the diverse ways in which encounters with wider structural forces unfold—and they all seek to challenge our understanding of how the political takes shape in these spaces of encounter.

De la Cadena's chapter addresses the core paradox of our time: the simultaneous commitment to economic growth and to environmental sustainability. Her description of the devastating environmental and human costs of the full-throttle extractivism that fuels the contemporary Peruvian economy quite clearly articulates a politics of contestation. However, the argument that de la Cadena puts forward is intended to unsettle such politics. She argues that liberal modern politics ("politics as usual") is not simply ill equipped to fight this battle but systematically reproduces the exclusions and separations that it claims to struggle against. She proposes an alternative: a politics in support of the "anthropo-not-seen," a politics that starts from the recognition that anthropos is neither singular nor universal. De la Cadena brings together two core strands of divergent political thinking: equivocation (after Viveiros de Castro 2004) and disagreement (after Rancière 1999). She develops the concept of equivocation to discuss the nonequivalence of human difference and the partial connections of human engagement that can form the basis for unexpected alliances between persons and groups with different ontological assumptions and orientations. Rancière's politics of disagreement evokes a more definitive act of refusal: the refusal to acknowledge the politics of another; the refusal to accommodate. At the core of the chapter is the example of a peasant woman determined to hold her ground, to refuse the separation of nature and culture on which extractivism depends. The land that the state is seeking to expropriate is not simply hers (as property and/or as resource); it is "her," integral to her being. To clear the ground for financial investment, the state, in turn, refuses this possibility and offers compensation in a register of equivalence that makes no sense to the woman. De la Cadena is at pains to point out that we should avoid seeing this case as an example of a dichotomy between those who separate nature from human being and those who do not. Her politics refuses that distinction. She talks, rather, in terms of excess: the peasant woman recognizes and uses idioms of ownership, and her land is property, but "not only"—land is a concept that exceeds the categories through which the state asserts its rights to control.

Questions surrounding the tensions between the structuring material-social-affective forces that support hegemonic and state power and the diversity inherent in such structures are Krohn-Hansen's central concern. In his chapter, he challenges the singularity and the universalism of anthropos in a quite different way. Krohn-Hansen insists that it is key to acknowledge capitalism's heterogeneity because it is in the spaces that exceed capital's control that possibilities can be found for collective political action, friendship, and human concern. The chapter draws on an ethnographic study of entrepreneurial Dominican livery-cab cooperatives in New York. Unable to break into the yellow cab market of central and lower Manhattan, Dominican migrants began working in northern Manhattan and in the Bronx, offering service to areas where the yellow cabs would not go. The livery-cab drivers formed cooperatives that instantiated familiar material conditions of entrepreneurial labor: low wages and long hours, with each driver carrying the risk of fluctuating markets and of uncertain regulatory demands. But these conditions do not sufficiently account for how these businesses work, or for why they take the form they do. The cooperatives are not simply a means of enabling work, nor are they held together solely by the payments that each member makes to the organization. The material relations that structure the working lives of these men are not abstracted from the affective relations that shape the social world of work. The cooperatives were formed using the same model as many of the Dominican voluntary associations or social clubs. They are social spaces where independence, autonomy, and specific modes of masculinity are recognized and valued, and where a passion for politics and for sport is assumed. Capitalism produces difference and makes use of difference, but it does not control the ways in which such differences become meaningful.

Krohn-Hansen's engagement with the structuring forces of global capitalism is complemented by Hoëm's chapter, which takes us to the Pacific atolls of Tokelau. Revisiting Marshall Sahlins's (1958) account of the structuring forces of sociopolitical organization, grounded in the combined material forces of landscape, technology, and resources, she interrogates the claim that these material conditions place an evolutionary ceiling on forms of political organization. Hoëm compares Sahlins's approach to the sociopolitical with Tsing's discussion of landscape as the extended material relations through which places and specific niches emerge and are sustained. This perspective is less structurally bound and more attuned to the comings and goings between the atolls, and between the atolls and other places. Here we begin to see that sociopolitical capacity is as emergent as it is structural. Tokelau is rich in resources even though it has little land and few people and, as a location, is extremely vulnerable to environmental forces. Indeed, these atolls appear for many as visible indices of climate change as the residents struggle to confront the challenges of rising sea levels, increasingly heavy storms that breach the division between sea water and the freshwater lagoon, and the consequences of economic growth and enhanced social connectivity, which feed desires for more consumer goods and ever-improving standards of living. Rising indices of poor health and the growing challenges of waste disposal are offset by the Tokelauan determination to remain where they are.

It is this third perspective that Hoëm emphasizes in her chapter. She argues that to focus solely on the material dimensions of Tokelauan life would be to miss the significance of the structuring forces of sociopolitical organization to which Sahlins draws attention. However, she argues that neither of these approaches gives sufficient emphasis to the significance of human action, the work and effort that go into creating and sustaining the networks of kin and associates through which access to resources—particularly the booming economy, which is driven by New Zealand state aid—is guaranteed. Structuring forces and material conditions are thus fundamental, but assuming agency in Tokelau is also about ensuring one's position in social networks that allow you to pass things on and, in turn, to receive from others. It is these networks that ensure Tokelauans have a place to stand.

Part II: Material Potential

The next section takes material potential as its starting point. Thinking history and landscape together is one way of connecting materializing structures to specific material formations. Recent research on ruins and ruination that explicitly starts from an interrogation of how imperial power occupies the present (Stoler 2013), or work on rubble that draws together the material, historical, and affective dimensions of debris (Gordillo 2014), serves as a useful site of connection between a focus on materializing structures and an investigation of the complex relational fields of specific object worlds. In addressing the challenge of how best to think material and human histories together, without an undue emphasis on the centrality of human agency, we could begin by acknowledging that humans necessarily engage the material, nonhuman world via their (historically and culturally varying) capacities of perception and imagination. Nevertheless, as Isabelle Stengers (2010) has argued, we can approach nonhuman agency with curiosity about how other-than-human forces "force thought" and, in so doing, extend our classical definitions of political agency. These broad discussions of material agency were the subject of the *Objects and Materials* collection (Harvey et al. 2014), which took as its starting point the "general agreement across the humanities and the social sciences that things are relational, that subject/object distinctions are produced through the work of differentiation, and that any specific material form or entity with edges, surfaces, or bounded integrity is not only provisional but also potentially transformative of other entities" (Harvey and Knox 2014, 1). This notion of agency assumes neither intention nor sentience, but it likewise does not rest with notions of cultural construction or relativist ontology. Rather, it opens a field of political interrogation, as Stengers suggests.

In a similar way, the growing levels of attention to infrastructural formations in anthropology and in science and technology studies also connect to an interest in finding ways to interrogate material forces without assuming a separation of human and nonhuman histories, thus allowing for contingency, affect, and the specificities of relational perspectives. Infrastructures constitute the material conditions of possibility for specific modes of life, including the movements and circulations on which such lives are built. They hold a particular fascination for the ways in which they so often combine the explicit intentions of designers, engineers, and politicians with the intrinsic uncertainty of complex systems, always connecting and/or disconnecting in unforeseen ways.[7] Ethnographic interrogations of material potential thus engage the relational capacities of the nonhuman as a complex field that embraces affective forms and meanings, feelings and desires, ideas about uncertainty and danger, ethical and moral values, and processes as well as outcomes, engagements, and separations.

The inherent tension between the material and the immaterial is another long-term preoccupation of anthropological research, which has a long tradition of scholarship that has focused on intimate encounters with the inner life of materials and things. To engage the material qualities of a nonhuman world—soils, forests, seeds, mushrooms, and the diverse flora and fauna that are constitutive of the worlds of hunters, gatherers, agriculturalists, or pastoralists—is to interact with the properties and the hidden dimensions of other living beings.[8] Shamanic, magical, and much religious practice typically involves this quality of close human encounters with highly charged nonhuman forces and forms. It is by means of historically and culturally specific sentiments, myths, desires, rules, taboos, and rituals that humans across the world interact densely with the world of things through work, magic, and other forms of activity.

At the same time, we need a critical focus on our use of conceptual distinctions. The conceptual distinction between subject and object is, in itself, the product of particular political histories, as is the fast-growing literature on the nonhuman that has given rise to lively theoretical debates on material vitality, object-oriented ontologies, and speculative realism.[9] Ethnographers are increasingly drawn to these discussions as they look for conceptual frames through which to explore realities that disrupt the assumptions of liberal humanism. However, anthropologists also point out that many societies, even the majority of those studied by classic twentieth-century anthropologists, never did assume a clear-cut distinction between human agency and a passive object world. And in the present day, contemporary science and technology studies also constantly comes up against the limits of such distinctions in the development of artificial intelligences, nanotechnologies, and many other prosthetic devices that extend and distribute "life" beyond the pulsations of organic bodies. In both of these contexts, ready-made distinctions between subject and object become obsolete—or, at least, difficult to stabilize. Like so many other important dichotomies that we employ, more or less routinely, to shape our questions and answers, these well-worn categories can no longer be taken for granted. The ethnographic challenge is rather to identify how such distinctions are drawn, in what circumstances, and to what effect. This interest in the human capacity to live with a paradoxical awareness *and* a partial disinterest in or ignorance of other-than-human agencies is key to the ethnographic accounts we present here.

The overlap between the "nonhuman turn" and ethnographic approaches more generally emerged in the various calls from within anthropology to move away from hermeneutic or semiotically oriented studies. A focus on how humans attach meanings and emotions to objects, or project force or agency into objects, was inflected by arguments that foregrounded alternative ontologies, and the notion that other-than-human beings and "things" might "speak for themselves" (Henare, Holbraad, and Wastell 2007).[10] In this volume, the chapters by Keir Martin, Marit Melhuus, Penny Harvey, and Knut G. Nustad step back from the notion that things might speak for themselves, but they also do not imagine materials as passive receptors of human intention. Studying materials in and through human worlds throws light on the interdependencies of human and other-than-human worlds that the challenges of the Anthropocene bring more sharply into focus. This brings us back to thinking natural and social history together, and the implications this has for how we conceive of diversity.

Martin's chapter moves from a discussion of the structuring forces of material relations to a consideration of the political agency of particular material forms. The topic is money. The chapter keeps one foot in the Pacific as Martin compares the *tabu* currency of Papua New Guinea with bitcoin. New technological possibilities allow bitcoin to offer a mode of exchange that can bypass the regulatory apparatus of banking systems, and thus of state control. Central to this capacity is the immateriality of the currency, with its circulation and its credibility established entirely through histories of online transactions. However, this is not an argument for technological determinism. On the contrary, Martin argues that while the immateriality of bitcoin could underpin a potential move to the pure market trade of the sovereign individual—anonymous and untraceable—it could also mark the beginning of a highly personalized transactional field where financial transactions could be embedded in closely monitored relationships of trust. His point is that the power of materials (and/or the condition of immateriality) to make or unmake human relations is a potential that needs always to be realized, and such realizations involve human action. The story of tabu currency follows a similar line: strings of tabu money can be divided, and there are debates as to whether it should or should not be allowed to circulate as money rather than as a ceremonial gift. The anonymity and the divisibility of the tabu strings also offer a potential that requires human action for its realization.

Melhuus is also concerned with how the potential that inheres in the materiality of reproductive substances (sperm and eggs) is limited, in practice, by specific forms of human action. The chapter has much in common with Martin's work on money. Sperm and eggs are materials that people do politics with. Central to her argument is the (technological) capacity for the detachment of reproductive substance, and the human concerns that accompany this technological possibility. The law is the structuring force, introduced in an attempt to limit the potentiality of these substances by categorizing and stipulating what can and cannot be brought into what relation. The substances are mobilized to create relationships between persons, but the social validation of such relations is central to the realization of such possibilities. Different national legislatures make different decisions at different times. Other laws concerning the rights of the child, gender equality, and limits on transactions in human substances create fields of open-ended possibility and paradoxical rulings. In Norway, for example, gay men can assume legal parentage of a child from a surrogate mother, while gay women cannot because the law stipulates the primacy of the birth mother, while sperm donation ensures legal fatherhood. In this way we can see how the state comes to inhere in the materials that might otherwise appear to exercise autonomous political agency.

Harvey's chapter on concrete and stone addresses the political dimensions of material vitality by exploring how the generative capacity of matter is engaged by state agencies, by artists, by engineers, and in everyday life. Drawing inspiration from an analysis of the processes of "grafting" through which stone structures were used to channel the vital forces of the Earth in the ceremonial architectures of the Inka state, Harvey considers the affective and material power of concrete in the modern world. In Peru, as in most other places, concrete supports state projects of ordering and stabilization. However, ethnographic attention to the work of civil engineers and of artists reveals the intrinsic instability of this material. Concrete is soft matter, one of those materials that has long fascinated scientists interested in soft solids and material flows but also artists interested in processes of entropy and unconformity. The experiences of those whose material engagements with concrete highlight the intrinsic fluidity of matter contrast strongly with more everyday uses of concrete as a material that can be counted on to fix things in place. The chapter explores this apparent paradox. Concrete is an emergent material that comes into being through the fusion of cement (a global commodity), aggregates (locally sourced stone and sand), and water. The chapter argues that the material vitality of concrete is directly related to the inextricable combination of intrinsic and extrinsic material relations. The diverse components react together to create specific synthetic forms, but these components and the resulting forms are always embedded in more extensive material and social relations. The chapter thus seeks to intervene in debates on material agency, arguing that we can address the vitality of matter without assuming or discounting the frameworks of animism. The material vitality of concrete emerges from the coming together of political and material agency, human projects, and other-than-human forces and provides an exemplary site for a consideration of the politics of human-material relations.

Nustad's chapter broadens our discussion of materials to a wider focus on disputed environmental values in St Lucia, on the east coast of KwaZulu-Natal, South Africa. Over the course of the twentieth century, this region became an important site for industrialized agricultural production, and toward the end of the apartheid era, a concession was granted for strip-mining. Postapartheid land reformers were faced with a choice about how best to realize the value of this land. Should it be used for mining, or should it be reclaimed from industry and protected as a nature reserve, valued for its separation from industrial productivity and managed as a resource for tourism and hunting? There were opposing views. Nustad tracks the terms in which the arguments were posed, noting the tensions between the conservationists, whose arguments rested on a romantic separation of nature from human activity, and the social scientists, who disputed the intrinsic value of nature and asserted that the value of the natural world is always socially constructed. Nustad is particularly interested in the political dynamics through which the relationship between anthropos and the material is forged in this case, and the vulnerabilities that emerge—vulnerabilities that affect the futures of specific humans and other-than-human beings. Key to Nustad's argument is a focus on the negation of preindustrial human presence in the region. The temporality of the conservation perspective erases the centuries of coevolution of human and nonhuman entities. Far from returning land to a prior state, conservation creates new relational landscapes in which rich tourists, but not local people, can reside, and in which human intervention is required to manage the emergent relationships among animals, land, and human beings. In these relationships the nonhuman world is not so much constructed as engaged by human agents, constantly pressing back against the desires to control and contain, and in turn stimulating new forms of intervention.

Part III: Material Uncertainties and Heterogeneous Knowledge Practices

Debates on the importance of the constitutive force of the nonhuman have implications for anthropology's traditional approach to human diversity and, by extension, for the ways in which researchers identify fields and objects of study. It is in this context that questions of ontological difference as opposed to cultural difference have arisen and become the subject of intense debate in recent years. At issue is a renewed discussion about the limitations of the concept of culture and the political consequences of the particular form of multiplicity that "culture" denotes.[11] The politics of multiculturalism posits difference as stemming from particular views on the world, the views of many cultures (understood as human constructs) on a singular world (nature). In this formulation difference appears as sui generis and as intrinsic to the human condition. The theory of perspectivism elaborated by Eduardo Viveiros de Castro (1998) and developed by advocates of the ontological turn (Holbraad, Pedersen, and Viveiros de Castro 2014) seeks to reverse this claim by positing the possibility that the diverse perspectives on the world are not lodged in the mind (as different ways of thinking) but in bodies (as sites of multinaturalism). Although the turn to ontology is often taken as reiterating the very sense of multiplicity that it seeks to dislodge (by the simple reversal of the nature-culture dichotomy), it is important to recover the difference that this turn could make in our attempts to rethink anthropos in relation to the material. The ethnographies from which the ontological approach developed have tended to be spaces of encounter where difference is marked not by mind but by bodily practice, often exemplified by the techniques of hunters or shamans (Viveiros de Castro 1998; Willerslev

2007; de la Cadena 2015; Pedersen 2011). The capacity to shift perspective from one's own body to the body of another opens radical possibilities for rethinking the terms of human relational engagement with the world. Interests in multispecies ethnographies (Kirksey and Helmreich 2010; Kirksey 2015), in embodied cognition (Toren 1999), and in the semiosis of other-than-human beings (Kohn 2013) all develop these insights in important ways.

Potential approaches to the political are also expanded by an ethnographic interest in the partiality of our engagements and understandings (Strathern 1991) and an appreciation of how human intention and human agency unfold in relations of uncertainty, systematic misunderstanding, and/or equivocation (Viveiros de Castro 1998; de la Cadena 2010). Rethinking the limits of the cultural in these ways brings us back to the foundational modern tension between parts and whole, and opens the possibility of transcending notions of singularity (more than one), without assuming an endless proliferation of difference (less than many). Despite the intensity of the debate, it is interesting to see how quite different (and sometimes overtly opposing) interventions have begun to work with this possibility. Ingold (2014), critical of the additive logics of multiculturalism and of the aggregations of the sociomaterial assemblages that characterize actor-network theory, chooses to think of life via discussions of voice rather than perspective. Vision, for Ingold, suggests a static positioning and a potential for a totalizing snapshot, picture, or view. Voice, for him, invokes what he refers to as an emergent "worlding" practice, where difference is constitutive of a whole, analogous to the ways in which a musical composition combines many parts, each discrete, yet each inflecting and inflected by the other voices (more than one and less than many). The argument is posed as a polemic, but when we look in some detail at the work of those to whom the critique is directed, we find considerable common ground. Morten Axel Pedersen (2011), for example, works with Viveiros de Castro's notion of perspectivism in his analysis of Mongolian not-quite-shamans. However, he also refers to ontology as "composition":

> The ontological turn amounts to a sustained theoretical experiment, which involves a strategic decision to treat all ethnographic realities as if they were "relationally" *composed*, and, in keeping with its "recursive" ambitions, seeks to conduct this experiment in a manner that is equally "intensive" itself. This is why the ontological turn contains within its conceptual make-up the means for its own undoing: it is nothing more, and nothing less, than a particular mode of anthropological play

designed with the all too serious aim of posing ethnographic questions anew, which already appear to have been answered by existing approaches. (2012; emphasis added)

Pedersen's use of "composition" thus suggests that ontologies are relational, emergent, and open-ended in very similar ways to the musical compositions to which Ingold refers.

The diverse ways in which ontologies are engaged perhaps simply reflect the very different starting points from which anthropologists come to pose questions and to mobilize theoretical frameworks to analyze the materials they gathered in the course of their empirical investigations. The question of how to engage politics is revealing in this sense. An online section of the *Cultural Anthropology* website (Holbraad and Pedersen 2014) gathered statements about ontological politics from a range of authors. Many articulated a suspicion of political certainties and expressed a desire to disrupt or move beyond the cul-de-sac of "politics as usual." Candea (2014), for example, supports the (Deleuzian-inspired) notion of a politics of permanent differentiation and warns against the use of representations of alterity that simply reproduce identity politics in a different (ontological) guise. The key issue here, on which many agree, has less to do with an ontological turn than with the limitations of modern, multicultural politics. Candea's intervention raised the question of what an appeal to the political brings into view. The articulation of alternatives offers little advance on a bland multiculturalism until we also articulate the kinds of struggles that are in play, until we can use our engagements to describe what and/or who flourishes, under what conditions, and at what expense. In this spirit, Blaser (2014) compares the investment of science and technology scholars in the enactment of reality (i.e., in the diverse ways in which realities are shaped through specific practices), as well as anthropological investments in the possibilities of alterity. Both approaches extend the possibilities for articulating the ways in which things could be otherwise, but neither assumes to know how such outcomes might emerge. In this respect we are confronted by our methodological commitment to uncertainty. As Blaser (2014) puts it, "Figuring out where, when and how to do difference and sameness as the circumstances require is to me the key challenge of doing political ontology." Thus, despite the sometimes quite strident terms in which the debate over ontological politics is conducted, the bottom line seems to be a call for anthropologists to question the terms of their own (theoretical) certainties, not in order to remain forever in doubt, but to "slow down thought"

(Stengers 2010) and to decide which tensions are generative, which to grasp and which to refuse (Verran 2014).[12]

Finally, we must acknowledge that ethnographic writing is a mode of storytelling that carries its own political promise and transformative ambition. Michael Jackson's recent work on the politics of storytelling engages Hannah Arendt's discussion of experience as the "subjective-in-between": "The entire field of experience is what Arendt calls the 'subjective-in-between,' since existence is never merely a matter of what I or you say or do but what we say and do together, interacting, conversing, and adjusting our interests, experiences, and points of view to one another" (2013, 15).

Jackson is primarily interested in how human sociality is constituted in and through the way we produce understandings of experience through our interpersonal engagements. However, the approach could quite easily be extended to include the nonhuman in our ethnographic accounts and to fold the nonhuman into our narratives of the subjective-in-between. This move does not require us to assume any subjectivity on the part of other-than-human being. Rather, it simply acknowledges that human interactions are not confined to an exclusive interhuman domain. Human experience is thus constituted through engagements beyond the human world, and it is in this sense that agency (plans, intentions, and projections) always implies something of a launch into the unknown and opens the political to an awareness of uncertainty.

Changing modes of material attention characterize Rune Flikke's account in this volume of colonial and contemporary efforts to control the flow of air, in what Peter Sloterdijk has referred to as a "politics of air conditioning." In Victorian England air was the object of such material politics, and efforts to control the flow of air as a means to prevent the spread of diseases such as cholera had clear material effects on urban design. "Miasma" was the noxious and contagious atmosphere emanating from dirt, rotting matter, and the bodies of the poor. Victorian settler communities took their fear of miasma to Africa, where a concern with air quality and the flow of air underpinned early segregation laws. Flikke's contemporary ethnography of Zulu Zionists in an African township on the outskirts of the South African city of Durban maps the enduring effects of these previous understandings of permeable bodies and circulating winds. Now reframed within the contours of sickness and healing, powerful winds are sought out by patients looking to counteract the negative bodily effects of other bodily boundary transgressions. Winds are sources of disease and of health in a politics of air conditioning that moves intangible substance across bodily membranes, carrying and channeling air, smoke, and breath. Noting that air is largely absent from contemporary discussions of the politics of matter, Flikke argues that social theory needs to foster a greater awareness of atmospheric forces and the modes of air conditioning that structure social worlds. Human experience emerges as an engagement with fluidity, flux, transformation, and transience.

The focus on instability is central to the following chapter, in which Marianne Elisabeth Lien and John Law discuss how ethnography can mobilize gaps and absences to speak to pressing political concerns. Their discussion centers on an inaugural ceremony held at a salmon farm on the west coast of Norway. A hatchery is about to expand, and the company assembles to celebrate. This process of assemblage is what interests Lien and Law, as they trace the particular way in which this ceremony enacts or conjures up overlapping social formations. The ceremony celebrates a moment of growth for the company as they expand their productive capacity, but Lien and Law are also attentive to other coexisting forms of growth—markets in fish and in pelleted fish feed, physical installations, jobs, parasites and diseases, regulations. Their ethnography follows the tensions among the intersecting scales of the global economy, industrial strategy, and community autonomy. Their analysis confronts the gaps and invisibilities that are constitutive of perspectives that cannot be rolled into one. Three ghosts, or manifest absences, haunt the celebrations: the ghost of bankruptcy in an unstable economic environment, the ghost of potential incapacity to sustain more intensive production, and the ghost of the potential fragmentation of social ties that might follow from the embrace of market competition. The chapter takes these three perspectives to show that while different relations come into view when we think about economic growth, the engineering challenges of industrial expansion, and the social effects of more intensive production, we should nevertheless remain attentive to what is occluded. Absences, invisibilities, and the unspoken garner ethnographic presence when the intrinsic instability of material relations are attended to.

Anna Tsing is also concerned with method and the politics of knowledge-making. Her chapter takes the form of a manifesto, bold and to the point. Tsing addresses those working at the interface of anthropology and science and technology studies. Acknowledging the necessary critique of positivist methods, she nevertheless calls for a renewed attention to the relational worlds of nonhumans. These worlds are classically the domain of the natural sciences, and the challenge is to think of these relations historically and thus to confound the separations of entrenched perspectives from the humanities (human focused) and from science (ahistorical). Tsing's suggestion, taken up in the ethnographic arguments of several of the other chapters in this volume, is to counteract the structuring, dichotomous frames of nature and culture by focusing on landscapes, ecologies, and assemblages that help attune our understandings of how entities make worlds together. Landscapes, approached as sites of material coordination, defy the dyads of nature and culture that have underpinned environmental degradation and offer spaces for analysis where geographic contours and historical process come together to fashion habitats for life other than human life. Here Tsing finds hope beyond the human, in those beings who live and thrive in the wreckage of human extraction.

NOTES

1. There is a broad and rich literature across the humanities and social sciences, drawing on diverse overlapping strands of Western philosophical thought. Key texts include Harman (2002, 2005); Haraway (2008, 2016); Meillassoux (2008); Helmreich (2009, 2016); Wolfe (2009); Bennett (2010); Coole and Frost (2010); Shaviro (2014); and Kirksey (2015). These diverse traditions are discussed later in this introduction.

2. Robert Macfarlane, "Generation Anthropocene: How Humans Have Altered the Planet Forever," *Guardian*, April 1, 2016, https://www.theguardian.com/books/2016/apr/01/generation-anthropocene-altered-planet-for-ever. Some of the academic texts mentioned are Timothy Morton's *Hyperobjects: Philosophy and Ecology after the End of the World* (2013), Elizabeth Kolbert's *The Sixth Extinction: An Unnatural History* (2015) and *Field Notes from a Catastrophe: Man, Nature, and Climate Change* (2006), Naomi Klein's *This Changes Everything: Capitalism vs. the Climate* (2014), Gaia Vince's *Adventures in the Anthropocene: A Journey to the Heart of the Planet We Made* (2014), Anna Tsing's *The Mushroom at the End of the World: On the Possibility of Life in Capitalist Ruins* (2015), Jedediah Purdy's *After Nature: A Politics for the Anthropocene* (2015), McKenzie Wark's *Molecular Red: Theory for the Anthropocene* (2016), Jason W. Moore's *Capitalism in the Web of Life: Ecology and the Accumulation of Capital* (2015), and Jeremy Davies's *The Birth of the Anthropocene* (2016).

3. These are highly controversial proposals to solve global warming through engineering. There are mainly two types of designs, either removing carbon dioxide from the air or limiting the amount of sunlight reaching the planet's surface. One proposal is to spray sulfate particles into the atmosphere to reflect radiation back to space. According to a *Guardian* article, these schemes are being treated seriously by key persons within the Trump administration as cheap ways of solving global warming. "Trump Presidency Opens Door to Planet-Hacking Geoengineer Experiments," *Guardian*, March 27, 2017, https://www.theguardian.com/environment/true-north/2017/mar/27/trump-presidency-opens-door-to-planet-hacking-geoengineer-experiments.

4. The distinction no longer holds for either history or science—a point that Tim Ingold has long since argued in his discussion of the "arbitrary" distinction between evolution and history, and also a point that Latour draws attention to his 2014 lecture.

5. We should perhaps note that we do not assume ethnography in the form that Ingold (2014) has recently criticized. Ingold argues that the contribution of anthropology lies in its ability to take part in unfolding lives and realities and not, as is often claimed by anthropologists, in ethnography. "Ethnography," a term he wants to reserve for its original meaning of a description of peoples, is, for him, the objectified, reified, and backward-looking construct that anthropologists make of their own ongoing learning and correspondence with others. We are not willing to tie ethnography to a version of the human in which anthropology is no longer invested (if it ever was). However, whether or not we want to reserve the term "ethnography" for these depositions, we agree with Ingold's insistence that one of the core strengths of anthropological fieldwork is the potential to be part of life and to follow it as it unfolds.

6. See Manganaro (1990) for a useful edited collection on this topic.

7. The key citation on infrastructures that captures much of what was written before 2013 is Larkin in *Annual Review of Anthropology*. Since then an edited collection and a monograph have gathered more recent work: Harvey, Jensen, and Morita (2017) and Anand (2017). See also a special issue of *Ethnos* from 2017 edited by Casper Bruun Jensen and Atsuro Morita.

8. Ferme (2001) is an engaging example of such a perspective or, more recently, Willerslev (2007) and M. Pedersen (2011).

9. The growing literatures on the nonhuman offer a detailed analysis of the shifts in Western philosophical approaches to material agency. However, as Richard Grusin (2015) notes, the genealogies of these literatures are diverse: "The nonhuman turn in twenty-first-century studies can be traced to multiple intellectual and theoretical developments from the last decades of the twentieth century: actor-network theory, affect theory animal studies, assemblage theory, cognitive sciences, new materialism, new media theory, speculative realism, and systems theory" (https://www.amazon.co.uk/Nonhuman-Turn-Center-Century-Studies/dp/0816694664).

10. This volume was one of several quite diverse interventions from scholars seeking to develop approaches to semiosis that went beyond the analysis of human language as a process of representation and interpretation. Key contemporary references include the influential work of Eduardo Kohn (2013) and Webb Keane (1997, 2007). Kohn develops the notion of semiosis as an embodied process that not only is not restricted to humans but is foundational to human life as a mode of engagement with the other-than-human world. Keane's ethnography of ritual language, politics, and religious practice in Indonesia works more specifically with the ways in which the power of speech is thoroughly entangled with the power of objects.

11. Debates around the culture concept are intrinsic to anthropological reflexivity and have taken different forms over the years. The current discussion of ontology differs from the "writing culture" debates of the 1980s (Clifford and Marcus 1986) and from the discussion of Roy Wagner's influential work *The Invention of Culture* (1975).

12. See the debate in "Fieldsights—Theorizing the Contemporary," special section, *Cultural Anthropology* online, January 13, 2014, https://culanth.org/fieldsights/461-the-politics-of-ontology.

REFERENCES

Anand, Nikhil. 2017. *Hydraulic City: Water and the Infrastructures of Citizenship in Mumbai*. Durham, NC: Duke University Press.

Appadurai, Arjun, ed. 1986. *The Social Life of Things: Commodities in Cultural Perspective*. Cambridge: Cambridge University Press.

Baca, George, Aisha Khan, and Stephan Palmié, eds. 2009. *Empirical Futures: Anthropologists and Historians Engage the Work of Sidney W. Mintz*. Chapel Hill: University of North Carolina Press.

Behrends, Andrea, Stephen Reyna, and Gunther Schlee, eds. 2011. *Crude Domination: An Anthropology of Oil*. New York: Berghahn.

Bennett, Jane. 2010. *Vibrant Matter: A Political Ecology of Things*. Durham, NC: Duke University Press.

Blaser, Mario. 2014. "The Political Ontology of Doing Difference . . . and Sameness." In "Fieldsights—Theorizing the Contemporary," special section, *Cultural Anthropology* online, January 13. https://culanth.org/fieldsights/474-the-political-ontology-of -doing-difference-and-sameness.

Boellstorff, Tom. 2015. *Coming of Age in Second Life: An Anthropologist Explores the Virtually Human*. Princeton, NJ: Princeton University Press.

Boellstorff, Tom, and Bill Maurer, eds. 2015. *Data, Now Bigger and Better!* Chicago: Prickly Paradigm Press.

Boyer, Dominic. 2014. "Energopower: An Introduction." *Anthropological Quarterly* 87, no. 2: 309–333.

Braun, Bruce, and Sarah J. Whatmore, eds. 2010. *Political Matter: Technoscience, Democracy, and Public Life*. Minneapolis: University of Minnesota Press.

Campbell, Ben, Jon Cloke, and Ed Brown. 2016. "Communities of Energy." *Economic Anthropology* 3, no. 1: 133–144.

Candea, Matei. 2014. "The Ontology of the Political Turn." In "Fieldsights—Theorizing the Contemporary," special section, *Cultural Anthropology* online, January 13, 2014, https://culanth.org/fieldsights/469-the-ontology-of-the-political-turn.

Chakrabarty, Dipesh. 2009. "The Climate of History: Four Theses." *Critical Inquiry* 35, no. 2: 197–222.

Clifford, James, and George E. Marcus, eds. 1986. *Writing Culture*. Berkeley: University of California Press.

Coole, Diana, and Samantha Frost, eds. 2010. *New Materialisms: Ontology, Agency, and Politics*. Durham, NC: Duke University Press.

Coronil, Fernando. 1997. *The Magical State: Nature, Money, and Modernity in Venezuela*. Chicago: University of Chicago Press.

Corsín Jiménez, Alberto. 2010. "The Political Proportions of Public Knowledge." *Journal of Cultural Economy* 3, no. 1: 69–84.

Davies, Jeremy. 2016. *The Birth of the Anthropocene*. Berkeley: University of California Press.

de la Cadena, Marisol. 2010. "Indigenous Politics in the Andes: Conceptual Reflections beyond 'Politics.'" *Cultural Anthropology* 25, no. 2: 334–370.

de la Cadena, Marisol. 2015. *Earth Beings: Ecologies of Practice across Andean Worlds.* Durham, NC: Duke University Press.

Epstein, Arnold Leonard. 1992. *Scenes from African Urban Life: Collected Copperbelt Papers.* Edinburgh: Edinburgh University Press.

Evans-Pritchard, Edward Evan. 1940. *The Nuer.* London: Oxford University Press.

Fabricant, Nicole, and Nancy Postero. 2015. "Sacrificing Indigenous Bodies and Lands: The Political-Economic History of Lowland Bolivia in Light of the Recent TIPNIS Debate." *Journal of Latin American and Caribbean Anthropology* 20, no. 3: 452–474.

Ferguson, James. 2015. *Give a Man a Fish: Reflections on the New Politics of Distribution.* Durham, NC: Duke University Press.

Ferme, M. 2001. *The Underneath of Things: Violence, History, and the Everyday in Sierra Leone.* Berkeley: University of California Press.

Finnström, Sverker. 2008. *Living with Bad Surroundings: War, History, and Everyday Moments in Northern Uganda.* Durham, NC: Duke University Press.

Fisher, Melissa S., and Greg Downey, eds. 2006. *Frontiers of Capital: Ethnographic Reflections on the New Economy.* Durham, NC: Duke University Press.

Gluckman, Max. 1958. *Analysis of a Social Situation in Modern Zululand.* Manchester: Manchester University Press.

Gluckman, Max. 1961. "Anthropological Problems Arising from the African Industrial Revolution." In *Social Change in Modern Africa: Studies Presented and Discussed at the First International African Seminar, Makerere College, Kampala, January 1959,* edited by Aidan William Southall, 67–82. London: Oxford University Press.

Gordillo, Gastón R. 2014. *Rubble: The Afterlife of Destruction.* Durham, NC: Duke University Press.

Green, Sarah F. 2005. *Notes from the Balkans: Locating Marginality and Ambiguity on the Greek-Albanian Border.* Princeton Modern Greek Studies. Princeton, NJ: Princeton University Press.

Gregory, Steven. 2014. *The Devil behind the Mirror: Globalization and Politics in the Dominican Republic.* With a new preface. Berkeley: University of California Press.

Grusin, Richard, ed. 2015. *The Nonhuman Turn.* Minneapolis: University of Minnesota Press.

Guyer, Jane I. 2004. *Marginal Gains: Money Transactions in Atlantic Africa.* Chicago: University of Chicago Press.

Haraway, Donna. 2003. *The Companion Species Manifesto: Dogs, People, and Significant Otherness.* Chicago: Prickly Paradigm.

Haraway, Donna. 2008. *When Species Meet.* Minneapolis: University of Minnesota Press.

Haraway, Donna. 2016. *Staying with the Trouble: Making Kin in the Chthulucene.* Durham, NC: Duke University Press.

Harman, Graham. 2002. *Tool-Being: Heidegger and the Metaphysics of Objects.* Chicago: Open Court.

Harman, Graham. 2005. *Guerrilla Metaphysics: Phenomenology and the Carpentry of Things.* Chicago: Open Court.

Harvey, Penny, Eleanor Casella, Gillian Evans, Hannah Knox, Christine McLean, Elizabeth B. Silva, Nicholas Thoburn, and Kath Woodward, eds. 2014. *Objects and Materials: A Routledge Companion*. Oxon: Routledge.

Harvey, Penny, Casper Bruun Jensen, and Atsuro Morita, eds. 2017. *Infrastructures and Social Complexity*. London: Routledge.

Harvey, Penny, and Hannah Knox. 2014. "Objects and Materials: An Introduction." In *Objects and Materials: A Routledge Companion*, edited by Penelope Harvey, Eleanor Casella, Gillian Evans, Hannah Knox, Christine McLean, Elizabeth B. Silva, Nicholas Thoburn, and Kath Woodward, 1–17. Oxon: Routledge.

Helmreich, Stefan. 2009. *Alien Ocean: Anthropological Voyages in Microbial Seas*. Berkeley: University of California Press.

Helmreich, Stefan. 2016. *Sounding the Limits of Life: Essays in the Anthropology of Biology and Beyond*. Princeton, NJ: Princeton University Press.

Henare, Amiria, Martin Holbraad, and Sari Wastell, eds. 2007. *Thinking through Things: Theorising Artefacts Ethnographically*. London: Routledge.

Hetherington, Kregg. 2013. "Beans before the Law: Knowledge Practices, Responsibility, and the Paraguayan Soy Boom." *Cultural Anthropology* 28, no. 1: 65–85.

Hinton, Devon E., and Alexander L. Hinton, eds. 2015. *Genocide and Mass Violence: Memory, Symptom, and Recovery*. New York: Cambridge University Press.

Holbraad, Martin, and Morten Axel Pedersen. 2014. "The Politics of Ontology." Introduction to "Fieldsights—Theorizing the Contemporary," special section, *Cultural Anthropology* online, January 13. https://culanth.org/fieldsights/461-the-politics-of-ontology.

Holbraad, Martin, Morten Axel Pedersen, and Eduardo Viveiros de Castro. 2014. "The Politics of Ontology: Anthropological Positions." In "Fieldsights—Theorizing the Contemporary," special section, *Cultural Anthropology* online, January 13. https://culanth.org/fieldsights/462-the-politics-of-ontology-anthropological-position.

Howe, Cymene, and Dominic Boyer. 2015. "Aeolian Politics." *Distinktion: Scandinavian Journal of Social Theory* 16, no. 1: 31–48.

Howe, Cymene, and Dominic Boyer. 2016. "Aeolian Extractivism and Community Wind in Southern Mexico." *Public Culture* 28, no. 2 (79): 215–235.

Ingold, Tim. 2014. "That's Enough about Ethnography!" *HAU: Journal of Ethnographic Theory* 4, no. 1: 383.

Jackson, Michael. 2014. *The Politics of Storytelling: Variations on a Theme by Hannah Arendt*. Copenhagen: Museum Tusculanum Press.

Jensen, Casper Bruun, and Atsuro Morita. 2017. "Introduction: Infrastructures as Ontological Experiments." *Ethnos* 82, no. 4: 615–626.

Johnstone, Philip, and Andrew Stirling. 2016. "Submerged Politics of UK Nuclear Power: Is Trident Renewal Influencing UK Energy Policy?" http://sro.sussex.ac.uk/65604/NGLI_Spokesman.

Juris, Jeffrey. 2012. "Reflections on #Occupy Everywhere: Social Media, Public Space, and Emerging Logics of Aggregation." *American Ethnologist* 39, no. 2: 259–279.

Keane, Webb. 1997. *Signs of Recognition: Powers and Hazards of Representation in an Indonesian Society*. Berkeley: University of California Press.

Keane, Webb. 2007. *Christian Moderns: Freedom and Fetish in the Mission Encounter.* Berkeley: University of California Press.

Kirksey, Eben S. 2015. *Emergent Ecologies.* Durham, NC: Duke University Press.

Kirksey, Eben S., and Stefan Helmreich. 2010. "The Emergence of Multispecies Ethnography." *Cultural Anthropology* 25, no. 4: 545–576.

Kirsch, Stuart. 2014. *Mining Capitalism: The Relationship between Corporations and Their Critics.* Berkeley: University of California Press.

Klein, Naomi. 2014. *This Changes Everything: Capitalism vs. the Climate.* London: Simon and Schuster.

Kohn, Eduardo. 2013. *How Forests Think: Toward an Anthropology beyond the Human.* Berkeley: University of California Press.

Kolbert, Elizabeth. 2006. *Field Notes from a Catastrophe: Man, Nature, and Climate Change.* London: Bloomsbury.

Kolbert, Elizabeth. 2015. *The Sixth Extinction: An Unnatural History.* New York: Picador.

Krohn-Hansen, Christian. 2015. "Political Anthropology." In *International Encyclopedia of the Social and Behavioral Sciences,* 2nd ed., edited by James D. Wright, 18: 335–341. Oxford: Elsevier.

Latour, Bruno. 2014. "Anthropology at the Time of the Anthropocene—a Personal View of What Is to Be Studied." Distinguished lecture at the Annual Meeting of the American Anthropological Association, Washington, DC, Dec. 3–7.

Lyons, Kristina Marie. 2016. "Decomposition as Life Politics: Soils, *Selva,* and Small Farmers under the Gun of the U.S.-Colombian War on Drugs." *Cultural Anthropology* 31, no. 1: 56–81.

Manganaro, Marc, ed. 1990. *Modernist Anthropology: From Fieldwork to Text.* Princeton, NJ: Princeton University Press

Martínez, Samuel. 2007. *Decency and Excess: Global Aspirations and Material Deprivation on a Caribbean Sugar Plantation.* Boulder, CO: Paradigm.

Masco, Joseph. 2006. *The Nuclear Borderlands: The Manhattan Project in Post–Cold War New Mexico.* Princeton, NJ: Princeton University Press.

Masco, Joseph. 2014. *The Theater of Operations: National Security Affect from the Cold War to the War on Terror.* Durham, NC: Duke University Press.

Mathews, Andrew S., and Jessica Barnes. 2016. "Prognosis: Visions of Environmental Futures." *Journal of the Royal Anthropological Institute* 22, no. S1: 9–26.

Mauss, Marcel. (1925) 1990. *The Gift: The Form and Reason for Exchange in Archaic Societies.* London: Routledge.

Mazzarella, William. 2009. "Affect: What Is It Good For?" In *Enchantments of Modernity,* edited by Saurabh Dube, 291–309. London: Routledge.

Mazzarella, William. 2010. "Beautiful Balloon: The Digital Divide and the Charisma of New Media in India." *American Ethnologist* 37, no. 4: 783–804.

Meillassoux, Quentin. 2008. *After Finitude: An Essay on the Necessity of Contingency.* Translated by Ray Brassier. London: Continuum.

Miller, Daniel. 1987. *Material Culture and Mass Consumption.* Social Archaeology. Oxford: Basil Blackwell.

Miller, Daniel, ed. 2005. *Materiality.* Durham, NC: Duke University Press.

Miller, Daniel. 2008. *The Comfort of Things*. Cambridge, UK: Polity.

Miller, Daniel. 2010. *Stuff*. Cambridge, UK: Polity.

Mintz, Sidney Wilfred. 1985. *Sweetness and Power: The Place of Sugar in Modern History*. New York: Viking.

Mitchell, Clyde J. 1956. *The Kalela Dance: Aspects of Social Relationships among Urban Africans in Northern Rhodesia*. Manchester: Manchester University Press.

Mitchell, Clyde J. 1969. *Social Networks in Urban Situations*. Manchester: Manchester University Press.

Mitchell, Timothy. 2013. *Carbon Democracy: Political Power in the Age of Oil*. 2nd ed. London: Verso.

Moore, Amelia. 2016. "Anthropocene Anthropology: Reconceptualizing Contemporary Global Change." *Journal of the Royal Anthropological Institute* 22, no. 1: 27–46.

Moore, Jason W. 2015. *Capitalism in the Web of Life: Ecology and the Accumulation of Capital*. London: Verso.

Moore, Jason W., ed. 2016. *Anthropocene or Capitalocene? Nature, History, and the Crisis of Capitalism*. Oakland, CA: PM Press/Kairos.

Morton, Timothy. 2013. *Hyperobjects: Philosophy and Ecology after the End of the World*. Minneapolis: University of Minnesota Press.

Ong, Aihwa. 2008. "Scales of Exception: Experiments with Knowledge and Sheer Life in Tropical Southeast Asia." *Singapore Journal of Tropical Geography* 29, no. 2: 117–129.

Pedersen, David. 2013. *American Value: Migrants, Money, and Meaning in El Salvador and the United States*. Chicago: University of Chicago Press.

Pedersen, Morten Axel. 2011. *Not Quite Shamans: Spirit Worlds and Political Lives in Northern Mongolia*. Ithaca, NY: Cornell University Press.

Pedersen, Morten Axel. 2012. "Common Nonsense: A Review of Certain Recent Reviews of the 'Ontological Turn.'" *Anthropology of This Century*, no. 5. http://aotcpress.com/articles/common_nonsense/.

Perreault, Tom. 2015. "Performing Participation: Mining, Power, and the Limits of Public Consultation in Bolivia." *Journal of Latin American and Caribbean Anthropology* 20, no. 3: 433–451.

Poggiali, Lisa. 2016. "Seeing (from) Digital Peripheries: Technology and Transparency in Kenya's Silicon Savannah." *Cultural Anthropology* 31, no. 3: 387–411.

Purdy, Jedediah. 2015. *After Nature: A Politics for the Anthropocene*. Cambridge, MA: Harvard University Press.

Rancière, Jacques. 1999. *Disagreement: Politics and Philosophy*. Minneapolis: University of Minnesota Press.

Rolston, Jessica Smith. 2013. "The Politics of Pits and the Materiality of Mine Labor: Making Natural Resources in the American West." *American Anthropologist* 115, no. 4: 582–594.

Sahlins, Marshall. 1958. *Social Stratification in Polynesia*. Seattle: University of Washington Press.

Schwenkel, Christina. 2015. "Spectacular Infrastructure and Its Breakdown in Socialist Vietnam." *American Ethnologist* 42, no. 3: 520–534.

Shaviro, Steven. 2014. *The Universe of Things: On Speculative Realism*. Minneapolis: University of Minnesota Press.

Stengers, Isabelle. 2010. "Including Nonhumans in Political Theory: Opening Pandora's Box?" In *Political Matter: Technoscience, Democracy, and Public Life*, edited by Bruce Braun and Sarah J. Whatmore, 3–34. Minneapolis: University of Minnesota Press.

Stoler, Ann Laura. 2013. "Introduction." In *Imperial Debris: On Ruins and Ruination*, edited by Ann Laura Stoler, 1–35. Durham, NC: Duke University Press.

Strathern, Marilyn. 1991. *Partial Connections*. Savage, MD: Rowman and Littlefield.

Striffler, Steve, and Mark Moberg, eds. 2003. *Banana Wars: Power, Production, and History in the Americas*. Durham, NC: Duke University Press.

Taussig, Michael. 1980. *The Devil and Commodity Fetishism in South America*. Chapel Hill: University of North Carolina Press.

Taussig, Michael. 2004. *My Cocaine Museum*. Chicago: University of Chicago Press.

Taussig, Michael. 2008. "Redeeming Indigo." *Theory, Culture and Society* 25, no. 3: 1–15.

Toren, Christina. 1999. *Mind, Materiality and History: Explorations in Fijian Ethnography*. London: Routledge.

Tsing, Anna. 2004. *Friction: An Ethnography of Global Connection*. Princeton, NJ: Princeton University Press.

Tsing, Anna. 2009. "Supply Chains and the Human Condition." *Rethinking Marxism: A Journal of Economics, Culture and Society* 21, no. 2: 148–176.

Tsing, Anna. 2015. *The Mushroom at the End of the World: On the Possibility of Life in Capitalist Ruins*. Princeton, NJ: Princeton University Press.

Van Velsen, J. 1967. "The Extended-Case Method and Situational Analysis." In *The Craft of Social Anthropology*, edited by A. L. Epstein, 129–149. London: Tavistock.

Verran, Helen. 2014. "Anthropology as Ontology Is Comparison as Ontology." In "Fieldsights—Theorizing the Contemporary," special section, *Cultural Anthropology* online, January 13. https://culanth.org/fieldsights/468-anthropology-as-ontology-is-comparison-as-ontology.

Vince, Gaia. 2014. *Adventures in the Anthropocene: A Journey to the Heart of the Planet We Made*. London: Chatto and Windus.

Viveiros de Castro, Eduardo. 1998. "Cosmological Deixis and Amerindian Perspectivism." *Journal of the Royal Anthropological Institute* 4, no. 3: 469–488.

Viveiros de Castro, Eduardo. 2004. "Perspectival Anthropology and the Method of Controlled Equivocation." *Tipití: Journal of the Society for the Anthropology of Lowland South America* 2, no. 1: 3–22.

von Schnitzler, Antina. 2013. "Traveling Technologies: Infrastructure, Ethical Regimes, and the Materiality of Politics in South Africa." *Cultural Anthropology* 28, no. 4: 670–693.

Wagner, Roy. 1975. *The Invention of Culture*. Chicago: University of Chichago Press.

Wark, McKenzie. 2016. *Molecular Red: Theory for the Anthropocene*. London: Verso.

Weston, Kath. 2012. "Political Ecologies of the Precarious." *Anthropological Quarterly* 85, no. 2: 429–455.

Weston, Kath. 2017. *Animate Planet: Making Visceral Sense of Living in a High-Tech Ecologically Damaged World*. Durham, NC: Duke University Press.

Willerslev, Rane. 2007. *Soul Hunters: Hunting, Animism, and Personhood among the Siberian Yukaghirs*. Berkeley: University of California Press.

Williams, Raymond. 1977. "Structures of Feeling." In *Marxism and Literature*, 128–135. Oxford: Oxford University Press.

Wolfe, Cary. 2009. *What Is Posthumanism?* Minneapolis: University of Minnesota Press.

Yanagisako, Sylvia Junko. 2002. *Producing Culture and Capital: Family Firms in Italy*. Princeton, NJ: Princeton University Press.

Yanagisako, Sylvia Junko. 2013. "Transnational Family Capitalism: Producing 'Made in Italy' in China." In *Vital Relations: Modernity and the Persistent Life of Kinship*, edited by Susan McKinnon and Fenella Cannell, 63–84. Santa Fe, NM: School for Advanced Research Press.

PART I

Materializing Structures

———

1. Uncommoning Nature

STORIES FROM THE ANTHROPO-NOT-SEEN

Marisol de la Cadena

A Preamble

On June 5, 2009, at dawn, near the northern Amazonian town of Bagua, a violent confrontation took place between police forces and a large group of Peruvian citizens self-identified as belonging to the Awajun Wampis indigenous group. This event, which resulted in more than thirty deaths, has marked the political imaginary, if with different emphases depending on one's position to the left or the right on the national political spectrum. In general, the narrative that circulates in the media goes more or less as follows: As part of a general strike, which started on April 9 (that same year) and was organized by several Amazonian indigenous groups, the Awajun Wampis had taken control of a highway in northern Peru at a place called "La Curva del Diablo"—the Devil's Curve. They were protesting several decrees with which the government had conceded their territory to corporate oil exploration without abiding by the ILO (International Labor Organization) agreement 169. This international legislation, to which the Peruvian government officially adheres, requires signatory states to consult the opinion of the inhabitants of territories that corporations request for exploration and exploitation. Because they had not been consulted, the concession was illegal, the protestors said. The police's objective was to break up the highway blockade; through unknown circumstances (which are under investigation), the confrontation got out of control. According to the official count, the clash—known as *el Baguazo* (in English, "the huge event in Bagua")—

resulted in more than thirty deaths among the Awajun Wampis and police. Two weeks later, on June 19—under enormous pressure from heterogeneous groups and against the will of then president Alan García—the National Congress canceled the decrees that allowed the concession of indigenous territories to oil companies and transgressed the ILO Convention 169. At the same time, the local state ordered the arrest of some indigenous leaders; they faced charges of murder and sedition. Following a long trial, they were finally acquitted in September 2016.[1]

Among those arrested was Santiago Manuin Valera, the most public individual among the Awanjun Wampis. The following quote is part of his testimony during the trial on April 10, 2014, five years after the event—at the time he faced life in prison: "The government is taking away *our territory, the territory of the Awajun Wampis people,* so that we become dependent on its [form of] development. The government never asked: do you want to develop? They did not consult us. We responded, 'Cancel the legislative decrees that *affect our existence as a people.*' Instead of listening to our complaint, the government wanted to punish us—other peoples surrendered, we did not. The government ordered our forced eviction" (emphasis added).[2] Two weeks after the trial, on April 26, he wrote:

> We will never accept that the Government does what it wants with . . . *the territory that our ancestors* assigned us before the Peruvian state was formed. Peru and the whole world should know that this place of thirty thousand [square] kilometers is ours and belongs to us; we will always defend it and will give our lives for it. [The Awajun Wampis] were defending *our right, our identity, our culture, a development of our own, our forest, our rivers, our cosmos, and our territory.*[3] (emphasis added)

Manuin ended the statement by declaring his innocence. Why would it be a crime to defend the ancestral territory of the Awajun Wampis against a usurping state? The criminal trial against Manuin and others may be interpreted as a conflict over sovereignty, and depending on where we stand, we can support the Awajun Wampis people's right to defend their territory or side with the state's prerogative to decide about the national territory and the use of natural resources. Taken to the court, this would already be a challenging legal problem. However, I intend to argue that at the inception of the conflict is a disagreement that would not find resolution within the rule of law—even in its fairest version—for it exceeds its existing domain.

Examining the confrontation, and writing in its aftermath, the anthropologist Shane Greene suggests "that there [was] more at stake than simply a defense of territory, a protest against capitalist expansion, or a concern over the fate of the environment. What [was] also at stake *is a distinct way of life*" (2009, 58; emphasis added). Explaining the confrontation in the midst of the strike, Leni—a young Awajun Wampis leader with his face painted in red and black, a bandana around his head—spoke words that may illustrate Greene's intimation:

> We speak of our brothers who quench our thirst, who bathe us, those who protect our needs—*this [brother] is what we call the river.* We do not use the river for our sewage; a brother cannot stab another brother. We do not stab our brothers. If the transnational corporations would care about our soil like we have cared for it for millennia, we would gladly give them room so that they could work here—but all they care about is their economic benefit, to fill their coffers with wealth. We do not understand why the government wants to raze our lives with those decrees.[4]

Taking Greene's cue and listening to Leni's words, I want to suggest that in the above statements, "territory" as referred to by Manuín may make reference *both* to a piece of land under the jurisdiction of the Peruvian state *and* to an entity that emerges through the Awajun Wampis' practices of life that may, for example, make people the relatives of rivers, as in Leni's statement. And kinship between people and water and forest may transform territory into Awajun Wampis, as in a recent public declaration by their leaders in which they said, "Territory *is* the Awanjun Wampis."[5]

This relation—where people and territory *are together*—exceeds the possibilities of modern humans and modern nature as well as modern relations between them, *without precluding any of them.* Nevertheless, it complicates the conflict: rather than an abuse of power that can be unmade (with difficulty, of course), the conflict becomes a misunderstanding that is impossible to solve without engaging in the terms that make territory other to the state's ability to understand and therefore other to its recognition. Erupting publicly, the conflict poses a challenge intolerable to the state, and its response might be the eradication of its roots: the denial of the existence of the terms of the Awajun Wampis. Thus viewed, the conflict is ontological. I draw on Jacques Rancière and Eduardo Viveiros de Castro to conceptualize it as a confrontation housing a historical disagreement (Rancière's term) *about* an equivocation (Viveiros de Castro's term) over *what territory is and what kind of relations make it.* Together these two concepts, disagreement and equivocation, may do work that each of them individually may not do; their joint analytic work may enable reflection about the *complexity* of the dispute expressed in Manuín's statements. It may also expose a conflict located *both* within *and* beyond the domain of the rule of law.

Viveiros de Castro is a Brazilian anthropologist; "equivocation" is his concept to explain the mode of communication among Amerindian inhabitants (humans and not) in the Brazilian Amazon. Equivocation, he says, houses "the referential alterity between homonymic concepts" (Viveiros de Castro 2004, 5) with which the entities that populate Amerindian worlds communicate with—or translate to—each other. Crucial to the concept is, first, that these entities—which we would regard as humans or animals— consider themselves human and see their "others" as animals; and, second, that what *is* results from the entities' point of view, which in turn results from their bodies. The almost canonical example to illustrate equivocation is that of the differences between jaguar and human: what the former sees as beer, the latter sees as blood. The reason for the differences between their points of view resides in their different bodies; the difference is not conceptual, for both entities share the notions beer and blood. Therefore, communication, and even the preservation of one's life, consists in "controlling" the equivocation (Viveiros de Castro 2004, 5) or understanding that while the concept (and therefore *the understanding* of the thing it refers to) may be shared, the *thing itself* may emerge as different if the concept is uttered by someone who is an other to the self in the interlocution. When equivocation is the mode of communication, concepts and things are only partially connected; the same word may refer to two different things depending on the world it is uttered from. In the case that concerns me here, territory may be both the piece of land that rests separate from the humans and the state that may have the right to it, and the entity that is with the Awajun Wampis— what territory is would depend on the world that is pronouncing the term, the relations that it emerges from.

Disagreement may have the appearance of an equivocation. Rancière, a philosopher of politics and aesthetics, conceptualizes disagreement as "the conflict between one who says white and another who also says white but does not understand the same thing by it." Yet while equivocation assumes that all participants in the interlocution are speakers (and thus can name things that are conceptually the same and "objectively" different), the misunderstanding that provokes disagreement (à la Rancière) results from "a contention over what speaking means"; it is "a dispute over the object of the discussion, and *over the capacity of those who are making an object of it*" (Rancière 1999, x, xi, xii). Moreover, *as a political interruption to alter the conventional order and establish equality*, disagreement is a dispute that confronts those who have (are granted) speech with those who do not have (are denied) speech—it is a dispute about the conventions that distribute capacities to define what is and how that is. Struggles for civil rights in the Americas would be an example of how disagreement established a new order of the perceptible. Thus, the difference between the two fellow concepts: equivocation is a misunderstanding in a relation among *equals* that *are* (i.e., ontologically) *mutually other*. The misunderstanding is an ontological relation; while the equivocation can be discerned (or controlled, to use Viveiros de Castro's term), it is also an inevitable condition that cannot be changed. In contrast, disagreement pits socially unequal individuals in a dispute to be *the same* (or socially equivalent) and from such a position to name and define what the same should be; here the misunderstanding is political and reflects an epistemic dispute seeking to change how the established order is perceived. To put it differently, and perhaps more clearly in terms of the argument of this article, the misunderstanding in equivocation emerges when bodies that belong to different worlds use the same word to name entities that *are not the same* because they too, like the bodies that name them, belong to different worlds; disagreement results from misunderstandings about the conditions for naming the same entities in a world that should be shared.

Impossible Politics, Silent War, and the "Anthropos-Not-Seen"

Thinking through Rancière's notion of disagreement, the "big event in Bagua" can be rendered as the eruption of politics: a historical event in which a subject emerges that disrupts the distribution of speech and the order it creates. In disagreement, this subject erupts in the established order (where he or she has no speech) to propose another distribution of the voices, ears, hands, and, ultimately, bodies that name what the French philosopher calls the perceptible. In the specific case of *el Baguazo*, the disagreement that the Awajun Wampis manifested would have interrupted the distribution of the speech that assigns the state sovereignty to decide about territory. Against it, the Awajun Wampis would have claimed their own sovereign voice. Understood as an extension of the country over which humans have the power of decision, the entity "territory" would have remained the same, and what and how it is would not be in dispute.

Conceptualized instead as a disagreement *that houses an equivocation*, the conflict can *also* be interpreted as a dispute around an entity—territory—that is not the same and *cannot be* the different things that it may emerge as in interlocutions between Awajun Wampis and the state. Thinking through territory as equivocation, Manuín's statements—and the trial from which they emerge—would *also* reflect a disagreement, the nature of which is ontological. Thus, the equivocation would also be a political dispute aggravated by the condition *of its impossibility*, for neither the state nor the law is able—let alone equipped—to recognize the equivocation or the political dispute around it. I am calling this condition the anthropo-not-seen. I conceptualize it as the world-making process through which heterogeneous worlds that do not make themselves through practices that ontologically separate humans (or culture) from nonhumans (or nature)—*nor necessarily conceive as such the different entities in their assemblages*—*both* are obliged into that distinction (and thus willfully destroyed) *and* exceed it. The anthropo-not-seen would thus be *both* the will that requires the distinction (and destroys whatever disobeys the obligation) *and* the excesses to that will: the collectives that, like the Awajun Wampis, are composed of entities that *are not only* human *or* nonhuman because they are also with what (according to the obligation) they should not be: humans *with* nonhumans, and the other way around.

The Anthropocene makes scholarly reference to the era when humans have become a geological force capable of planetary destruction. The "anthropo-not-seen" makes obvious reference to the term, and the suffix is equally obviously intended as a pun on -*cene*. However, the not-seen may be deceptive, for in using it, my intention is not to evoke the invisible of a visible realm under which it exists bearing the duress of power. In fact, the not-seen does not mainly refer to a regime of visibility. Rather, it aims to make reference to what *is* within a historically formulated hegemonic condition of impossibility, and hence, included in the anthropo-not-seen are antagonistic partners and their antagonistic relationship. On one hand, the anthropo-not-seen comprises the practices and practitioners of the will that granted itself the power to eradicate all that disobeyed mandates to be "human" as modernity (in its early and late versions) sanctioned. On the other hand, it includes the disobedient practitioners of collectives composed of entities recalcitrant to classification (and individuation) as *either* human *or* nonhuman. Complexly, the anthropo-not-seen includes both the anthropos that embodies the self-granted will to make the world as he or she knows it, and the disobedient anthropos, the one that is inherently-with-others and thus *not only* human. Both inhabit the not-seen, yet they do so in antagonism: in the case of the first anthropos, what is not-seen (as such) is its constitutive will to destruction, which in turn cancels the possibility of disobedient beings and therefore makes for their not-seen condition. As an organized process of destruction—sometimes through benevolently offered assimilation—the anthropo-not-seen included, and continues to include, a silent war waged against entities and world-making practices that ignore the separation of entities into nature and culture.[6]

Dating from the early sixteenth century in what became the Americas, the war was initially loud and clear; fighting for their God, Christian clerics walked the Andes from Colombia to Argentina and Chile, "extirpating idolatries," a political practice that the friars conceived against "devil-induced worship." Extirpation required dividing the participating entities into God-made nature (mountains, rivers, forests) and *naturales*, or incipient humans with a soul still to be saved. The invention of modern politics secularized the antagonism: the war against the recalcitrance to distinguish nature from humanity was silenced; yet it continued in the name of progress and against backwardness, the evil that replaced the devil. Making it not-seen, war practices included forms of making live. Inferior humans became the object of benevolent and inevitable inclusion, enemies that did not even count as enemies: the war was waged through silent means. This last phrase paraphrases Michel Foucault's inversion of Carl von Clausewitz's classic aphorism ("War is a continuation of politics through other means"): "Politics is the continuation of war by other means" (2003, 15). Unpacking the phrase, he explains, first, that the relations of force through which modern power works were established in and through war at a given historical moment; and, second, that while politics "pacifies" "it certainly does not do so in order to . . . neutralize the disequilibrium revealed by the last battle of the war"; but, third, that instead "the role of political power is perpetually to use a sort of silent war to reinscribe that relationship of force, and to inscribe it in institutions, economic inequalities, language, and even the bodies of individuals" (15–16). I tweak Foucault a bit to indicate, first, that the signature of the war that established modern power was its colonial will to destroy—or assimilate, which amounts to destruction yet has hegemonic potential—that which was not in its image and likeness; second, that the "last battle" is always ongoing; and, finally, that rather than being waged *through* politics, modern war may be a mechanism *against* the *demand for politics* posed by those collectives against whom the war is waged. When these collectives pose such a demand—when the disagreement around equivocations becomes public, and collectives press for recognition of that which the state cannot recognize—the silent war may translate into overt battle. The state would wage it in the name of the common good; disobedient collectives respond to defend their survival.

Extractivism or the End of the Silent War (and of the Not-Seen)

Extractivism is a concept that circulates quite profusely in Latin America and that, quite literally, makes the Anthropocene materially present as a human-geological force, while at the same time foregrounding its articulation through financial capital and in connection with infrastructural growth. This term is currently used in environmental circles in the region; critical contributors trace the start of extractivist practices back to Spanish colonial mining (see Gudynas 2015; Bebbington 2015; Svampa 2015). The extraction of silver from the Cerro Rico de Potosí and Huancavelica (currently in Bolivia and Peru, respectively) is an infamous example of the death and destruction caused by the extraction of minerals for circulation in Iberian metropolitan markets. Guano, rubber, cotton, and sugar plantations and perforation for oil (mostly in coastal areas with access to small ports) followed in the late nineteenth century. Then, enabled by the construction of railways, the growth of ports in size and numbers, and the creation of a merchant naval industry, a great number of mines were opened throughout the twentieth century, attracting US and British capital. Throughout, these activities contributed to the general national income, to ecological "transformation," and to the death of populations (needless to say, these were mostly indigenous and slaves of African origin).

Many features make extractivism a different venture compared to earlier (also extractive) practices. Some obvious ones are the corporate character of the practice; the worldwide ubiquity of the model and its interconnectedness; the unprecedented rate of expansion of markets for minerals, oil, and energy; and the magnitude of new technologies that allow for quick and profitable extraction.

Former "tunnel mining"—the perforation of mountains following the vein of minerals—has been replaced by open pits that destroy mountains, creating crater-like formations that extend over hundreds of hectares and reach depths of more than a thousand meters.[7] Multiple-well platforms have substantially increased the number of barrels and the speed of production, and relatively new technologies like inland and offshore fracking and the production of oil from tar sands are responsible for the unprecedented territorial expansion of oil extraction. The magnitude of the so-called environmental impacts is also unprecedented. An example: between 2006 and 2011, Bolivia produced 5,600 tons of silver, which required the removal of more than 44 million tons of rocks (removing the rocks from where they were and then dumping them elsewhere is destructive). And while the tremendous amounts of water used in mining are not exactly destroyed, it becomes so full of contaminants that it is rendered useless for consumption by any living being. In the case of oil: fracking uses extraordinary amounts of water and releases large volumes of toxic and radioactive waste and dangerous air pollutants, and it thus affects bodies of all sorts in vast areas.[8] Soybean and oil palm plantations (among others) join in the production of what Uruguayan biologist and politician Eduardo Gudynas has labeled "ecological amputations" (2015, 25). The construction of infrastructure (necessary to market the resources) sponsored by central financial institutions like the International Monetary Fund, the World Bank, and new regional financial entities such as the Latin American Development Bank, enables the extraction to reach the remotest territories. All this propels what appears to be an unprecedentedly unstoppable and mighty removal of resources in these territories as they are also transformed into spaces for financial investment.

As immense an ecological concern as it is, extractivism has become a central component of the economic strategies of all governments in the region, left and right, without exception. Perhaps the only difference is that while the first, guided by a nationalist agenda, declare that they prefer to execute the extraction themselves, the latter have decidedly opened their territories to transnational corporations. *Appropriation through Pollution* is the subtitle Michel Serres (2011) gives to the little book in which he discusses the planetary ecological crisis we live with—to pollute is to possess; it is to exclude others from access to the resources that the polluter appropriates. And, of course, appropriation through pollution also kills those humans whom the destructive anthropos does not care to see—and therefore neither pollution nor deaths matter, for not infrequently (if implicitly), ecological amputations are deemed necessary "geographies of sacrifice," to adopt Valerie Kuletz's (1998) phrase and adapt it to the ethos of extractivism. Accordingly, forms of life that continue to exist in the spaces from which resources can be extracted are disposable because those forms of life ought to have disappeared long ago. Moved by a well-funded race for progress and promoted by economic growth, the reach of the current destruction of indigenous worlds is historically unparalleled, and news about it is not exactly scarce; it takes no effort to learn about appalling incidents at any given time. Consider this commentary published on March 23, 2016, as I was writing this piece:

it narrates the slow death of an indigenous group recognized in Colombia as the Wayúu at the hands of an infamous coal mine.

> Everything has been taken away from them. They have stolen their land, their water, even their names. . . . And the spoliation continues. The draught that burns them with thirst is neither nature's whim, nor a consequence of global warming: it is that the great coal company from El Cerrejón, built the dam El Cercado, which the state inaugurated with great publicity, and it sucked the water for the needs of the immense mine. The mine grows, and as it does, it evicts the Wayúus into the desert in La Guajira. [Before the dam] El Cerrejón had already diverted for its own ends the course of several streams that fed the Río Ranchería, and now it insists on building a new riverbed, thus taking the whole river away in order to reach the immense coal deposits that lie under the water.[9]

Denunciations like the above find a public beyond the indigenous peoples whose life is at stake, and among those more generally concerned with the distribution of ecological conflicts and human rights. Digging a mountain to open a mine, drilling into the subsoil to find oil, damming all possible rivers, and razing trees to build transoceanic roads and railroads are tools for the transformation of territories into grounds for investment—but extractivism's hegemony is hard to achieve. Extractivism has met a relentless opposition that articulates, if in complex and irregular ways, unexpected alliances across the heterogeneous demands of a vast array of collectives. Centrally, in all its diverse complexity, the alliance defies the monopoly of the state and corporations to make, inhabit, and define nature—and, at times, the challenge it poses touches states' nerves, producing the feeling that sovereignty over the territories they rule is challenged and that their hopes for economic growth (founded on extractivism) are jeopardized. So far, the reaction of national states (from the left and the right) has been to waver between accepting and rejecting their opponents' demands for negotiation. When rejection happens, what I have been calling the "silent war" moves onto an open battlefield—in the name of progress, as always. The confrontation in 2009 in La Curva del Diablo is an emblematic event of the end of the silent war: those who oppose the transformation of universal nature into resources oppose the possibility of the common good as the mission of the nation-state and are thus the state's enemies, deserving jail at the very least.

The alliance against extractivism is complex. Politically relevant, it has a capacity to attract public attention opposing the participation of the state in human rights violations and corporate ecological amputations; while performed through modern notions (environment, rights, biodiversity), the reality-making practices of the alliance continue the anthropo-not-seen. Yet the complexity does not end here—and following it up, we may find that the alliance deserves care. Defending themselves, the spokespersons of worlds experiencing destruction—this time at the hands of extractivism—have revealed their practices through television stations and newspapers. Challenging the legitimacy of the will to destroy, they have shared that nature or the environment—the matter of public concern—is not only such. Revelations of unimaginable beings and their destruction can be as ubiquitous as the war against those who oppose what the state considers (at least so far) its mission to provide for the common good. The one-world world that Christianity and modernity collaboratively built and sustained is being challenged—perhaps at an unprecedented rate since its inauguration five hundred years ago. Here I propose that the moment the anthropo-not-seen, *as the destruction of worlds*, seems to have acquired a might and speed that early extirpators of idolatries and nineteenth-century explorers (turned rubber and sugar plantation investors) would envy is also the moment when, from the other side of the coin—the anthropo-not seen *as worlds defending themselves against their destruction*—stories emerge that may bring into existence a public that does not yet exist (Warner 2005). Thus, even if what becomes public is a translation into environmental and human rights concerns, the denunciations (and the alliances that make them possible) offer a possibility for ontological openings that deserves attention.

Stories from the Anthropo-Not-Seen

We need stories (and theories) that are just big enough to gather
up the complexities and keep the edges open and greedy for
surprising new and old connections.
—DONNA HARAWAY, "Anthropocene, Capitalocene, Plantationocene,
Chthulucene: Making Kin"

Analogous to the Awajun Wampis people's claim of *being* their ancestral territories, and their assertion of kinship with the forest, in a dispute about petroleum extraction at a site called Vaca Muerta (Argentina), a Mapuche group wrote in a communiqué, "Our territories are not 'resources' but lives that make the Ixofijmogen [life of all lives] of which we are part, not its owners."[10] In contrast, this is how Vaca Muerta is defined by developers from Neuquén, one of the provinces included in the hydrocarbon deposit at issue: "Vaca Muerta is an immense *páramo* [a barren cold plateau]. A desert that extends beyond what the eyes can see. . . . It is a hostile territory that shelters enough energy to make Argentina self-sufficient and even export gas and oil to the world."[11] The stark contrast between these statements suggests that the public dispute is *not only* about petroleum extraction. The Mapuche declaration reveals the inherent relationality between the entities that compose Ixofijmogen, which therefore cannot be easily divided into territory and the resources extracted from it. What the oil company enacts as nature and humans, the Mapuche do not only enact as such.[12] Their interruption of the hegemonic partition is a political worlding event that is also conceptual: it performs an ontological opening into that partition that makes possible the enactment of humans *with* nature. This condition (which is not simply a mix of humans *and* nature) makes each more than just one of them. What is more, entities may emerge as materially specific to (and through) the relation that inherently connects them. An example from my own work in the Andes of Cuzco: *runakuna* (the local Quechua word for people) with *tirakuna* (earth beings, entities that are also—yet not only—mountains) are together in complex materiality and liveliness as they jointly fabricate place and are fabricated by it (de la Cadena 2014, 2015); in contrast, the materiality in and of the relation between modern lively humans *and* inert mountains makes them distinct from each other.[13]

Runakuna with earth beings are, of course, not a requirement of the processes that have emerged to question the universality of the partition of the sensible into nature and humans. Here is another example: In the northern Andes of Peru, a mining corporation plans to drain several lagoons to extract copper and gold from some, and to drain mineral waste in others. In exchange, reservoirs with a water capacity several times that of the lagoons would be built. Opposing the plan, environmentalists argue that the reservoirs will destroy the ecosystem of which the lagoons are part: a landscape made of agricultural land, high-altitude wetlands, cattle, humans, trees, crops, creeks, and springs. The local population adds that the lagoons *are* local life: their plants, animals, soils, trees, and families *are with* that specific water, which cannot be translated into water from reservoirs, not even if, as the mining corporation promises, they would provide more water. It would not be the *same* water; to defend it, they have organized themselves as "guardians of the lagoons." Many guardians have died in this defense, making public another instance of the war against those who oppose the translation of nature into resources. Yet the guardians of the lagoons have never said that the water is a being; what they say is that it is local water: the water *with which* they, their plants, their animals, and, ultimately, "their natures" *are*. As such, it is untranslatable to H_2O and cannot be used for the general common good. Rather, transpiring through local bodies (human and other-than-human), through the political practice of its guardians, the water from these lagoons emerges as it emplaces entities and makes itself uncommon nature, or nature already occupied by local bodies and therefore unavailable for transformation into the state or the corporation's interests if they do not coincide with those of their bodies.

This lagoon water, and the "nature" it is, is a complex boundary object in this conflict. On one side, nature is half of a dualism; on the other, encompassing human and other-than-human heterogeneities, nature is an almost meaningless term. Complexly, then, lagoon water is itself *not only* natural, and nature *is not* only Nature.[14] The politics that it—the lagoon water—proposes are equally complex and elude the kind of either-or analyses that require ontological agreement about what *is*.

An iconic guardian of the lagoons is a peasant woman whose plots the corporate mining project wants to buy to fully legalize its access to the territories it plans to excavate. The woman, whose name is Máxima Acuña, refuses to sell—and probably for an amount of money that she would otherwise not ever see in her lifetime. Countless times, the national police force, hired by the mine, has destroyed the family's crops and attacked her and her children and even her animals; influenced by the mine, several judiciary courts have ruled against the woman. She has also won some legal battles: as I wrote this piece, a judiciary court ordered the national police force to protect the woman and her family from the mine. The woman's plots have been under siege for more than three years now. "I fight to protect the lagoon" has been one of her responses. And, asserting attachment to place, she adds, "I am not going to stop; they will disappear me. But I will die with the land" (personal communication).

Her refusal to sell is incomprehensible to the dominant market-oriented rationality. It may also remind us of similarities between Máxima and Bartleby, the scrivener in Herman Melville's ([1853] 2007) story, whose refusal to do as requested by those who surrounded him has provoked numerous philosophical musings.[15] Bartleby says that he "would prefer not to" do as his superiors ask. Because the requests seem logical and because the scrivener does not explain why he "prefers not to," he drives his superiors crazy. Similarly, Máxima's refusal to sell has driven more than one person crazy: she prevents the mining company from accomplishing their goal. Yet she is not necessarily agrammatical, at least not in the sense of disengagement from the social that Gilles Deleuze (1998) accords to Bartleby's agrammaticality.

Through the lens of modern politics (and using the grammar that separates humans and universal nature), we can interpret this woman's actions as defending the ecosystem: an environmentalist, and thus an enemy or an ally, depending on who speaks. Driven to exasperation, supporters of the reservoirs (and also "rational" politicians) see her as a cunning manipulator awaiting a better price for her plot; to those on the other side of the political spectrum—the complexity of which I will explain and where I include myself—she is a hero willing to sacrifice herself to prevent ecological damage.[16] In the language of both detractors and supporters, she is a subject in relation to an object—and thus perfectly grammatical as she acts in response to conditions imposed on her. However, the "refusal to sell" may include another relation: one from which woman-land-lagoon (or plants-rocks-soils-animals-lagoons-humans-creeks—canals!!!) emerge inherently together: an entanglement of entities needy of each other in such a way that pulling them apart would transform them into something else.[17] Refusing to sell may also refuse the grammar that transforms the entities into individual bodies, units of nature or the environment, which when they are part of each other, they are not. Thus analyzed, Máxima's refusal would be the act of a private thinker, one who thinks with her own forces (see Deleuze and Guattari 1994, 62) to enact a locally ecologized nature (entities interdependent on each other) that simultaneously coincides with, differs from, and even exceeds (also because it includes humans) the object that the state, the mining corporation, *and* the environmentalists translate into resources to be exploited or defended. Carving out "a kind of foreign language within language" (Deleuze 1998, 72), she *also* makes herself agrammatical to the subject and object relation and to the social thus made. Her response is driven by a logic that exceeds both that of profit and gain, and that of the environment and its defense. In this sense, Máxima's response might be like Bartleby's formula as proposed by Deleuze: a response that exceeds any known or expected logic, one that may muddle any attributed social position, while at the same time self-asserting composite positions that communicate with usual grammars and at the same time open them up to other possibilities.

If she is an environmentalist—and I think she is—she is *not only* an environmentalist. Defending herself, and also going beyond herself, she declares her stewardship of the lagoons and all that their waters are and allow—and she does that in more than one way. She confronts the mine by arguing that the land is her property—she even shows the legal documents that prove her ownership. However, when Máxima explains how her being with the land is impossible to detach or break apart, how their *being together* is through/ with crops, rain, soil, animals—entities that make/are the relation—her explanation, I propose, exceeds the limits of the property concept, where she nevertheless *also* meets the mine in the confrontation. She stays because she *is* by staying; that this reads like a redundancy marks the agrammaticality of the woman's decision. When I asked why she stayed (as many others have done before me, and I am sure after), she replied, "What can I be if I am not *this*? [And the word "place" is not uttered—instead, she stomps her feet.] This is who I am, how can I go? I will die [The word "here" is not uttered.] who I am, with my bones I will be [Once again "here" is not uttered.] like I am now." Of course we can read her sentences through a habitual subject and object grammar, which I have suggested with the words in brackets; but the need for the brackets—the nonutterances in Máxima's answers are not blanks to be filled—also suggests that there is *not only* one grammar in her refusal to sell the land that the mine wants. Because we do not need help with our habits, I remark on the unusual.

Not only is a phrase that we (scholars or not) frequently use in our analysis—I have already used it in several paragraphs above. I learned to give this phrase conceptual status from conversations with Mariano Turpo, a friend with whom I collaborated on the ideas that came into a book I published not long ago (de la Cadena 2015). A Quechua speaker and a commuter across some of the worlds that make our country (Peru), he would insist that what to me *was* (or the thing that was to me, for example, a mountain or an archive) was *not only* that. And what *it* not only was, I had no figure or form for until it became *that* to me—or until, through laborious and patient practice, I was able to work my thought out of the habit of needing to grasp (many times barely) the entity or the practice. Grasping what was "not only" what emerged through my habitual practice of thought, in addition to taking time, required working at a permanent interface where Mariano's worlding practices and mine were both seemingly alike and at the same time different (de la Cadena 2014, 2015). And what emerged at the interface, rather than "the" entity or practice in question, was a mutual "redescription" (Strathern 1988) of each other's (Mariano's and mine) concepts, forms, or figures in ways that always exceeded each other, even as they also overlapped. Drawing from this ethnographic-conceptual experience, I propose to think Máxima's refusal to leave through the notion of property (and its relations) and also through what may be *not only* property and the relations (or lack thereof) that may emerge to make her (with-those-she-is). Considering both relations simultaneously, their mutual excesses may also be considered. I explain more below.

Concepts do their work in an ecology. They perform with the concepts they find themselves in the company of (Strathern 2011, 23)—and when Máxima practices her refusal to leave, "property" may emerge as a concept-multiple as she switches from becoming with "land" to legally defending herself vis-à-vis the corporation's attempt to evict her. The first, "becoming with land," exceeds the legal notion of property and emerges at its limit (i.e., when the legal concept *is not* anymore). "Refusing to leave" may be moti-vated by an ideological rejection of the mine's desire to destroy lagoons, and it may also be a practice that defies commensuration—it renders land unoc-cupiable by the market, for it is integrally occupied by and occupying "the woman who will not leave." This last phrase—which circulates mostly in oral commentary—indicates Máxima's inconceivable defiance to the mine and may also translate her agrammaticality: the enactment of a relation that modern property cannot sustain. This would include her capacity to become with the collective: the human guardians of the lagoons but also the other-than-human entities they guard. Intriguingly, her lawyer—also a woman and acquainted with the practices of the guardians of the lagoons—understands this and, with it, her own inability to *fully* translate into the legal language of property Máxima's insistence on staying. In one of the many interviews Máxima has given, she mentions that a "company man" (*un hombre de la compañía*) threatened her, saying, "A flea will never defeat an elephant."[18] Belying that refrain, "the woman who will not leave" has gone to trial and with the help of her lawyer has defeated the mining corporation on at least two occasions. Explaining these women's success, pundits in central news media emulate the "company man" and express their surprise in narratives that liken the fight to that of David against Goliath. Indeed, there is a public for this story; what is not public in this undoubtedly surprising story is that the concepts that the flea and the elephant (or David and Goliath) employ are both the same and *not only* the same.

Along with surprise, complexity is relentless in this story: Máxima's lawyer, a woman of impeccable professional ethics and astute professional practice, both trusts the veracity of the titles that represent the woman's ownership to the land and is convinced that the mine is using fraudulent tactics to discredit those documents—yet she also thinks that Máxima's will to stay on the land exceeds legal argumentation. In a recent work, Isabelle Stengers writes, "What is proper to every event is that it brings the future that will inherit from it into communication with a past narrated differently" (2015, 390). If we attend to Máxima's refusal to sell as an excess to modern property (rather than as a mining conflict that can be solved so that all can go back to normal), she may also be inscribing an event: she may be creating a refuge for life (including rocks and water and much more, for without them life is not) away from the destruction on which what currently passes for progress is predicated. She may be creating possibilities for an alternative future, one that, inheriting from Máxima's stubbornness to stay and defend life, would be able to narrate the past—that is, our present—in a different way.

A Hopeful Ending: Uncommoning Nature or a Commons through Divergence

Máxima's story, like those of the Mapuches, the Awajun Wampis, and runa-kuna, is a story from the anthropo-not-seen; while such stories seem to occur everywhere, the events are local. Told attending to place, the narratives may expose complexities that unsettle linear grammars and push concepts to their limits. Listened to with care, they reveal that the conflicts they narrate may include a disagreement that cannot find easy resolution because it exceeds the existing domain of the rule of law, namely, the conception and regulation of nature as resources. If we consider (rather than deny) the possibility of excess—namely, the assertion that nature is *not only* such, or that the materials that make it are *also* specific to place and may include humans—these stories could open thought and feeling to that which is *not only* what to our common senses *is*. The requirement for this opening may be a disposition to give equivocation a political chance. This means a disposition to consider that what *is* hegemonically—for example, nature (to continue with the same theme)—may also be other than nature even if it occupies the same space: not only a river, also a person; not only universal water, also local water; not only mountains, also earth beings; not only land, also Ixofijmogen.[19]

In the pages that follow, I conclude this intervention with a speculation about the composition of a political alliance that welcomes agreements that accept the possibility of equivocation, not agreements made across different viewpoints about the same world, but those made taking into consideration that the viewpoints may correspond to worlds that are *not only* the same. I speculate using the story of the guardians of the lagoons that Máxima's recalcitrance has made famous, and fruitfully hopeful. It illustrates Donna

FIGURE 1.1. Complex alliances against extractivism: The man driving the excavator says to the peasant family, "You are poor. If you sell your mountain and your lagoon to me, you will have money." The peasant family replies, "Once the money is spent, we will have neither mountain nor lagoon." The man responds, "Ignorant!!" *Diario La República* (Lima), July 16, 2012. Used by permission of artist Carlos Tovar Samanez, also known as Carlín.

Haraway's wish for stories "just big enough to gather up complexities and leave edges open for surprising new connections" (Haraway 2015, 160) to happen.

Confronted with the mining company's proposal to desiccate the lagoons, a heterogeneous network of environmentalists has backed the local guardians against the mining corporation. The cartoon I include here reflects the alliance: a participant in the alliance, the cartoon's author mocks the corporation's efforts to convince a rational peasant family who, confronted with the choice between finite money and long-lasting land, uses a subject and object grammar and economic benefit logic to reasonably choose the latter (figure 1.1). Similarly, through a global extension of this network, Máxima received the Goldman Environmental Prize, a highly important award honoring grassroots leaders.[20] These alliances are, however, complex. Occupying the same space (which "cannot be mapped in terms of a single set of three-dimensional coordinates"; Mol and Law 2002, 1), heterogeneous forms (universal nature, the environment, water that resists translation to H_2O, land that is object and not, entities that I am calling ecologized nature—or nature recalcitrant to universality) converge in the network through agreements that do not preclude differences. For example, in comparison to the cartoonist's depiction, the economic security of her family may not figure as definitely in Máxima's refusal to sell; yet they share a support for not selling.[21] Similarly, the interest that environmentalists and the guardians of the lagoons share—to defend nature, or the environment—may be not only the same interest: the locally ecologized nature of the guardians and the biologically defined nature of (global and national) environmental activists may indeed exceed each other as it is *not only* the same nature. However, both cases house the possibility for an agreement that, rather that converging on identical interests, would be underpinned by "uncommonalities": interests in common that are not the same interest. This agreement speaks of the possibility for an alternative alliance, one that along with coincidences may include the parties' constitutive divergence: they may converge without becoming the same. Such an agreement could include discussion about the one-world world as an ontological condition that participants in the alliance do not share homogeneously and that, consequently, may be a source of friction among them.[22]

Underpinned by terms that could alter politics as usual, this alliance would also house hope for a *commons* that does not require the division between universal nature and diversified humans. A commons constantly emerging from the uncommons as grounds for political negotiation of what (resulting from the latter) would become the interest in common, and thus the commons. This commons (always ephemeral and subject to change) would not be without uncommons: rather than (only) the expression of shared relations and stewardship of nature, this commons would (also) be the expression of a worlding of many worlds ecologically related across their constitutive divergence. As a practice of life that takes care of interests in common, without requiring that these be the same interest, the alliance between environmentalists and local guardians (of lagoons, rivers, forests) could engage in (and become through) a conversation that considers the hegemony of the ontological distribution of the world into universal nature and locally differentiated humans *without, however, considering such a distribution a requirement.* The alliance would thus express a confrontation with the agreement that made the anthropo-not-seen and would question the legitimacy of the war against those who disagree with that distribution. The partition of the world into diversified humans and homogeneous nature— or, rather, and more radically, the making of the world into one through the imposition of the homogeneity of such a partition—could become a matter of political concern. Thus, the ontological sameness that modern politics requires could be questioned, and along with it a novel consequence would be inaugurated: disagreement concerning ways of world making (i.e., ontological politics) could even take place *among those who share ontological sameness* (i.e., those who world in similar ways). Illustrative of this possibility is the disagreement between the mining corporation that wants to evict "the woman who does not want to leave" and the lawyer who defends her. The alliance between the two women is the other side of the same coin. In an alliance across worlds that are not only the same, what brings them together is an interest in common that is not the same interest: their interests mutually exceed each other's, as the two women converge in a complex notion of property—one that upholds their divergent ways of being with water, land, animals—to contend with the mine.[23]

Similar unexpected alliances may have emerged as extractivism, stimulated by the prices of minerals and neoliberal policies, became apparently unstoppable and accelerated the definition of nature as resources, which it also makes ubiquitous. The paradox could be that the ruthlessness of extractivism has made public collectives that oppose the (extractivist) destruction of who they are (and not only of nature) making alliances with environmentalists (for whom nature may be only nature). Extractivism is the trope through which the Anthropocene makes itself present in Latin America, and like on the planetary scale, it threatens with the destruction of what makes it possible, ending with the gradual annihilation of life itself. Seen through extractivism (including the opposition to it), the Anthropocene might be a historical moment of implosion, when the war against disobedient worlding practices turned against the world that waged it and, in so doing, also revealed the impossibility of the destruction of worlds that exceeded, first, the word of God and, later on, the word of the modern human—capitalist and socialist alike. Defending themselves against the current destruction, the collectives that exceed the divides between "human" and "non-human" have become visible, manifesting their excess. The resistance to the not-seen war erupts in public, excessive collectives asserting their being and demanding politics beyond the rights the state might (or might not) benevolently grant through culture. A far cry from being a "conflict as usual," their disagreement with the state may be about territorial sovereignty, *and not only* about that. It may express the public demand to allow in politics conditions of "no nature, no culture" (Strathern 1980) that have been historically denied being. The silence that cloaked the war against disobedient worlding practices may be coming to an end; their destruction (and the fight against it) can be ubiquitously seen on all types of screens. Paradoxically, the era of the Anthropocene may witness the historical end of the not-seen.

NOTES

I am grateful for comments by Judy Farquhar, Cristiana Giordano, Stefanie Graeter, John Law, Casper Bruun Jensen, and Brit Winthereik.

1. Contribution by Mia Mayixuan Li, September 29, 2016, http://www .rainforestfoundation.org/53-indigenous-leaders-in-perus-2009-baguazo-acquitted-of -all-charges/Rainforest Foundation.

2. Santiago Manuin Valera, "Red Cooperacción," April 16, 2014, http://www .cooperaccion.org.pe/noticias/10-noticias/2140-pronunciamiento-de-santiago-manuin -contra-la-peticion-de-cadena-perpetua-contra-su-persona.

3. Santiago Manuin Valera, "Red Cooperacción," April 16, 2014, http://www .cooperaccion.org.pe/noticias/10-noticias/2140-pronunciamiento-de-santiago-manuin -contra-la-peticion-de-cadena-perpetua-contra-su-persona.

4. Los Sucesos de Bagua, http://www.servindi.org/producciones/videos/13083. Also quoted in de la Cadena 2010, 363.

5. Servindi, Comunicación intercultural para un mundo más humano y diverso, "Para Perico La territorialidad no era sólo un concepto," Video Audio de Shapiom Noningo, January 29, 2016, http://www.servindi.org/actualidad-noticias-radioteca -videos/29/01/2016/para-perico-la-territorialidad-no-era-solo-un.

6. In a similar vein, Bruno Latour (2002, 25, 26, 27) conceptualizes these wars as "latent," "never declared," "considered simple police operations."

7. For example, Chuquicamata, a copper mine in Chile, extends over eight hundred hectares and has a depth of 1,250 meters (Gudynas 2015).

8. One of the greatest current fracking threats in South America is located in the Entre Ríos region of Argentina and the neighboring area of Uruguay, in the Paraná Chaco, where the extraction of shale oil and shale gas is planned. In Santiago Navarro and Renata Bessi, "Fracking Expands in Latin America Threatening to Contaminate World's Third Largest Aquifer," December 11, 2015, http://www.alternet.org/fracking /fracking-expands-latin-america-threatening-contaminate-worlds-third-largest -aquifer.

9. Antonio Caballero, "Miseria artificial," *Arcadia*, March 23, 2016, http://www .revistaarcadia.com/opinion/columnas/articulo/antonio-caballero-escribe-sobre-la -guajira-y-saqueo-a-los-indigenas-wayuu/47708.

10. Puerta E Red Eco, "Vaca Muerta una situación Urgente que no da para más," Argenpress, Info Prensa Argentina para todo el mundo, October 7, 2014, http://www .argenpress.info/2014/10/vaca-muerta-una-situacion-urgente-que.html.

11. "Un viaje a las entrañas de Vaca Muerta, el future energético del país," March 7, 2015, *Misiones Online*, http://misionesonline.net/2015/03/07/un-viaje-a-las-entranas -de-vaca-muerta-el-futuro-energetico-del-pais/.

12. I have explained this in other works. When persons live across more than one, less than many worlds, their practices may enact entities that are *not only* what they also are. For example, across the world of mining and the world of earth beings, the latter may emerge also as mountains and not only as earth beings (or vice versa of course.) See de la Cadena (2010) and (2015). John Law (2015) calls this the capacity for *both-and* (rather than *either-or*).

13. As runakuna and earth beings become together as place, they embody the materiality of human and geological bodies *and exceed it*. Their liveliness (see Tsing, this volume) is an intrarelation, a mutual enactment that does not depend on the human only as being such—only human—it is not a runakuna condition. Rather, closer to what Anna Tsing suggests could be a modern analytical mode of attention, runakuna *are* attuned to the ways of earth beings (which includes soil, water, pebbles, and rocks that are not only such) but also vice versa: they *are* together (and with plants and animals). And this differs from Tsing's proposal.

14. "Boundary object" is a term coined by Star and Griesemer (1989)—I thank Judy Farquhar for conversations that fed this paragraph.

15. See also Harvey and Knox (2015) for a similar description of an Andean Bartleby.

16. One article that portrays her as a manipulator is Ricardo Uceda, "El Pantanoso caso Chaupe," *La República*, February 24, 2015, http://larepublica.pe/24-02-2015/el -pantanoso-caso-chaupe.

17. Another example of a similar relational materiality: peasants in the Isthmus of Tehuantepec (Oaxaca, Mexico) have rejected the installation of windmills, which would transform the relationship between air, birds, ocean water, fish, and people (Howe and Boyer 2015).

18. Máxima Acuña, "Me dijeron: Una pulga nunca le va a ganar a un elefante," Mamágrande Films, posted October 16, 2013, 7 mins., https://www.youtube.com /watch?v=5dFm5JuUz1A.

19. "Divergence"—the final word of the subhead above—is a notion I borrow from Stengers (2005). It refers to the constitutive difference that makes practices what they are *and* as they connect across difference, even ontological difference.

20. Máxima Acuña, "Galardonada del Goldman Environmental Prize 2016 para Sur y Centroamérica" (Goldman Environmental Prize), April 19, 2016, 5.30 mins., http:// www.goldmanprize.org/recipient/maxima-acuna/.

21. For example, in a recent interview Máxima declared, "I'd rather not have money. My land makes me happy, money does not." Máxima Acuña interviewed by Joseph Zárate, *Revista Etiqueta Negra*, April 24, 2015, http://etiquetanegra.com.pe/articulos /maxima-acuna-la-dama-de-la-laguna-azul-versus-la-laguna-negra.

22. The argument that the one-world world is heterogeneously shared is one of the main ideas in Law (2015). What I add here is that the alliance houses the possibility for the discussion of this condition.

23. Penny Harvey (this volume) examines the vitality of none other than concrete, an exemplar of what a "material" might be, and using it to think with the material of "the woman who will not leave" may seem far-fetched. However, the politics of the guardians of the lagoons, in step with the invitation that this volume makes, compli-

cate distinctions between human and material politics. Thus, I want to propose an interpretation of the alliance between Máxima and her lawyer that is similar to Harvey's analysis of the vitality of concrete, which, she explains, is composed as its intrinsic components combine with conditions that extend beyond concrete. Analogously, the alliance between Máxima and her lawyer against the corporation takes into consideration the separation between humans and nature that the law requires; yet their nonseparation also needs to be seriously considered as an intrinsic component in the negotiation between the two women.

REFERENCES

Bebbington, Anthony. 2015. "Political Ecologies of Resource Extraction: Agendas pendientes." *European Review of Latin American and Caribbean Studies* 100 (December): 85–98.

de la Cadena, Marisol. 2010. "Indigenous Cosmopolitics in the Andes: Conceptual Reflections beyond 'Politics.'" *Cultural Anthropology* 25, no. 2: 334–370.

de la Cadena, Marisol. 2014. "Runa: Human but *Not Only.*" *HAU: Journal of Ethnographic Theory* 4, no. 2: 253–259.

de la Cadena, Marisol. 2015. *Earth Beings: Ecologies of Practice across Andean Worlds.* Durham, NC: Duke University Press.

Deleuze, Gilles. 1998. *Essays Critical and Clinical.* New York: Verso.

Deleuze, Gilles, and Félix Guattari. 1994. *What Is Philosophy?* New York: Columbia University Press.

Foucault, Michel. 2003. *"Society Must Be Defended": Lectures at the Collège de France 1975–1976.* New York: Picador.

Greene, Shane. 2009. "Making Old Histories New in the Peruvian Amazon." *Anthropology Now* 1, no. 3: 52–60.

Gudynas, Eduardo. 2015. *Extractivismos: Ecología, economía y política de un modo de entender el desarrollo y la naturaleza.* La Paz: Centro de Documentación e Información Bolivia.

Haraway, Donna. 2015. "Anthropocene, Capitalocene, Plantationocene, Chthulucene: Making Kin." *Environmental Humanities* 6: 159–165.

Harvey, Penelope, and Hannah Knox. 2015. *Roads: An Anthropology of Infrastructure and Expertise.* Ithaca, NY: Cornell University Press.

Howe, C., and D. Boyer. 2015. "Aeolian Politics." *Distinktion: Journal of Social Theory* 16, no. 1: 31–48. http://dx.doi.org/10.1080/1600910X.2015.1022564.

Kuletz, Valerie. 1998. *The Tainted Desert: Environmental and Social Ruin in the American West.* New York: Routledge.

Latour, Bruno. 2002. *War of the Worlds: What about Peace?* Chicago: Prickly Paradigm Press.

Law, John. 2015. "What's Wrong with a One-World World?" *Distinktion: Scandinavian Journal of Social Theory* 16, no. 1: 126–139.

Melville, Herman. (1853) 2007. *Bartleby, the Scrivener: A Story of Wall Street.* London: Hesperus.

Mol, Annemarie, and John Law. 2002. *Complexities: Social Studies of Knowledge Practices.* Durham, NC: Duke University Press.

Rancière, Jacques. 1999. *Disagreement: Politics and Philosophy.* Minneapolis: University of Minnesota Press.

Serres, Michel. 2011. *Malfeasance: Appropriation through Pollution?* Stanford, CA: Stanford University Press.

Star, Susan Leigh, and James Griesemer. 1989. "Institutional Ecology, 'Translations,' and Boundary Objects: Amateurs and Professionals in Berkeley's Museum of Vertebrate Zoology, 1907–39." *Social Studies of Science* 19, no. 4: 387–420.

Stengers, Isabelle. 2005. "Introductory Notes on an Ecology of Practices." *Cultural Studies Review* 11, no. 1: 183–196.

Stengers, Isabelle. 2015. *In Catastrophic Times: Resisting the Coming Barbarism.* London: Open Humanities Press/Meson Press. http://openhumanitiespress.org/books/titles/in-catastrophic-times.

Strathern, Marilyn. 1980. "No Nature, No Culture: The Hagen Case." In *Nature, Culture and Gender*, edited by Carol MacCormack and Marilyn Strathern, 174–221. Cambridge: Cambridge University Press.

Strathern, Marilyn. 1988. *The Gender of the Gift: Problems with Women and Problems with Society in Melanesia Studies in Melanesian Anthropology.* Berkeley: University of California Press.

Strathern, Marilyn. 2011. "Sharing, Stealing and Borrowing Simultaneously." In *Ownership and Appropriation*, edited by Veronica Strang and Mark Busse, 23–42. Oxford: Berg.

Svampa, Maristella. 2015. "Commodities Consensus: Neoextractivism and Enclosure of the Commons in Latin America." *South Atlantic Quarterly* 114, no. 1: 65–82.

Viveiros de Castro, Eduardo. 2004. "Perspectival Anthropology and the Method of Controlled Equivocation." *Tipití: Journal of the Society for the Anthropology of Lowland South America* 2, no. 1: 3–22.

Warner, Michael. 2005. *Publics and Counterpublics.* Brooklyn, NY: Zone Books.

2. Contemporary Capitalism and Dominican New Yorkers' Livery-Cab Bases

A TAXI STORY

Christian Krohn-Hansen

How might anthropologists usefully conceptualize the structure of contemporary capitalism? In an article from 2009, "Supply Chains and the Human Condition," Anna Tsing has theorized supply chains as a model for understanding both the "bigness" and the inherent heterogeneity of global capitalism. In sharp contrast with theories of growing capitalist homogeneity, she argues that cultural diversity is structurally central to capitalism, and not an epiphenomenon. She develops her argument by putting to use a form of anthropology of labor.[1]

In this chapter, I draw on Tsing's views at the same time as I seek to discuss and develop a couple of her central ideas. There are two elements of her argument that particularly interest me. First, she underscores, as mentioned, that heterogeneity is part and parcel of contemporary capitalism. She summarizes this in the following manner: today's supply chain capitalism utilizes diverse social-economic niches across the world through which goods and services can be produced more cheaply. Such niches are reproduced in performances of cultural identity. Such performances, in turn, are necessarily given form by the character of the workforce—the workers' gender, race, nationality, religion, and so on—and are nowadays constantly encouraged by new (mystifying) imageries of work or labor power in which making a living appears not so much as "work" but, instead, as entrepreneurship or management, or, quite simply, as a search for independence and freedom, or the construction of space for self-making. In brief, difference is completely inherent in the mobilization and employment of labor, resources, and capital, or the capitalist process.

Second, against the background of these views, Tsing discusses a fundamental question: if capitalism uses diversity, does that mean that it is in control of diversity at a global scale? Tsing does not claim that cultural values and imageries shape diverse capitalisms. Instead, her argument is that capitalism makes use of and helps give form to diversity. But its power is not absolute. On the contrary, she maintains that because diversity is both "inside" and "outside" the capitalist configuration, it constantly "both makes supply chain capitalism work *and*, upon occasion, gets in its way," creating and sustaining unforeseen effects or working against it (2009, 171; emphasis added). Today's supply chains entail and reproduce grotesque forms of exploitation and massive inequalities in wealth and power. But even the most exploitative conditions also manifest sources of hope. As she puts it, creative alternatives and new projects of identity can appear "from within the interstices between capitalist and noncapitalist spaces. . . . There are possibilities for a more livable world here as well as perils" (172).

Her attempt to theorize capitalism is based on reading but seems above all to be an outcome of her ethnographic work among a group of independent mushroom pickers in forests in central Oregon. The North American matsutake is harvested in Canada and the northwestern United States for export to Japan (Tsing 2015). At first sight, it may appear far-fetched to seek to model the structure of capitalism based on fieldwork among a number of pickers of a wild mushroom in some forests. For my part, I will be equally bold. Most of what I shall present and maintain here is a result of fieldwork undertaken among Dominican immigrants who support themselves through working as livery-cab drivers in New York City. Twentieth-century anthropologists mostly worked in this manner to produce their understandings, through forms of strongly localized participation and observation, and as I wish to demonstrate, we have an efficient tool, namely, the ethnographic examination of labor mobilization and work activities. The following includes two parts, which discuss more closely each of the two lines of reasoning sketched above.[2]

Supply chains are not the only contemporary form of capitalism—but they offer a window or a model for conceptualizing central features of the human condition today. Such chains connect putatively independent economic agents, rendering it possible for commodity processes to extend across the world.[3] As said, Tsing's focus is on the mobilization of labor. Real labor is never abstract; on the contrary, all work is concrete right through. If we look at how actual labor forms are produced, it is easy to see that these are created and sustained with (are unthinkable without) the diverse constituents of culture, including imagination and hope. To mobilize labor power, or quite simply to perform work, is to simultaneously contribute to the production of identities and self-understandings. With this I agree. In brief, I support Tsing when she claims that we must recognize the full implications of maintaining that all labor forms are inextricably associated with the production of understandings of self and other, differences. But I think at the same time that it is necessary to add something to what she invites us to think with and about. We ought to seek to dig deeper into the issue of *why* it apparently has been so common, so easy, to go on operating with capital and labor as abstract figures in attempts to theorize capitalism.

An important reason that capital and labor survive and thrive as supposedly universal categories has to do with the fact that large parts of social theory for a long time have operated with a little-problematized, supposedly universal motivation: "interest." Modern economic (rational) actions in general and forms of moneymaking in particular are interest-driven activities—a long series of authors from Max Weber to Talcott Parsons have underscored this for us. What interest is, beyond not being influenced by feelings, is most often fairly taken for granted, fairly unspecified. Interest has been produced as an undifferentiated thing. Capitalists and laborers are thought to work based on their noncultural, nonemotional interests. One of the best attempts to historicize and thereby deconstruct hegemonic thinking about interest and interests that I know of is found in Albert O. Hirschman's *The Passions and the Interests: Political Arguments for Capitalism before Its Triumph* ([1977] 2013). His story is replete with historical irony. He asks, How did moneymaking pursuits become honorable at some point in the period from the sixteenth to the eighteenth century after having stood condemned or stigmatized as avarice for centuries past? European thinkers in the sixteenth and seventeenth centuries saw humans as hopelessly dominated by their passions. Thus, the affair of state (or political problem) arose of how to control these passions. While various methods were suggested, one gained ground. This entailed seeking and identifying a strong countervailing passion. Only a passion could secure the taming of the unreasonable, socially destructive passions. Paradoxically, this countervailing passion was the lust for money: avarice. This desire had been called the deadliest of all sins in the Middle Ages (Hirschman [1977] 2013, 41). As a countervailing force, though, this passion, avarice, was given a new name, that is, (commercial) "interests." Subsequently the semantic changes continued, and the term "interest" was cleared of any affective content. What was "lust of wealth" in Niccolò di Bernando dei Machiavelli's and Thomas Hobbes's day has become "rational self-interest." No matter how one chooses to consider the nuances of Hirschman's work, he demonstrates convincingly how completely historical and how little self-evident the concept of interest is.

We need a different thinking about motivation. As I see it, we ought to seek to combine investigations of labor regimes with a more general preoccupation with the role of affective forces in social life. I am influenced by a range of various sources—from Hirschman, to the anthropological concern with feelings and emotions that emerged in the 1980s and the 1990s, to parts of the more recent affective turn in the social sciences (Hirschman [1977] 2013; Williams 1977; Rosaldo 1984; Yanagisako 2002; Mazzarella 2009; Richard and Rudnyckyj 2009; Freeman 2014; Weston 2017). I understand the interest in "sentiments" or "the affective" as a wide, flexible focus. I use these terms to attempt to get away from unproductive divisions between thought and feelings. Affective forms include beliefs, emotional tendencies, and embodied dispositions. The category "the affective" also includes notions of identity. The affective is thoroughly historical and socially produced. Under particular historical conditions, affective forms foment particular economic and social moves. Another way of formulating this is to say that affective ideas and ideas with affect work as forces of production. When Karl Marx used the term *Produktivkräfte*, or "forces of production," Sylvia Yanagisako (2002, 11) insists, he was referring mainly to "human capacities"—and not primarily to things outside human beings.[4] Human capacities include skills, knowledge, and not least sentiments, and they enable, shape, and constrain specific forms of material production.

Let me sum up so far. Two ideas ought to shape our thinking. First, it is necessary to acknowledge that all real forms of work mobilization under capitalism are concrete—they are therefore by definition permeated by particular forms of identity making (performances of gender, age, race, nationality, religion, and class). Second, if we wish to understand labor forms, we need to study the affective ideas and forces that incite, energize, and shape specific forms of work (with their accompanying configurations of identity production). *Why* is this of significance? My answer is that I think it is with this double focus—on labor mobilizations as shot through with constructions of ideas about self and other, *and* on socially produced forms of affective life as forces of production—that we best can see and maintain Tsing's basic point, that diversity *is* entirely inherent in the structure of today's capitalism.

In the remainder of this section, I seek to substantiate and develop these views with the aid of an ethnography of small businesses and labor forms among Dominican immigrants who support themselves through working as livery-cab drivers in northern Manhattan and in the southwestern parts of the Bronx. Large-scale emigration from the Dominican Republic began in the early 1960s, with most Dominicans settling in New York City. Since then the growth of the city's Dominican population has been staggering, and they now account for around 7 percent of the total populace. Here I shall be content to look at only a part (although an important part) of this history; I will discuss the history of the many Dominicans who ended up in the city's taxi industry. According to the US Census Bureau, in 2007 more than two-thirds of the city's Dominicans lived in the Bronx (38.9 percent) and Manhattan (28.8 percent). Most Dominicans residing in Manhattan live north of the Harlem area, that is, in Washington Heights and Inwood, and most Dominicans residing in the Bronx are found in the borough's southern and western parts.

In the 1960s and 1970s, a significant number of the Dominicans in New York were factory workers, employed in light manufacturing (Grasmuck and Pessar 1991). But during the 1980s, Dominican immigrants in the manufacturing industry declined. In 1979, 49 percent of all Dominican workers were engaged in manufacturing. In 1989, only ten years later, this number had declined to 26 percent (Hernández, Rivera-Batiz, and Agodini 1995, 42–45). After that, the figure continued to drop. But more and more Dominican New Yorkers were found in other parts of the economy. An increasing number found jobs in the service sector, and more became self-employed. In 1991 around twenty thousand businesses in the city were owned and operated by Dominican immigrants. Dominicans in particular owned cab operations, grocery stores, restaurants, travel agencies, beauty parlors, and sweatshops (Portes and Guarnizo 1991, 61).

When I conducted my field research from 2002 to 2008, the company Uber had not yet been established, and New York had three categories of taxis: the familiar yellow taxis that patrol Manhattan's most central areas, black cars, and livery cabs.[5] Black-car services are mostly used by corporate clients. Livery cabs offer most of the taxi services outside Manhattan's central and lower areas—in northern Manhattan, the Bronx, Queens, and Brooklyn. In Upper Manhattan and the Bronx, Dominicans completely dominate the industry: a majority of the drivers are Dominican, and Dominicans own the livery-car companies. While a few of these Dominican-controlled livery-car services are individually owned, the great majority are cooperatives. Each was founded, and is owned and run, by a group of Dominican drivers together. Owners and drivers call their company *la base*, or "the base." The group of owners is called *los socios*, or "the owners" or "the partners." The number of socios varies—from as many as sixty to eighty to only ten or twelve. Most socios themselves work as livery-cab drivers. In addition, each base has a number of drivers who belong to the company without being socios. Large Dominican-owned bases include three hundred to four hundred socios and drivers.

In the 1960s New York's yellow cabs, the majority of the city's legal taxis at the time, hardly drove outside the "nice" parts of Manhattan. African Americans, Puerto Ricans, and immigrants started to drive legal and illegal cabs where the yellows would not venture, in the city's lower-income neighborhoods. Eventually, there were so many unlicensed, or "gypsy," cabs that the city enacted new ordinances in the 1980s to bring the unregulated cars under its control. In 1987, when the livery-car services were required to register with the New York City Taxi and Limousine Commission, there were almost forty thousand livery and gypsy cabs (compared with 11,700 yellow taxis) (Schaller Consulting 2006, 30; Sanjek 1998, 187).

I asked veteran Dominican drivers in Washington Heights how the Upper Manhattan livery industry was created. They said that the founders and pioneers had been Puerto Rican. In the late 1970s and early 1980s, Dominican drivers entered a group of Puerto Rican–owned bases. For a few years, Puerto Ricans and Dominicans built the industry together.[6] Subsequently, it came to be dominated entirely by Dominicans, while the number of bases, most of them cooperatives, skyrocketed.

In New York, liveries were a source of contention from their birth. While a number of elected officials defended them as community businesses providing needed transportation, the yellow-taxi industry attacked them as illegal and unsafe and claimed they were encroaching on yellow taxis' rights. More than other groups of Dominican immigrants with whom I worked, the community of Dominican base owners and drivers embodied a history of struggle and resistance. From the beginning, livery drivers were on the outside; not only were they involved in a day-to-day battle to make money, but many also took part in a larger struggle. Base owners and drivers were forced to endure, and face, what they viewed as an unfair and hostile environment: representatives of the police, the Taxi and Limousine Commission, the yellow-taxi industry, and the cab-insurance industry. These forces, in the livery industry's eyes, sought to prevent base owners and drivers from exercising a basic right: to survive and provide food, clothes, and a home for one's family.

In Dominican Upper Manhattan, many explained that people chose to become livery drivers because they did not want to work in a factory. Working in a factory—in New Jersey or elsewhere—left people with too little money and too little freedom. A man who drove a livery cab was basically his own boss. He owned or rented his own vehicle but paid a weekly sum, around $50, to his base for being able to work—but he could work when he wanted to, and he could travel back to the island, stay for two or more months if he needed to, and thereafter return to his work in New York. When a livery driver manages to earn enough, though, it is primarily because he works a lot. Most drivers made between $450 and $600 a week—provided that they worked six or seven ten- or twelve-hour shifts. A factory worker or an employee in a supermarket or a restaurant made significantly less. Nearly all Dominican base owners and drivers are men. But there are exceptions. A few Dominican immigrant women work as livery drivers.

This niche in today's New York economy has been, and continues to be, reproduced through a myriad of practices that in reality are performances of identity. Put differently, work mobilization here has depended on the practice of migrant and citizenship status, ethnicity, and gender. The language in the Dominican bases was (Dominican) Spanish. In addition, Dominican base owners and drivers played games—softball, basketball, or dominos—together. The glue that held the bases together was friendship relations between groups of Dominican immigrant men. Silvio, a Dominican in his mid-forties, headed a large base in Upper Manhattan. One day early in my fieldwork, he tried to explain to me how bases are created. His generalized description went like this: two or three friends who are all livery drivers have lunch together or go to the same Dominican restaurant and start talking about establishing or purchasing a base together. They invite other drivers they know to join them. Each of the two or three friends recruits three or four people. If the group includes around ten drivers, they may contact a lawyer. With the aid of the lawyer, they manage to have the necessary paperwork done. Above all, they need the necessary licenses. Let us suppose that they are twenty men, Silvio said. Each of the twenty becomes a socio by buying a share, perhaps for $1,000. The capital is used to rent a location and establish the base station with offices, phones, and the rest of what is needed to start working.

The Dominican bases have been built through vernacular thinking about masculinity—and this comes from the island, though migration brings changes. For instance, an important image of masculinity on the island is that of the *hombre independiente*, the free, autonomous man. This ideal says that a man should be able to make his own decisions. Compared to a factory worker or other wage earner, a man who works as a livery driver is "free." Dominican livery drivers call themselves *independientes*, or "independent contractors." Another set of central ideas revolves around an image of the man as one who should *compartir*—spend time and share resources with his male comrades. Closely linked to this is the image of a man as one who dedicates himself to politics (in a wide sense of the word) and/or sports. Politics and sports and games are Dominican passions. The country's political processes—and sports activities—are based on patronage or mutual exchanges between friends. It is easy to see that these ideals have been important in New York also. The bases have provided Dominican immigrant men with an arena for the production of comradeship among men. But there is more. These systems of reciprocity have not just made it possible for many to make a living; they have also made it feasible for many to take part in sports and games and political life—quite simply, to be a man.

Many in the bases showed a striking discipline. They worked six or seven days a week, often between nine and twelve hours a day. Most of those I met in the bases believed that a man typically worked harder in New York than on the island. One consequence is that many drivers have less time to spend on their male friends, compared to (urban and rural) working-class men on the island. As an example of this type of self-discipline, one man I knew who was keen on softball and on partying after a game always drove some extra hours the day before he played, so that he did not lose work or money.

In this whole history, we can see the products of a particular set of affective ideas and ideas with affect that have worked as forces of production. Being able to work and spend time with other Dominicans, speak the mother tongue, eat Dominican meals—all this arouses and represents feelings just as much as thoughts and images. Dominican immigrants in Washington Heights felt Dominican. Take Miguel, for example, a livery driver around forty who had been living in New York for fourteen years. Asked how he saw himself, he said, "Well, I'm Dominican. In my view, a person's nationality doesn't change a bit depending on where one lives. You, if you live here, you have to comply with the laws of the United States. What happens? I'm a Dominican, because I feel Dominican—[but] I live here."

The same is true for the powerful Dominican myths of what it means (and should mean) to be a man. Being sufficiently *independiente* (that is, being one's own boss) and being able to compartir are sentiments, passions, and have, in brief, a strongly mobilizing emotional dimension. The desire to be a man is, in the last instance, a desire to feel personal dignity, self-respect (see, in addition, Ferguson 2013).

The Dominican livery drivers' activities form part of New York's service production. But in what ways are the Dominican bases with their practices an integral part of the larger order that creates and sustains enormous economic inequality?

The US capitalist regime has been, and remains, based on granting cheap labor to capital; it achieves this by various means. On one hand, the legal minimum wage has been kept extremely low.[7] On the other hand, the United States guarantees cheap labor by securing and accepting streams of undocumented and documented poor migrant workers and by failing to provide an indirect wage—in other words, by not offering a solid welfare net—and by engaging in a massive outsourcing of risk. The Dominican livery bases and their services must be understood as incorporated into a much wider network of income-producing activities, survival strategies, and work-related patterns in those parts of the city that David Harvey in his *A Brief History of Neoliberalism* (2005) has chosen to call working-class and ethnic-immigrant New York.[8] These cab operations offer transportation services in neighborhoods where most lack money but nevertheless need to go to work, travel to a hospital, see to it that their son or daughter gets from home to school and back home safely, and so on. People in these parts of the city depend on the livery-car services to be able to function, work, and live.

Much of the Dominican livery drivers' labor has the character of self-exploitation. They have become their own bosses but are forced to work long hours. If a driver needs money badly, he can get some by deciding to drive particularly long shifts. As one man explained, a driver may go out determined to make $200. He does not stop driving until he has reached his goal, even if he has to work twenty hours before the job is done. Some do this. But as the same man acknowledged, few can do this more than occasionally; it is too exhausting. The self-exploitation has been shaped by a hybrid set of cultural, affective forces. The drivers' will to work has, as said, been a product of, among other things, the celebrated popular Dominican desire to be able to be sufficiently independent. But their will to work has also found resonance in the powerful, neoliberal American myths that strongly value and encourage personal economic autonomy, entrepreneurship, and liberty.

Two influential authors on the connections between contemporary capitalism and affect are Michael Hardt and Antonio Negri. These theorists maintain that the processes of economic restructuration that have been in course since at least the mid-1970s have placed "immaterial labor," and especially "affective labor," in a role that not only directly produces economic value but also is at the very top of the hierarchy of laboring forms. Immaterial labor has, the argument goes, assumed a dominant position with respect to the other forms of work in the global capitalist economy (Hardt 1999, 2005; Hardt and Negri 2000). Let me be clear. The perspective that I seek to convey here differs from that of these two authors in two significant ways.

The first important difference has to do with our understanding of the part played by affective forms. Since the production of services results in no durable good, Hardt and Negri choose to define the work involved in this production as immaterial labor—that is, labor that creates an immaterial good, such as a service, knowledge, or feeling. Today, they maintain, affective work (in the production of health services, in the culture and entertainment industries, etcetera) is economically of enormous and increasing significance. The products of affective labor are intangible, they claim: a feeling, a relief, well-being, excitement—even a sense of belonging or community. What is new, they insist, is the degree to which affective work is now directly productive of profit and the degree to which it has captured wide parts of the economy. But as I see it, their use of the categories "immaterial labor" and "affective labor" is problematic and misleading (see also Yanagisako 2012; Bear et al. 2015). It leaves an impression that only *some* forms of labor are material—and that there are some historical and contemporary labor forms that have a decisive component in the form of affect, while there are others that do not have this. It contributes, in brief, to a reproduction of veiling dichotomies—between material and immaterial labor forms, and between industrial labor (and/or agricultural labor, informal labor, and so on) and affective labor. Instead, my own view is as follows: all labor forms have a crucial affective component. Sentiments have *always* been basic forces of production—in all economic systems, and from the global capitalist system's inception. Historically specific affective forms have always helped to constitute and drive the production activity of concrete producers and laborers.

The second important point concerns our understanding of the relationship between capitalism and diversity. Hardt and Negri tell a large-scale history of capitalist changes—and convey hope. Their story of empire expresses not only that profound political change is imperative but also that such change is possible. The problem is that their story draws a picture of global capitalism as a far more uniform and homogenizing historical process than it is; in other words, their history shows little interest in, and consequently silences, one of capitalism's most central characteristics, its inherent variety.

Capitalism and Politics

Tsing argues that cultural diversity is both inside *and* outside capitalism—and that precisely because capitalism is made, remade, and transformed in, and through, a diversity that is both inside and outside it, capitalism lacks a form of constraining force or power. Global capitalism makes use of differences—but its power isn't absolute, and it isn't in control of diversity. On the contrary, she maintains that because the cultural diversity is not completely created by capitalists or employers, "it offers a wealth of resources, for better or worse, that workers use without considering the best interests of their employers"—and that creative alternatives and new projects of identity can emerge from within the interstices and the tensions "between capitalist and noncapitalist spaces" (2009, 171, 172).

This perspective is one I share. But which possibilities for a more livable world, which alternatives, and which dangers might we trace if we choose to leave the most abstract level of discussion? Might we comprehend more of contemporary capitalism's power over diversity through continuing to examine the history of New York's Dominican-controlled car services? In the following, I look at the conditions for creating and building what Sian Lazar (2008, 178) has described as "neoliberal collectivities"—or forms of mutual help among groups of workers, or the poor, in the era of neoliberalism. The question is, what kinds of creative survival strategies and what kinds of limitations does the Dominican collectively owned base embody? To provide answers, it is necessary to first explain more about the microsociology of the bases.

In most bases, there is an annual election in which the partners elect the base's board and leadership for the next year. Two of the socios are elected base president and vice president. In addition, they elect a treasurer, an auditor, and a *presidente del departamento de disciplina*, or "president of the base's internal discipline"; the latter is responsible for seeing to it that the base's particular rules are followed by the partners and drivers. The base president manages and runs the entity's commercial and other operations on a day-to-day basis. Bases rent a small commercial site that functions as the base station. In the base station, one finds the president, one or two secretaries, dispatchers, and a few drivers who have stopped by on an errand or for a chat. Legally, livery-cab drivers are not allowed to pick up passengers who hail them on the street but can only respond to telephone calls to a licensed dispatch service or livery-car service. Yet, in practice, they cruise for street hails. The president, secretaries, and dispatchers are paid salaries. A base does not own vehicles. Instead, each driver is responsible for obtaining access to a vehicle; each owns or rents the car used as a cab.

Each week, the drivers pay a fixed sum to their base. The money is used to run the base and is regarded by the base and the drivers as payment for the base's product or commodity: the right to respond to telephone calls to the base station. A customer who calls the base is connected with one of the drivers. The passenger pays in cash, and the whole payment belongs to the driver. This system means that a base's income is limited. Any surplus has to be divided among all the socios. Bases that operate as cooperatives are, therefore, essentially a means. The goal is to make it possible for each driver affiliated with the base to produce a sufficient livelihood.

The Dominican car services reproduce many of the forms of voluntary associations formed by migrants in New York (Sánchez Korrol 1994, 131–166; Jones-Correa 1998, 132–136), including Dominicans, who have created an impressive number of voluntary associations in the city (Georges 1984; Torres-Saillant and Hernández 1998, 80–85). Dominicans call these associations *clubes*, or "clubs." The Dominican Republic has for a long time had an enormous number of clubs. While some have been formed with a political purpose, most have mainly had social, cultural, or recreational aims.

Dominican clubs in New York have a recognizable structure with common organizational features that have been imitated and adapted in the Dominican collectively owned car services. Dominican clubs in the city share some features. (1) They usually begin as networks of friends, acquaintances, and families. (2) After a club has been founded, the members are registered. The members are called *socios*, and they pay a small registration fee. Thereafter, each socio pays a certain amount—often a monthly sum—to the club. (3) With the aid of the money the club receives from its socios, it rents a space where the socios meet and cultivate sports or other activities and organize ceremonies, fiestas, and such for the socios' families and others. (4) The club is founded by a group, not one person, and is also administered by a group.

Each year, or every two years, the club's socios elect a board; this is headed by a president and also includes a vice president, a treasurer, a president of the club's internal discipline, and other positions.

This overlap in organizational forms is not strange, however. The heart of the Dominican immigrant club is friendship, and this also applies to the typical Dominican-owned car service. Like most of the clubs, the car services remain short of money and are maintained and energized by networks of relatives, friends, and acquaintances.

A large proportion of the Dominican bases appeared during the 1980s and 1990s. They were built to run a car-service operation, and their sole source of income was what the drivers paid to the base each week. Yet since the early or mid-1990s, a growing number of these enterprises have begun to change somewhat. Some of the bases now manage more than one source of income. A few have become property owners. Others have established businesses, such as a car-repair shop, a coffee shop, or a small multiservice agency. The motives behind this economic diversification have been complex: in some cases, the socios have mainly sought to increase the base's income; in others, they have wanted to spread or reduce risk. This diversification has produced a certain differentiation. A few have managed to strengthen their economic position. But the vast majority remain either wholly or almost wholly dependent on the weekly sums paid by the drivers.

Dominican drivers often referred to their base as *la compañía*, or "the company," and as one driver once put it, "the point of the company is, like in any company, the work," or making money. But as both this driver and the rest of those I met in the Dominican livery community acknowledged, la compañía is, nonetheless, also about something more than making a living. As the same driver explained to me, "The point is the work, but, well, we consist of various parts. . . . Me, for example, I've always had a passion for sports." He went on to describe how being part of a base and working as a livery driver had made it possible for him to continue to cultivate his passion. In the base, he and other drivers played softball and basketball regularly and organized and participated in tournaments. Sometimes he and his teammates from the base traveled to a city like Boston or Miami to meet another Dominican team or a team composed of Puerto Ricans or Cubans. Or they met a team on the island; as he reiterated, he loved this. It formed an important part not only of his everyday routines but also of his feeling of belonging.

The Dominican car service resembles a "total" phenomenon (in the Maussian, or classic anthropological sense of this expression; Mauss 1923–

1924). Just like Dominican clubs, Dominican car services organize sports, social gatherings, and picnics. And just like the voluntary associations, the bases have political functions. These cab operations with their total arrangements and processes are both inside and outside of contemporary global capitalism. Or, better put, perhaps, the total stuff that they contain, embody, and articulate is both capitalist *and* noncapitalist. The car services make capitalist processes possible; in this sense, they are capitalist. But many of the bases' processes and forms have little to do with what we often associate with capitalism's spirit or discipline, and in this sense the bases, or these sites, are noncapitalist.[9] The capitalist logic isn't in full control of them. In sum, these outcomes of entrepreneurship, these collectively operated cab operations, have meant alternative roads to work, livelihood, and forms of (limited) personal freedom, and have offered new sites for cultural and political production and experiences of dignity. The activities in the bases have helped build and sustain a (male) popular New York City Dominican, or one might say Dominican American, identity. Many of the Dominican bases have joined forces and protested and struggled politically together. Between 1998 and 2002, New York's livery industry saw the appearance of two new interest organizations that quickly established themselves as the most important in the business. While most of the members of the New York State Federation of Taxi Drivers were Dominican drivers who belonged to bases in the Bronx and Brooklyn, the New York City For-Hire Base Group was almost exclusively based in Dominican Upper Manhattan. With these organizations, New York's Dominican and other livery drivers strengthened their political position; they managed more than before to make themselves heard (in the press, in political processes and negotiations, and elsewhere)—in brief, they came to a greater extent to constitute a voice in the city.

Many Dominican livery drivers have a wife or partner—and bilingual children who go to public schools in Upper Manhattan, the Bronx, Queens, or Brooklyn. In a way, this typically makes their economic and social situation more vulnerable, more precarious. But the family situation may also offer hope. Silvio, the base president in Washington Heights whom I mentioned previously, had five children. At the time of the fieldwork, his oldest son had finished high school and had landed a good job with the communications company Verizon. The four others were still in school.

But there is no reason to fantasize or be naive. From a form of radical or leftist, not to say anticapitalist, perspective, these Dominican bases have limitations. These entities do not resemble the more or less socialist-inspired cooperatives or collectivities that existed in many places in the 1970s. Rather, they look like products of sentiments and modes of thinking that in those days were often rejected as those of petits bourgeois. As said, the base is the means; the goal is that each socio can be economically independent through running his or her own business.

The cases of a couple of the bases, Seaman and High Class, are instructive. These bases had bought property. When I carried out the fieldwork, both dreamed of being able to assist their socios, or some of them, in obtaining apartments, and perhaps small businesses, in the same tenements (in a part of the Bronx). Friendship continued to serve as the idiom for their activities and projects, even after the base had capitalized and improved its economic standing—but so did the wish for private property, capitalist success, and individual mobility.

Let us briefly look at the story of Seaman. Seaman was founded by a hundred drivers in the late 1980s; each of them paid $300. The base station is located in a six-story tenement in the northernmost part of Manhattan. At first, the socios paid rent. Subsequently, Seaman bought the entire building sometime in the first half of the 1990s. The socios financed the purchase by means of a mortgage. After becoming the owners of the building, the partners no longer had to pay rent.

At the time of the fieldwork, Seaman consisted of three firms—Seaman Radio Dispatcher (or the base), Seaman Realty, and Seaman Mechanical Services. All three were controlled by the socios and were administered by the base's president. Seaman Realty, a property firm, had been created when the socios bought a second building, this time in the Bronx. In this building, they established a car-repair shop. To run this, they founded Seaman Mechanical Services. Seaman Realty managed the base's buildings. In the Bronx, Seaman had tenants, for example, other immigrants who operated small businesses. In northern Manhattan, the socios had invested a significant sum in the base's offices. On the building's second floor, they had just opened a hall for ceremonies, fiestas, and seminars. The hall could be rented.

Of Seaman's (at the time) forty-five socios, about twenty continued to drive a livery cab for the base. The others had different jobs. Four had studied and later moved back to Santo Domingo, where they now worked for the Dominican state; they remained socios. Many of the others had obtained their own small businesses in New York; a few had become owners of repair shops, and others ran parking lots. When a socio bought his own business, the base assisted him in obtaining a bank loan by helping him with the documents and application.

The base had just sent off an application to New York City's authorities. Seaman wanted to purchase four or five buildings in the Bronx. The buildings were owned by the city but were abandoned and dilapidated. The base offered to buy them but also demanded that the city spend money on the buildings' remodeling and restoration. The goal was to offer apartments in the buildings to socios and others and to hire out space for small-business development.

The bases mirror and incorporate hierarchies. Some help to reproduce exploitation. Most bases have hired one or two secretaries—usually women, often Dominican immigrants in their twenties or thirties. The secretaries receive the drivers' weekly payments, write letters and create certificates, and take part in the base's ongoing administration. Silvio's base needed a new secretary and hired Dabril, a single mother in her thirties. She had moved from the Dominican capital to New York twelve years earlier. Before she left, she had studied medicine for a year and a half. In New York, she had worked for a number of years in a doctor's office. When she was offered the job in Silvio's base, she had been unemployed for over a year but had just started to study business administration at Baruch College. Dabril and the other secretaries worked from nine to five, five days a week. Her payment was so miserable that it embarrassed her. She would not tell me what the base paid her, only that her wage was low. She hoped for an increase after a while; meanwhile, she tried to do her best.

These Dominican car services have been, and continue to be, the outcome of a number of poor migrants' entrepreneurship and forms of friendship and solidarity. They have created alternative sources of income—and have provided sites for the production of belonging and a male, popular New York City Dominican/US Latino identity that were unavailable through other, more conventional types of work and employment. The existence of the bases has been contested, and base owners and drivers have therefore constantly acted, protested, advanced demands, and struggled politically. In the 1980s and 1990s, their voice was like a cry in the desert. Since then, they have strengthened their political position in the city a little.

But considered as political voices and forces, the bases have clear circumscriptions. These Dominican migrants are not particularly radical. Their operations and activities have created a form of collectivities. But these—and their two interest organizations, the federation and the New York City For-Hire Base Group—work politically in close dialogue with representatives of the American establishment; large parts of their political work have been carried out in cooperation with a number of New York's elected officials (members of the city council and state assembly), mostly Latino and white Democrats but also Republicans.

The story could have been different. As should be evident, I'm not a determinist. Global capitalism harnesses niches—but the processes and sites that the capitalist order utilizes in the search for profits are both inside and outside it, capitalist and noncapitalist. There are domains and dimensions that are not entirely governed through capitalist political-economic transactions. In this we ought to see the continual existence of possibilities— possibilities for the creation of alternatives. New York's Dominican livery bases have appeared through a concrete history and through a myriad of choices. Choices are precisely choices. The general problem of politics in the real world, including today's capitalist one, may be outlined in the following manner: political action is above all a matter of forging connections and building alliances and forms of community that cut across important differences (tied to gender, age, race, ethnicity, nationality, citizenship status, class, religion, and political-economic doctrines). But given that capitalism's reach or power is, in a certain sense, limited—or that there is social-cultural stuff in most places that is mainly outside or beyond it (as if it were irrelevant or superfluous)—it *is* possible to construct political relations and entities that challenge capitalism's apparently self-evident truths and dominance. Historically and culturally produced differences are constitutive of the configurations of power and knowledge that we call contemporary capitalism. The existence of diversity is therefore among the conditions for the exercise of politics. This makes political work hard. But, again, the core of most forms of politics revolves precisely around the efforts to create and sustain ties and alliances that cross boundaries and differences. Politics, or political action, *is* possible.

Conclusion

Powerful thinking (among intellectuals, politicians, and citizens) has operated, and continues to operate, with a mystifying separation of the economic and the social; the contemporary global economy is studied as if it is outside of society, or, if one prefers, outside of social and cultural processes. The historical materialist tradition has been different. Marxists have insisted on the need to understand the economic and the social as entwined. The problem has been that the interest in the significance of the social too often has been reduced to almost only a matter of the class relationships; society, or the social as interconnected with the economic, became class.

The argument here has instead been that labor is concrete; performance of work is never abstract and can never articulate only class. Labor practices are unthinkable without complex cultural resources and components. Capitalist labor practices depend therefore on a series of apparently non-economic processes. One effect is that work in a capitalist system is woven together with the production of concepts and feelings of self and other, differences. Society's variety is inherent in and constitutive of global capitalism. This makes capitalism's figure a good deal messier than is often thought or argued; yet it seems also to open capitalism more to the anthropological project, to make capitalism to a larger extent an open field that can, and should, be studied with ethnographic methods.

I have maintained that we need a focus on the "job" done by forms of affective life as forces of production. If we want to understand capitalist labor forms, we have to study the affective ideas that give shape to specific labor activities with their accompanying forms of identity making. Globally, the affective includes tremendous cultural diversity. To see affective forms as *in* capitalism, as decisive to it, is therefore only to deepen and reinforce the basic assertion that differences are built into contemporary capitalism. Put another way, the argument here rests on a claim about *anthropos*. If we study human histories and practices, we always find that affective, material, and social processes are entangled—they work together and are folded into one another. Material determinism is a dead end. The materialism that I back is instead the sort of extended materialism that has been formulated by David Graeber (2001, 54)—his materialism is one that sees history and histories "as arising from creative action, but creative action as something that can never be separated from its concrete, material medium [such as the body with its labor power, the car or the taxi, and features of the city landscape]."

Capitalism is made and remade through shifting, creative uses of niches. In this we rightly see possibilities for desired changes. But it is also a reality that contemporary capitalism strongly restricts and undermines many possibilities and that much of the actual use of creativity and identity projects with which today's capitalism is associated shows a gloomy picture: universes shot through with intolerance, grotesque exploitation, and violence. Two authors, among many, who have provided examples are Jean and John Comaroff (1999, 2001). They use the term "millennial capitalism" not only to place the practices and processes that they discuss in concrete, historical time but also to attempt to draw attention to the formidable, awful, frightening meanings associated with the turn of the millennium. Employing material from South Africa and a series of other countries, they have examined the past decades' growth of "occult economies," fantastic (by way of, for example, wealth-extracting zombies or brutalization of children) and quite practical (by way of, for example, aggressively speculative investment in the world's stock markets or pyramid schemes) ways of making a lot of money apparently without productive work. While recognizing that it is almost impossible to calculate whether there is any real increase in the frequency with which stories of, and practices related to, the mystical or the occult are appearing, they maintain all the same that the preoccupation with the occult, and especially with the possibility of rapid enrichment through largely invisible methods, has become part of society in ways that are altered or new and that have taken on new significations in a global capitalist system where massive speculative financialization has become part of the normal. Their studies demonstrate how forms of (transformed) cultural diversity are part and parcel of the (changed) contemporary global economy. But they let us also see depressingly clearly the extent to which symbolic and affective forms, or the diversity outside and inside neoliberal capitalism, may be associated with undermining and destructive processes—suspicion, fear, accusations of sorcery, dissolution of relations and solidarity, witch hunts, ritual murders. It is essential not to romanticize the basic condition in many places. But capitalism is not only evil or destructive. It can also open productive possibilities and alternatives and offer (small) social improvements and hope. It is equally important not to trivialize these potentials, or the significance to many people of tiny improvements.

NOTES

1. For other versions of the same basic argument, see also Tsing (2012, 2015).

2. During the past four decades, there has almost everywhere been a significant turn toward neoliberalism in political-economic practices and thinking (Harvey 2005; Ortner 2011). Forms of deregulation, privatization, and pullout of the state from many areas of social provision have represented a pattern. Most states, from Chile to the United States to China, have adopted some version of neoliberal theory and action (but see Ferguson 2015). When I speak of "contemporary global capitalism" in this chapter, I refer to the capitalist history in the decades from about the 1970s until now.

3. Supply chains "are not new; they extend back in various forms as far as trade itself. What is new is the hype and sense of possibility that supply chains offer to the current generation of entrepreneurs" (Tsing 2009, 149).

4. Yanagisako's (2002, 11) argument is inspired by her reading of Donald L. Donham (1990) and Gerald Allan Cohen (1978).

5. The San Francisco–based Uber, founded in 2009, expanded into a new city each month starting in mid-2011, including New York City, and the company is undoubtedly

transforming the transportation dynamics and parts of the taxi business in New York while I write this. See, for example, Ryan Hutchins and Dana Rubinstein, "Bill to Protect Car Services from Uber Raises Questions," *Politico New York*, January 14, 2015, http://www.capitalnewyork.com/article/city-hall/2015/01/8559999/bill-protect-car-services-uber-raises-questions; Danielle Furfaro, "Uber Cuts Rates in Escalating NYC Cab Wars," *New York Post*, January 28, 2016, http://nypost.com/2016/01/28/uber-cutting-rates-in-nyc-amid-escalating-cab-wars/; and Dan Rivoli, "Uber Cars Rack Up Violations for Illegal Street Hails as NYC Proposes Crackdown," *New York Daily News*, April 6, 2016, http://www.nydailynews.com/new-york/nyc-proposes-crackdown-uber-cabs-picking-street-fares-article-1.2591233. But as I see it, the "Uberization" of New York's and the world's taxi industry, and, more generally, the contemporary service economy, helps only to support and further strengthen the most basic argument about the role and the significance of affective-cultural differences that I seek to convey here. To illustrate, Uber contracts with their driver partners under legal arrangements as contractors, and not employees. Uber and other companies using "e-hail" services use, and help to give shape to, cultural diversity; they do not undermine or reduce it.

6. For more on these connections and exchanges between Puerto Ricans and Dominicans, see Krohn-Hansen (2013, 69–81).

7. Until 2007 the nation's minimum wage was just $5.15 per hour. The Fair Minimum Wage Act of 2007 raised the federal minimum wage rate to $5.85 per hour, effective July 24, 2007; $6.55, effective July 24, 2008; and $7.25, effective July 24, 2009.

8. "The aftereffects of New York City's fiscal crisis in 1975 . . . and other consequences of fiscal austerity . . . defined the condition in the city for over two decades. Overall, the city's budget shrank 22 percent between 1975 and 1983, and service cuts affected every aspect of the masses' everyday life" (Sanjek 1998, 93). To quote Harvey, "Working-class and ethnic-immigrant New York was thrust back into the shadows" (2005, 47).

9. As Tsing (2012, 41) underscores, "Noncapitalist is not 'precapitalist' or 'premodern'; evolutionary frames are out of line here."

REFERENCES

Bear, Laura, Karen Ho, Anna Tsing, and Sylvia Yanagisako. 2015. "Gens: A Feminist Manifesto for the Study of Capitalism." In "Fieldsights—Theorizing the Contemporary," special section, *Cultural Anthropology* online, March 30. http://www.culanth.org/fieldsights/652-gens-a-feminist-manifesto-for-the-study-of-capitalism.

Cohen, Gerald Allan. 1978. *Karl Marx's Theory of History: A Defence*. Oxford: Clarendon.

Comaroff, Jean, and John Comaroff. 1999. "Occult Economies and the Violence of Abstraction: Notes from the South African Postcolony." *American Ethnologist* 26, no. 2: 279–303.

Comaroff, Jean, and John Comaroff, eds. 2001. *Millennial Capitalism and the Culture of Neoliberalism*. Durham, NC: Duke University Press.

Donham, Donald L. 1990. *History, Power, Ideology: Central Issues in Marxism and Anthropology*. Cambridge: Cambridge University Press.

Ferguson, James. 2013. "Declarations of Dependence: Labour, Personhood, and Welfare in Southern Africa." *Journal of the Royal Anthropological Institute* 19, no. 2: 223–242.

Ferguson, James. 2015. *Give a Man a Fish: Reflections on the New Politics of Distribution*. Durham, NC: Duke University Press.

Freeman, Carla. 2014. *Entrepreneurial Selves: Neoliberal Respectability and the Making of a Caribbean Middle Class*. Durham, NC: Duke University Press.

Georges, Eugenia. 1984. "New Immigrants and the Political Process: Dominicans in New York." Occasional Paper 45, Center for Latin American Studies, New York University, New York.

Graeber, David. 2001. *Toward an Anthropological Theory of Value: The False Coin of Our Own Dreams*. New York: Palgrave.

Grasmuck, Sherri, and Patricia R. Pessar. 1991. *Between Two Islands: Dominican International Migration*. Berkeley: University of California Press.

Hardt, Michael. 1999. "Affective Labor." *boundary 2* 26, no. 2: 89–100.

Hardt, Michael. 2005. "Immaterial Labor and Artistic Production." *Rethinking Marxism: A Journal of Economics, Culture and Society* 17, no. 2: 175–177.

Hardt, Michael, and Antonio Negri. 2000. *Empire*. Cambridge, MA: Harvard University Press.

Harvey, David. 2005. *A Brief History of Neoliberalism*. Oxford: Oxford University Press.

Hernández, Ramona, Francisco Rivera-Batiz, and Roberto Agodini. 1995. *Dominican New Yorkers: A Socioeconomic Profile, 1990*. New York: City University of New York Dominican Studies Institute.

Hirschman, Albert O. (1977) 2013. *The Passions and the Interests: Political Arguments for Capitalism before Its Triumph*. Princeton, NJ: Princeton University Press.

Jones-Correa, Michael. 1998. *Between Two Nations: The Political Predicament of Latinos in New York City*. Ithaca, NY: Cornell University Press.

Krohn-Hansen, Christian. 2013. *Making New York Dominican: Small Business, Politics, and Everyday Life*. Philadelphia: University of Pennsylvania Press.

Lazar, Sian. 2008. *El Alto, Rebel City: Self and Citizenship in Andean Bolivia*. Durham, NC: Duke University Press.

Mauss, Marcel. 1923–1924. "Essai sur le don: Forme et raison de l'échange dans les sociétés archaïques." *Année Sociologique* 2, no. 1: 30–186.

Mazzarella, William. 2009. "Affect: What Is It Good For?" In *Enchantments of Modernity: Empire, Nation, Globalization*, edited by Saurabh Dube, 291–309. London: Routledge.

Ortner, Sherry. 2011. "On Neoliberalism." *Anthropology of This Century* 1, May. http://aotcpress.com/articles/neoliberalism/.

Portes, Alejandro, and Luis E. Guarnizo. 1991. *Capitalistas del trópico: La inmigración en los Estados Unidos y el desarrollo de la pequeña empresa en la República Dominicana*. 2nd ed. Santo Domingo: Programa FLACSO—República Dominicana; Baltimore: Johns Hopkins University Press.

Richard, Analiese, and Daromir Rudnyckyj. 2009. "Economies of Affect." *Journal of the Royal Anthropological Institute* 15, no. 1: 57–77.

Rosaldo, Michelle. 1984. "Toward an Anthropology of Self and Feeling." In *Culture Theory: Essays on Mind, Self and Emotion*, edited by Richard A. Shweder and Robert A. LeVine, 137–157. Cambridge: Cambridge University Press.

Sánchez Korrol, Virginia E. 1994. *From Colonia to Community: The History of Puerto Ricans in New York City*. Berkeley: University of California Press.

Sanjek, Roger. 1998. *The Future of Us All: Race and Neighborhood Politics in New York City*. Ithaca, NY: Cornell University Press.

Schaller Consulting. 2006. *The New York City Taxicab Fact Book*. New York: Schaller Consulting. http://www.schallerconsult.com/taxi.

Torres-Saillant, Silvio, and Ramona Hernández. 1998. *The Dominican Americans*. Westport, CT: Greenwood.

Tsing, Anna L. 2009. "Supply Chains and the Human Condition." *Rethinking Marxism: A Journal of Economics, Culture and Society* 21, no. 2: 148–176.

Tsing, Anna L. 2012. "Empire's Salvage Heart: Why Diversity Matters in the Global Political Economy." *Focaal* 64: 36–50.

Tsing, Anna L. 2015. *The Mushroom at the End of the World: On the Possibility of Life in Capitalist Ruins*. Princeton, NJ: Princeton University Press.

Weston, Kath. 2017. *Animate Planet: Making Visceral Sense of Living in a High-Tech Ecologically Damaged World*. Durham, NC: Duke University Press.

Williams, Raymond. 1977. *Marxism and Literature*. Oxford: Oxford University Press.

Yanagisako, Sylvia. 2002. *Producing Culture and Capital: Family Firms in Italy*. Princeton, NJ: Princeton University Press.

Yanagisako, Sylvia. 2012. "Immaterial and Industrial Labor: On False Binaries in Hardt and Negri's Trilogy." *Focaal* 64: 16–23.

3. *Anthropos* and *Pragmata*

ON THE SHAPE OF THINGS TO COME

———

Ingjerd Hoëm

To account for "the shape of things to come"—to understand what the future may hold in the face of increasingly complex and fraught relationships between people (*anthropos*) and things (*pragmata*)—we need to better understand what factors are at play in shaping future livelihoods.[1]

In this endeavor, it may help us to step back from the present. A reflexive distance may be furthered either by anthropological comparison or by historical analysis. In this essay, I will make use of both methods. In this, I follow the approach outlined in the introduction to this collection, where a collapse of the opposition of "anthropos" and the "material," as implied by much of the thinking associated with the naming of our present epoch as the Anthropocene, is presented as a challenge to politics and as a challenge to anthropology. If we go back only a few decades in the history of our discipline to examine the anthropological analyses of the relationship between people and things developed in the early 1950s and 1960s, we see how the issues of systems of production, access to resources, and political distribution of goods were framed in interestingly different ways than their current iterations. I shall draw on these differences to show how things have changed since then, in ways that affect the relationships between people and things, from the vantage point of a Pacific perspective. I use ethnography from the atoll society of Tokelau to discuss some of the factors that contribute to a situation where the relationship between people and things can only be described as increasingly troubled.

Among the burning issues informing the early stages of our anthropological discipline were those phrased as explorations of the relative determining forces of the material and sociopolitical organization. One well-known example of these approaches is the perspective developed by the early Marshall Sahlins (1958, 1963). His approach was based on the premise that the material determines, or somehow shapes, sociopolitical structures. In this perspective, "the material" is defined as comprising landscape and access to resources, and includes the technological means to access and exploit those resources.

In what follows, I shall discuss the insights that this "materialist" perspective may provide us with today, in particular its approach to what we today would call the relationship between people and things. This discussion is followed by a presentation of the more recent materialist perspective of Anna Tsing (this volume, 2015) on the complex relationship among landscape, people, and animate and nonanimate things. The landscape chosen for this comparative exploration is one of the ethnographic cases used by Sahlins in his early analysis: the Polynesian atoll society of Tokelau.

On the Changing Relationship between People and Things—as Seen from a Very Small Place with an Increasingly Global Reach

Based on ethnographic studies in Tokelau since the mid-1980s (see, for example, Hoëm 1999, 2004, 2005, 2015), the local perspective on agency operates on the assumption that political institutions, including their social constituency, may work to determine or shape the material (in the sense defined above, as a combination of landscape, technology, and resources). By bringing in the Tokelau variant of a pan-Austronesian orientation, we gain a comparative contrast to the different materialist perspectives of the early Sahlins and the later Tsing. The gist of the Tokelau account is to show how political institutions and social organization may also work as forms of technology, or what we may call a form of sociotechnology, in processes of relating to the material. Throughout, I challenge the opposition of the sociopolitical and the material. In doing so, I highlight a practice of place making that in the past few decades has expanded globally through the extension of its network of kin relationships, while still culturally anchored in the atoll environment. I use the approach developed by Tsing (this volume) as an aid in this exploration that aims to view the complex relationships of landscape, technology, and resources anew.

Juxtaposing the earlier perspective represented by cultural material-ism with the more recent representation of landscape as specific constella-tions of living and inert matters allows us to consider more closely how—overlooking for the moment the terminology employed by these respective perspectives—what we may call the margins of lifeworlds are constantly being shaped and challenged.[2] The access to resources is crucial to this con-tinuous shaping and reshaping of a specific lifeworld. It is important that, to this way of thinking, an atoll environment represents the most marginal, resource-poor environment of all island habitats in the Pacific Ocean. I shall problematize this picture of marginality in the discussion that follows.

In the earlier perspective of Sahlins (1958, 1963), the relationship between political organization and material environmental factors is conceived of as a dynamic of cultural adaptation, and the defining parameters are de-scribed as *evolutionary ceilings*. The limits posed by evolutionary ceilings are thought to have an impact on social development, but at the same time they seem to emerge as unintentional by-products of the underlying model. The model presents a complex interplay among environmental factors, tech-nological development, and the redistributive capacities of sociopolitical organization.

In the more recent perspective of Tsing (this volume, 2015), the relation-ship between the political and the material is conceived of in such a way that her empirical descriptions bring to mind the issue of what used to be called a niche's "carrying capacity," but in her analysis this is seen as an on-going and transformative interaction between living and inert matter. The limits emerge as observable instances of what she calls "crowding," as well as tensions between crowding and "coordination" (Tsing, this volume). In her chapter in this collection, she illustrates the phenomenon of crowding by reference to a steadily growing herd of red deer gathering in an abandoned mining area. Enclosed by farmland, the deer are left to multiply in the aban-doned mine area without threats from humans or (other) predators. Tsing uses the term "crowding" to describe and discuss the actual process of over-population in this partially enclosed area but also to refer to the effects of this enclosure on the landscape, in particular on the coordination among the fir trees, mycelia, and the sandy ground being churned by the animals. These processes of (over)crowding and interspecies coordination are also traceable as consequences of political decision-making. While this is not the explicit focus of Tsing's analysis in her chapter in this volume, this reading presents us with a possible connection between the perspectives of Sahlins and Tsing that may bring about a more nuanced understanding of certain parameters, "ceilings," or "limits" of the lifeworlds that we inhabit. Such situations of relative temporal isolation (such as that caused by the interventions of the abandonment of a mine, accompanied by the planting of firs and the feeding of red deer) or openness (such as the conditions ages ago in the area that Tsing describes, before the mines or before intensive farming) are highly relevant for a comparison with the assumed marginality of the Tokelau environment that I referred to above.

On High and Low Islands: The Premise of Locality

The famous article "Poor Man, Rich Man, Big-Man, Chief: Political Types in Melanesia and Polynesia," written by Marshall Sahlins and published in 1963 following his monograph *Social Stratification in Polynesia* (1958), discusses factors inherent to relations of production and political organization. In Sahlins's terminology, these factors amount to what he calls an "evolutionary ceiling." In the Melanesian case, political evolution is limited by the so-called big-men's dependence on their faction (consisting of close kin and associates) to provide the means of distribution of goods and services to the population at large—which is necessary to earn renown. In the Polynesian case, the "ceiling is higher," and a definite limit is reached when and if the population rebels against the extraction of their surplus (goods, labor) by the chiefly strata. Sahlins's comparison concludes that the two models of political leadership "not only reflect different varieties and levels of political evolution" but are indicative of different degrees of capacity "to generate and to sustain political process" (1963, 300).

These differing degrees of capacity are linked to scale, that is, to the number of people connected through an overarching political system; to communication techniques, such as oral transmission, canoes, travel by foot, and so on; and, ultimately, to the resource situation provided by the local environment. While Sahlins here discusses the material in terms of a particular set of labor relations and practices in relation to the environment, the model comes across as heavily dependent on the limits on access to resources represented by a particular locality. The so-called high islands of Polynesia (Tahiti, Hawaii, Tonga, and Samoa, to mention a few) are rich in resources and represent examples of chiefdoms, which merits their characterization as highly evolved in terms of political structure and organization. The "low," resource-poor atoll societies of Polynesia show the same social organization, but in a minimal fashion, constrained as they are by their marginality.

Following the Material: An Exploration into the
Land- and Seascape of Tokelau

The "world" in Tokelauan is *lalolagi*, a word that translates as "under the sky." The image in figure 3.1 can be used to illustrate common habitual ways of perceiving landscape. The image can be taken to represent a very small, isolated piece of marginal land, a tiny chain of islets surrounded by a large ocean. This is the dominant perception of the image by outsiders, that is, people who are not familiar with the environment. For those with local knowledge, as famously expressed by the late Pacific scholar Epeli Hauʻofa (1994), what one sees is a sea of islands. In this perspective, the sea is the dominant figure, not the land, and the ocean is perceived as a connecting force, not as a separating one.

To come to Tokelau is to enter a lifeworld that for long stretches of time exists largely on its own. Because it is geographically distant from its nearest neighbors, the rhythm of village life is interspersed with the flurry of activities that follow the infrequent (monthly or fortnightly) boat visits. The three atolls are a day and a half's boat ride away from Samoa. The land area of the atolls is altogether approximately twelve square kilometers, with the highest point of the islets reaching 1.524 meters above sea level. At times of rough seas, the ocean washes over the islets, taking with it quantities of the sandy village soil. It is not possible for boats to moor alongside the reef, so any visitors and all cargo must be taken ashore in aluminum dinghies running through a narrow human-made passage and onto land. On each of the three atolls, a village is situated on one of the numerous small islets (on Fakaofo, there are two adjacent islets). In the village, population density is high, and at its narrowest the village islet is two hundred meters across from the ocean to the lagoon side.

The surrounding ocean is bountiful and has provided the people living in the three villages of Fakaofo, Atafu, and Nukunonu with most of their food for generations. There is very little fertile soil. Pandanus and coconut palms are native to the atolls, and breadfruit, *pulaka* (swamp taro), and banana palms have been introduced and survive with some care. The freshwater lens is shallow, and water had been a scarce resource until a development project ensured the installation of concrete cisterns as the foundation of most houses. The climate is humid, and because Tokelau is close to the equator,

FIGURE 3.1. Fakaofo atoll seen from the open-ocean side. Atolls are very low islands.
Photo by author.

the sun, reflected by the sea and the white ground, is intense at midday. Apart from the drying of fish, preservation of food is difficult. Other, more durable goods—for example, outboard motors and freezers made of metal— rust and decay very quickly.

In short, this is not an environment conducive to the long-term accumulation of material objects. It is not even possible to find much material to create valuable, long-lasting objects from. In contrast to valued treasures (in Maori, *taonga*, "treasure," is a term that includes valuable items of material and immaterial culture) from other parts of Polynesia—such as the New Zealand greenstone, from which pendants and weapons are made; the Tongan *tapa*, fine dyed bark cloth made from the mulberry tree; and so on— Tokelau valuables are made out of three materials: hard *kanava* wood (used to make *tuluma*, boxes for fishing gear, as well as *vaka*, canoes), mother-of-pearl shell (turned into *pa* or *tifa*, fishhook pendants that are presented at weddings), and *kie*, the highly valued fine type of pandanus (from which are produced fine mats, also transferred at life-cycle ceremonies). In contrast, the immaterial culture—Tokelau forms of sociality, oral literature, and performative arts—is truly where the riches of Tokelau are to be found.

Despite the combined challenges of a harsh climate and a marginal on-land environment, the period since the mid-1980s, when I started my fieldwork on Tokelau, has seen massive external financial investment in the atolls. This investment has resulted in the presence in the villages of two-story houses, aluminum boats with outboard motors, computers, phones, trucks, aluminum cans, solar panels, freezers, washing machines, and more—all kinds of things that were absent, largely absent, or few and far between as recently as thirty years ago.

Dump Sites and Things of No Account

The islets that make up each of the three Tokelau atolls encircle a lagoon. The lagoon has coral heads on which the *fahua*, the colorful and very tasty giant clams *Tridacna maxima* (*fahua nao*) and *Tridacna squamosa* (*fahua taka*), grow. These clams, fish, *feke* (octopus), and other edible species harvested from the reef and the lagoon are important parts of the local diet. Supplementing the produce from the open ocean and the plantations on the outer islets, what can be harvested from the lagoon is a safe fallback when the open ocean is too rough for fishing.

Along the beachfront, facing the lagoon, are the outhouses, which are popular same-sex gathering places. The small pandanus-thatched huts and huts covered with corrugated iron are outhouses situated directly over the water and catch the cooling breeze, making them pleasant places for a game of cards, a shared smoke, or a snooze. Human waste enters the lagoon water, and hepatitis B is endemic among the population. Attempts to rectify this situation have been made. In Samoa the first priority of the Peace Corps was to install sheds of corrugated iron containing a water closet in every village, earning them the local name *fale pisikoa* ("Peace Corps houses"). To use them, buckets of salt water were most commonly used, as running water was not commonly installed. As the introduction of water closets in Tokelau further threatened the freshwater lens, alternative methods of waste treatment were sought.

A solution was proposed by the resident representative of the South Pacific Regional Environment Programme (SPREP). The model chosen was an advanced yet easy-to-maintain composting toilet, which had the advantage of producing much-needed soil in addition to presenting a potential solution to the hepatitis threat. During one of my visits to Nukunonu, I saw what seemed to me to be a concrete tower, perhaps for water storage, placed near the convent and close to the school. I asked my host family about this construction. They laughed in response: "Oh, that? That is [the name of the SPREP representative]'s throne." Their manner of speaking indicated that there was a story to this. The construction that towered over the low convent and school buildings was indeed the remaining shell of the toilet project. What had happened? As was obvious from what I could see, the project had failed to catch on. It turned out that the seat, or, as they called it, the "throne," was placed physically higher than the seating of the political leadership, the village council representatives. Therefore, it could not be used. However, the villagers let the SPREP representative carry out the project, and only after the first construction was completed did it become apparent to all involved that it would never be put to use.

Why did they let the representative go on using time, energy, and money in this wasteful manner, and why was the "throne" left standing? My impression is that people had a wait-and-see attitude at first, and when they saw the resulting object, they found it a hilarious monument to a man with good intentions but little local understanding. Also, I believe that this construction was taken as one among many things of no account (*mea tauanoa*), and hence it was not even considered important enough to need to be dismantled.

And what about the water situation, the danger of catching hepatitis, and the potential depletion of the freshwater lens? In addition to the outhouses over the lagoon, water toilets are still used and are more common now than thirty years ago; they are serviced from water tanks placed on roofs. The management of waste is placed outside of the village center, which is associated with respectful, decorous behavior and the exercise of political power. At the far end of the village islet is the *vao*, the bush area, which was transformed from a place to gather *lu* (bird's-nest fern, an edible green) to a large rubbish dump, the designated disposal area for nondegradable waste.

As may be inferred from the example of the "throne," hierarchy is kinetically marked. This is also evident in that different areas in the villages are treated differently depending on how close they are to the centers of power. This centripetal spatial model is universally applicable: for example, it makes it possible to view Tokelau as the "back," or outskirts, and powerful overseas countries as centers. "Now I understand," a man exclaimed happily during a workshop on food security conducted in Tokelau. "We are a dump site!" In other words, and as analyses of the correlation between the low quality of imported food and increased health risks in the Pacific have shown, for approximately fifty years Tokelau has been on the receiving end of an increasing volume of low-quality goods, ranging from the notorious turkey tails (Singer 2014), corned beef, and other fatty produce, to goods with high sugar content (mainly soft drinks), to tobacco and alcohol. As a result of these imports, nondegradable waste has piled up and is currently shipped to

Samoa on a regular basis. The low-quality imported food has taken a toll on health: hypertension, diabetes, and kidney failure have become increasingly common, even among the younger part of the population.

From this brief description of life on the ground, we learn that the local landscape is divided into zones of different value: the important central areas and the areas of no consequence at the back, on the outskirts of the villages. Things are also divided following a similar conceptual distinction into things that are of importance, valued, inalienable things that are cared for, and things that are of no importance, alienable things that are treated with indifference and passed on. Examples of the first category are the fine mats and tuluma boxes made of the precious kanava tree. Examples of the second are the concrete toilet described above, soft drink and beer cans, computers, clothes, books, watches, passports, and other ephemeral things. The description of Tokelau as a dump site should be read as drawing on these concepts and values. The man from the workshop says, in other words, that from a relational perspective Tokelau is treated as "the back" to a powerful place's "center." From this premise it follows that the center will distribute its "things of no account," its waste products, to its "back side" (or, as he put it, its dump site), in this case Tokelau.

Forceful Matters

This relational perspective, as illustrated by the "sea-of-islands" image, represents a spatial orientation that is modeled on wind directions and ocean currents. The name Tokelau is itself a metonym for this kind of map: meaning "wind from the north," it situates the atolls relative to their closest neighbors. The skilled navigators and fishermen of Tokelau are familiar with the yearly cycle of winds, and they time their activities accordingly (Macgregor 1937; Hoëm 1993; Hooper and Tinielu 2012). To venture outside the reef and enter the deep ocean is always dangerous; inexperienced persons are not allowed to do so, but with a skilled leader, the danger is greatly reduced.

Tokelau has always considered the ocean its greatest source of livelihood. Until recently, it has not been considered endangered by the ocean (at least not in the sense that Fiji has been for a long time), because Tokelau is on the northern edge of the hurricane belt that runs across the Pacific, with a main center close to the Philippines. The atolls commonly experience high seas and strong winds with regularity during the wet season between November and March. The ongoing construction of seawalls by piling up coral stones and cement blocks and encaging them in chicken wire was initially begun as a land-claim project. Until 1990 Tokelau had experienced only three recorded hurricanes; however, Hurricane Tusi in 1987 was followed in 1990 by Hurricane Ofa, which contaminated the freshwater lens and prevented plant growth for months.

The fact that the severe damage resulting from tropical hurricanes may provide an occasion for political intervention and social engineering became apparent in the aftermath of the hurricane that struck Tokelau in January 1966. The New Zealand government at the time had envisioned a plan for the resettlement of the Tokelau population to New Zealand, because the villages on the atolls were considered too costly to maintain. The atolls, in this plan, could better be used as coconut plantations. The resettlement scheme met with little success, as people were strongly opposed to abandoning their homeland. However, in the aftermath of the hurricane in 1966 and the subsequent famine and hardship, three extended families (*kaiga*) agreed to resettle, and for the first time, migration outside of Samoa (and other local movements for shorter or longer periods) took place. The diagnosis was food shortage and overpopulation, and assisted migration was proposed as the solution. In consequence, population numbers in Tokelau fell from approximately 2,000 to 1,546 between 1966 and 1982, and in New Zealand the number of people from Tokelau increased to 2,762 individuals (Smith, Sauer-Thompson, and Lyons 1997, 54).

Hurricane Ofa in 1990 was followed by a rapid succession of hurricanes—Val in 1992 and Percy in 2005—and villagers and scientists increasingly came to attribute the current weather pattern to climate change, that is, regarding it as a result of global warming. In this perspective, the construction of seawalls took on a new significance and a new sense of urgency. Given the likelihood of rising sea levels and more unpredictable wind patterns, the new way of thinking became "Tokelau needs all the protection it can get." In 2014 the first international climate demonstration ever conducted by Tokelauans took place; a team joined the Pacific Warriors in a peaceful protest against the continuation of coal extraction in the Australian harbor of Newcastle.[3] The representation of Tokelau leaders in international meeting fora has increased rapidly, and the villagers complain that their leadership spends more time away from the islands than on them. At the same time, since in its two most recent referenda Tokelau decided to continue its relationship of dependency with New Zealand, Tokelau no longer has a voice in fora dedicated to climate issues. They are, at present, effectively cut off from those networks and are mainly forced to rely on New Zealand's representation.

FIGURE 3.2. Outhouse over the lagoon. Photo by author.

FIGURE 3.3. Modern two-story building, Nukunonu. Photo by author.

As evidenced in figures 3.2 and 3.3, over the past few decades, more houses, most of them multistory and with closed walls, have been built than ever before—to the point of almost universally replacing the low, open-walled thatched housing. An obvious advantage is the increase in water collection and storage capacity provided by the combination of corrugated iron roofs and cement tanks in the houses' foundations. In terms of climate change, Tokelau has been the first Pacific nation to shift from diesel-powered generators to a total reliance on solar power. Investment in satellite communications has diminished Tokelau's isolation remarkably quickly, although transport, and hence access to the outside world, still involves a lengthy journey by boat (see Hoëm 2015).

The Wind as an Instrument of Control

Rune Flikke, in this volume, describes how locally anchored understandings of the relationship between atmospheric phenomena and issues of health and well-being are used as instruments of social control and, in the historical case of South Africa, racial segregation. In the Pacific perspective discussed here, the relationship between air, wind, and storms, on the one hand, and the well-being and fecundity of people and the landscape, on the other, is dependent on morally correct social action (see also Hoëm 2015). The residence of the pre-Christian god of storms and hurricanes, Fakafotu, was placed directly in the center of the politically dominant village, on the *malae* (ceremonial meeting ground) of Fakaofo. Thunder was considered the manifested anger of Fakafotu. Since the conversion of Tokelauans to Christianity as Roman Catholics and Protestants in the 1860s–1870s, the old gods have receded into the firmament—literally. The megalithic stone slabs that were the seats of the high god of the heavens (Tui Tokelau), the god of the ocean (Hemoana), and the god of the winds (Fakafotu) were dismantled and incorporated into the seawall surrounding the village islet of Falé on Fakaofo. However, people still make a connection between the gods of old and political power, and the remains of the slab of Tui Tokelau have been recovered and placed in the present-day meetinghouse in Fakaofo. Ensuring that the people act as one body with a common purpose is both the expected duty of leadership and a precondition for survival in the ocean environment. Given the experience of risk connected with open-ocean fishing and the scarcity of resources on land (ranging from lack of water to lack of arable soil), a preoccupation with ways of ensuring fertility would seem to follow. Socially correct action results from a concern with the well-being of the group over and above individual needs. Most tasks are divided following gender: the most socially important distinction is the brother-sister relationship, in addition to the dimension of age (Hoëm 2015). The line between life and death, fecundity and famine, is narrow, and it is the responsibility of the village and family leaders (*pule*) to ensure that the balance is on the right side of the margin. The elders—family heads, male as well as female—achieve this by orchestrating the coming together of a harmonious whole (*maopoopo*), the basis for any task-oriented group. The hearts (*fatumanava*, a compound word of the two terms "stone" and "breath") of the members of a group are cleared of any internal dissent through a public ritual apology, and only then can the wind (*matagi*) enter and bring joy (*fiafia*) and inspiration (*matagia*), as they are joined in a common movement elevated in experience through speeches, dance, and celebration. Breaches of this ideal conduct bring about famine and death, but this outcome can be avoided, for example, through the ritual redress described above and through public apologies (*ifoga*) (Hoëm 2005, 2015). In other words, the cognitive model of causality, and hence the responsibility for natural events, is related to moral values. One man, describing the hurricane of 1966, explained how the church compound was spared the onslaught of the waves. He attributed its protection to the dignity of the behavior in this area, which ensured God's protection.

Forceful Effects: Different Perspectives but Only One Future

We see here a perspective where the wind—soothing and refreshing but also devastating and hurricane causing—is identified with the heart of the social and human body, as in the case described by Flikke in this volume. In general, villagers acted, and still act, on the assumption that there is a causal relationship between human action and the material environment, in that the manifestation of natural phenomena such as the wind occurs in coordination with human agency (see Hoëm 2015). How this agentive relationship is perceived represents a third perspective alongside those of Sahlins and Tsing, who both seem to place the weight of causality (or, in Tsing's case, perhaps rather the weight of analysis) more on the material environmental side than on the side of the human or the sociopolitical organization (see Flikke, this volume). Knut G. Nustad's chapter in this volume describes conflicting understandings of what landscape is (in his case, that of St Lucia in KwaZulu-Natal). The Tokelau landscape, in the early Sahlins model, is poor in resources, and the ocean sets a barrier to sociopolitical development. In the Tsing perspective, the Tokelau landscape, in a more recent incarnation characterized by more frequent interaction with the world outside of the atolls, shows a great influx of things, some of which are harmful to the environment in ways not previously encountered. In the Tokelau perspective, however, these things are of no particular significance in themselves, but the fact that they speak of Tokelau as being placed relationally as a dump site is! The approach advocated by Nustad (this volume), to "pay attention to the material traces of landscapes, as well as to the political economies embedded in them," is of relevance here.

Taking the atoll landscape and what is found there—that is, the relationship between anthropos and pragmata, between people and things—as the focus of my exploration in the two previous sections has brought to the fore the consequences of changing constraints (that is, what I, using the perspective developed by Tsing, call areas of relative isolation or openness). By drawing out the possible tensions associated with the phenomena of crowding and coordination, we may be able to see some contours of what the future has in store for us—in other words, to trace "the shape of things to come." Considering the atoll landscape, the effects of what Tsing calls crowding (this volume) are apparent. One example is the situation before the hurricane of 1966 when, on the island of Falé in Fakaofo, the population was identified by outside experts as having reached a ceiling for what the environment could sustain. Other examples of crowding are found in my descriptions of slowly degradable and nondegradable things piling up in the atoll landscapes, where we see how environmental margins shift. To illustrate further, before 1966, the incursions of saline water that occur because of more frequent hurricanes would have meant famine and certain death for many. Today, the water tanks in the basements of family houses present a solution and a transcendence of that margin. The increases in hepatitis infection of the seafood in the lagoon, malnutrition, and health problems are accompanied by better access to hospital care. And, most important, the marginality of local food resources matters less and less as access to outside resources increases.

So far, this description of the land- and seascape, with an eye to sustainability, represents a different perspective on political process and the resources it engages, a perspective where the significance of the relationship between shifting scales (in the sense of increased access to things) and what used to be called "limits to growth" (Meadows, Randers, and Meadows [1972] 2004) or "viability" (Stenning 1969) comes to the fore. However, an important issue raised by the early Sahlins perspective is whether sociopolitical capacity is affected by increased access to resources. This is not answered by the Tsing-inspired exploration of the atoll land- and seascape. To answer this question, we need to turn to the third, Tokelau, perspective on the relationship between people and things, their sociotechnology. In particular, we need to return to their take on the relationship between what are often taken to be opposing forces of material and human agency. If we transpose Tsing's concepts of crowding and coordination onto the Tokelau perspective, it is possible to see how the past thirty years' expansion of Tokelau's social network (Hoëm 2004, 2015) of coordination that reaches beyond the local also attracts more goods, which in turn results in crowding and deterioration of the atoll land- and seascape. As such, an expansion of scale has clear effects on sustainability if defined as local self-sufficiency.

Comparing the earlier analysis of Tokelau's sociopolitical organization and material environmental factors, as presented in Sahlins (1958, and modified by Hooper in 1968), with the contemporary situation brings out some major differences between the two scenarios. The first scenario allows for a study where the material environmental factors can be relied on to provide a stable ground from which one can assess how the economy, defined as a system of distribution based on accessible resources, affects political organization. In light of the historical development and more recent research, initially on relationships between localities and beyond regions (such as the later Sahlins) and, later, on globalization processes, it is increasingly difficult to sustain the notion of invariant environmental factors existing in isolation from other niches. As climate research progresses, it even becomes difficult to count on an environmental niche maintaining its stability over a period of time.

The first outside notice of crowding, described at the time largely in demographic terms, was seen, as I have said, as an opportunity for social engineering—one that led to what is today a diaspora of approximately six thousand Tokelauans living outside of Tokelau. In a recent Tokelau address to the international dialogue on climate, held in Kiribati in October 2015, the Tokelau representative Paula Faiva, speaking on behalf of the *ulu o Tokelau* (literally, head of Tokelau, that is, the political leader), explained that while Tokelauans appreciated that the issue of relocation had been dealt with favorably by New Zealand, allowing them access to their shores, the preference for Tokelauans is to also maintain a living community in the atolls for as long as it is at all possible.[4] This option, Faiva explained, provides Tokelauans with control over their own livelihoods; in short, it gives them a place to stand (*tulaga*).

In the atolls, as we have seen, access to resources (and contact with the outside world) has increased dramatically from 1966 until today. These translocal and transnational networks clearly represent a resource and alternative "places to stand," ultimately providing other places for the atoll population to reside (as Sahlins also noted, to have access to resources and also to places to reside through translocal networks is common to the Pacific in his article "Goodbye to Tristes Tropes: Ethnography in the Context of Modern World History," published in 1993).

While wind patterns grow more erratic and tidal waves wash over the atolls with greater frequency, investments in house construction and high-maintenance machinery, ranging from computers to motorized vehicles, continue to grow exponentially (as apparent in figures 3.2 and 3.3). Whether these investments are viable over time, or whether the two curves will eventually meet, is impossible to say. For now, people invest heavily in making their environment attractive and safe to live in. Even if the standards for what is considered attractive include aspiring to a lifestyle that might not be viable in an atoll environment, this standard is familiar from other places around the world where Tokelauans now live. With political ties to New Zealand, meaning that Tokelau citizens have free access to New Zealand, and with networks of kin overseas, the atoll population is in a different situation than the inhabitants of Tuvalu or Kiribati, for example, who have no obvious places to move to should their atoll landscapes become uninhabitable. These political and kin ties also provide Tokelauans with access to overseas goods to a hitherto unprecedented degree.

The local conception of the relationship between sociopolitical organization and material environmental factors in Tokelau makes no distinction between the two dimensions. It may be described as a sociotechnology that ensures flexibility in relation to changes in the material. The concept of tulaga (see Hoëm 1999) means an opportunity, a position, and a place to stand. To have a place to stand is dependent on being part of a network of kin and associates; it is necessary to have access to resources such as food, and it is the means to having a political voice. To be able to command, to have agency, it is necessary to coordinate with the network in such a way that things pass on. It is, as Arne Perminow has described for Tonga, the way of the hand that lets go [of things] (2003, 157–177). This letting go does not preclude the accumulation of goods; it demands only that it is done in such a way that the network benefits and remains vital. This way of being amounts to an inbuilt flexibility, in the sense that it represents a coping mechanism during both times of scarcity and times of plenty. The main difference lies in the scale of the network: it contracts locally in resource-poor times and expands globally in times of resource abundance (see also Schwimmer 1990). The address by the Tokelau leaders to the dialogue on climate change asks that this network be extended to include those island nations, such as Kiribati, that currently have no such safety net for an eventual relocation. An international "climate change displacement coordination facility" has been suggested.

As anthropological studies of globalization and localization processes have shown, it is important to include relationships that reach beyond a specific area or place of study. More significantly, if we study in-depth the relationships that make places and niches within one location, it is possible to see how seemingly external macro factors may be deeply embedded in the processes of making the local landscape. In the case that I have presented here, the changing weather patterns are the most obvious sign of such external forces acting locally; the strong winds and tidal waves are met with activities such as replacing diesel-fueled power generators with solar panels and investing increasingly more time and labor in the construction of seawalls. Most important in terms of my discussion in this chapter, however, it does not make sense to describe the weather as an external force. The force of Fakafotu, the god of storms and hurricanes, may be harnessed for political purposes, as shown by the climate warriors of Tokelau in the demonstration in Newcastle. Whether the margins represented by the landscape of Tokelau will maintain their flexibility (see note 3), and whether the limits or thresholds of niches may be continually transformed or transcended, as in the examples discussed above, remains to be seen. At present, Tokelau spokespeople maintain that they would rather "fight and adapt" than relocate.

In terms of the perspectives that we apply to further our understanding of the interactions among the environment, technology, and access to resources (understood broadly as the material), the discussion shows that a narrow focus on the material misses the importance of sociopolitical organization—perhaps the most significant factor when it comes to dealing with shifting margins. We need to include in our analyses the forceful relationships among places, people, and the things that gather in specific landscapes. Such a model is found in Tokelau conceptions of environmental sociality in terms of the relationship between people and places. In the face of dramatically shifting margins, such a perspective provides a viable basis for life and political action.

NOTES

I would like to thank the following people for helpful comments on earlier versions of this article: all the participants in the international workshop Engaging the Material, November 13–14, 2014, at Soria Moria, Oslo, Norway, in particular Marit Melhuus and Anna Tsing. Furthermore, I received constructive comments from reviewers Penny Harvey, Knut G. Nustad, and Christian Krohn-Hansen, and, finally, Keir Martin commented extensively on my draft article.

1. *The Shape of Things to Come* is a science fiction work by H. G. Wells. Written in 1933, it envisions an alternative history to the events that came to unfold with World War II and depicts the realization of a world state.

2. I take the term "margins" here in the sense used by systems theory—that is, as "flexibility," as defined by Gregory Bateson (1973, 473); as uncommitted potential for change; and, in the more common definition within ecological/biological anthropology, as the "limits" for a species represented by the specific niche it inhabits.

3. See Government of Tokelau, "Tokelau Warriors on Their Way to Stop Coal Industry in Australia," October 7, 2014, http://www.tokelau.org.nz.

4. See Government of Tokelau, "Tokelauan's Prior Relocation Highlighted in Kiribati" (address by Paula Faiva), October 10, 2015, http://www.tokelau.org.nz.

REFERENCES

Bateson, Gregory. 1973. *Steps to an Ecology of Mind*. St. Albans: Paladin.
Hau'ofa, Epeli. 1994. "Our Sea of Islands." *Contemporary Pacific* 6, no. 1: 147–161.
Hoëm, Ingjerd. 1993. "Space and Morality in Tokelau." *Pragmatics: Quarterly Publication of the International Pragmatics Association* 3, no. 2: 137–153.
Hoëm, Ingjerd. 1999. "Processes of Identification and the Incipient National Level." *Social Anthropology* 7, no. 3: 279–295.
Hoëm, Ingjerd. 2004. *Theater and Political Process: Staging Identities in Tokelau/New Zealand*. Oxford: Berghahn Books.
Hoëm, Ingjerd. 2005. "Stealing the Water of Life: On the Historicity of Contemporary Social Relationships." *History and Anthropology* 16, no. 3: 293–305.
Hoëm, Ingjerd. 2015. *Languages of Governance in Conflict: Negotiating Democracy in Tokelau*. Amsterdam: John Benjamins.
Hooper, Antony. 1968. "Socio-economic Organization of the Tokelau Islands." *Proceedings VIIIth Congress of Anthropological and Ethnological Sciences, 1968, Tokyo and Kyoto*. Edited by International Union of Anthropological and Ethnological Science, 238–240. Tokyo: Science Council of Japan.
Hooper, Antony, and Iuta Tinielu, eds. 2012. *Echoes at Fishermen's Rock: Traditional Tokelau Fishing. By Elders from Atafu Atoll*. Knowledges of Nature 4. Paris: UNESCO.
Macgregor, Gordon. 1937. *Ethnology of Tokelau Islands*. Honolulu, Hawaii: Bernice P. Bishop Museum bulletin.
Meadows, Donella, Jørgen Randers, and Dennis Meadows. (1972) 2004. *Limits to Growth: The Thirty-Year Update*. White River Junction, VT: Chelsea Green.
Perminow, Arne. 2003. "The Other Kind: Representing Otherness and Living with It on Kotu Island in Tonga." In *Oceanic Socialities and Cultural Forms: Ethnographies of Experience*, edited by Ingjerd Hoëm and Sidsel Roalkvam, 157–177. Oxford: Berghahn.

Sahlins, Marshall. 1958. *Social Stratification in Polynesia*. Seattle: University of Washington Press.

Sahlins, Marshall. 1963. "Poor Man, Rich Man, Big-Man, Chief: Political Types in Melanesia and Polynesia." *Comparative Studies in Society and History* 5, no. 3: 285–303.

Sahlins, Marshall. 1993. "Goodbye to Tristes Tropes: Ethnography in the Context of Modern World History." *Journal of Modern History* 65, no. 1: 1–25.

Schwimmer, Eric. 1990. "The Maori Hapu: A Generative Model." *Journal of the Polynesian Society* 99, no. 3: 297–317.

Singer, Merrill. 2014. "Following the Turkey Tails: Neoliberal Globalization and the Political Ecology of Health." *Journal of Political Ecology* 21: 436–454.

Smith, Joseph Wayne, Gary Sauer-Thompson, and Graham Lyons. 1997. *Healing a Wounded World: Economics, Ecology, and Health for a Sustainable Life*. Westport, CT: Praeger.

Stenning, Derrick J. 1969. *Household Viability among the Pastoral Fulani*. Indianapolis: Bobbs Merrill.

Tsing, Anna. 2015. *The Mushroom at the End of the World: On the Possibility of Life in Capitalist Ruins*. Princeton, NJ: Princeton University Press.

Wells, Herbert George. 1933. *The Shape of Things to Come*. London: Hutchinson.

PART II

Material Potential

4. *Tabu* and Bitcoin

FLUCTUATING (IM)MATERIALITY IN TWO
NONSTATE MEDIA OF EXCHANGE

Keir Martin

The extent to which the material form that money takes is key to ensuring that it successfully serves as a means of circulation that enables economic growth and stability has been a matter of political debate for centuries. In the last decade of the nineteenth century, US politics was dominated by a debate between "silverites" and advocates of the gold standard, with each side blaming the other's preferred metal for the great Panic of 1893. This debate revolved around particular material forms' capacity to encourage hoarding. This hoarding of money tied up the value that it stored in illegitimate ways. The silverites claimed that gold encouraged anticirculatory accumulation on the part of the rich, as exemplified in William Jennings Bryan's famous "Cross of Gold" speech to the Democratic Convention of 1896 that secured him the party's presidential nomination:

> Upon which side will the Democratic Party fight; upon the side of "the idle holders of idle capital" or upon the side of "the struggling masses"? . . . Having behind us the producing masses of this nation and the world, supported by the commercial interests, the laboring interests, and the toilers everywhere, we will answer their demand for a gold standard by saying to them: "You shall not press down upon

the brow of labor this crown of thorns; you shall not crucify mankind upon a cross of gold." (quoted in Kazin 2006, 61)

Bryan went on to lose the subsequent presidential race, but his contribution is widely claimed to have been one of the most important speeches in US political history (see, for example, Williams 2010), and the debate over gold has continued to have a marked political importance in the years since. The United Kingdom's final withdrawal of sterling from the gold standard marked a major tipping point in that nation's withdrawal from global political and economic leadership, being seen at the time as a moment that "it is safe to predict . . . will become an historic date . . . the definite end of an epoch in the world's financial and economic development."[1] Forty years later, the abandonment of the US dollar's $35-an-ounce gold standard peg ushered in a new global economic era that Christopher Gregory (1997) came to characterize as the era of "savage money"; in 2011, yet another forty years on, the financial journalist Edmund Conway described this move as "one of those seminal moments whose significance has only gradually become apparent. . . . The more one examines economic history, the more obvious it is that this was one of the most important policy decisions in modern history. Were it not for that decision, it is quite feasible that we would not have suffered the financial crisis of the past four years."[2]

This concern with the effects of money's different material forms is reflected in anthropological debates. At the heart of many of these debates is a concern about the limits of human agency versus the power of particular material exchange media to re-create human sociality in their own image. This potential is often feared with regard to state currency and is likewise often hopefully embraced with regard to other media of exchange. In this article I argue that, despite the strongest statements of such expectations, conscious human intervention remains central to shaping the outcomes of particular materializations (or seemingly dematerializations) of exchange relations.

Most of the twentieth-century anthropological debate about the nature of money tended to assume that money was a particular kind of material object. From a perspective that stressed the contextual social creation of meaning and value, the material itself often seemed to be given a power that was worryingly fetishistic. This particular emphasis on placing the impact of the material forms of money within the proper context of the wider networks of social relations that appear to give them power formed the basis of Maurice Bloch and Jonathan Parry's (1989) famous critique of both Paul Bohannan's (1959) and Igor Kopytoff's (1986) analyses of the "impact" of money on the Tiv. From Bloch and Parry's perspective, both Bohannan and Kopytoff seemed to view money objects as having an almost magical power to simply destroy customary distinctions between different spheres of exchange in a manner that did not adequately explore the wider political-economic context within which money circulated, a position derided by Bloch and Parry (1989, 16) as a form of "technological determinism." Likewise, Jane Guyer (2004) was skeptical about the assumption that the introduction of Western money to West Africa simply replaced existing networks of exchange with a singular commodified mode of value. The simplistic position attributed to Bohannan is now rarely advanced except as a foil against which to define our now apparently more sophisticated understandings (e.g., Maurer 2006). Instead, when the focus is on the form that money takes, it is now less on the extent to which it is a mistake to ascribe social effects to particular material objects (as, in different ways, Bryan and Bohannan could be accused of doing by their opponents) than on the extent to which a move to apparently less tangibly material forms (such as credit cards and online banking) changes the ways in which money can shape our world.[3] But whereas money's predominant impact, in the older literature, was the power to cut the ties of custom and relational obligation and to usher in a new age of individual agency, agreement about the effect of the move toward less obviously materialized forms of money has not been so forthcoming. Daniel Miller, for example, argues that the emergence of money that can be traded electronically and instantly without constraints of place means that "money is the one form that is coming to correspond to what up to now has been the fantasy of the discipline of economics, a virtual asocial economic fact, and thereby a building-block of pure capitalism" (1997, 43).

Keith Hart (n.d.), by contrast, claims that the revolution ushered in by virtual currency lies in its repersonalizing effect. Virtual transactions leave a personalized footprint in a way that previous material technologies of exchange did not, meaning that every time I spend, I build up a personal history as a consumer. Virtual currency when seen from this perspective becomes a highly personalized medium of exchange that builds ongoing relationships with other actors (businesses) and, in the context of that relationship, shapes my ongoing behavior and nature as a personal consumer. For Hart, this has a number of potentially utopian outcomes:

> The idea that the communications revolution contains some potentially redeeming features rests on one overwhelming fact: that large

amounts of information concerning the persons involved in economic transactions at any distance can now be processed cheaply, thereby making possible the repersonalization of complex economic life. . . . Rather than be overwhelmed by money as an external object of un-known provenance, however, people may come to express themselves subjectively through it. Money would then be seen as the preserve of neither states nor anonymous markets, but rather as the ongoing in-vention of people seeking to measure the consequences of some of their interactions. (chap. 1)

We are thus given two utopian visions for the future in which demateri-alized money enables a previously unimaginable freedom: one in which its dematerialization finally makes possible the dream of pure depersonalized free-market capitalism, and another in which precisely the same material shift enables the polar opposite of repersonalized monetary transactions.

Contested Currencies and the Bitcoin Revolution

In this article I compare two media of exchange whose monetary status is contested: Tolai *tabu* (often referred to as "shell money" or "shell wealth") and bitcoin, the most widely circulated and best-known form of non-state-backed virtual currency. Tabu and bitcoin have very different histories and scopes of circulation. However, for both it is, in part, their nature as a par-ticular kind of electronic or material medium of exchange that is advanced by many users as underpinning particular potential social effects, but only provided that the possibilities offered by their unique form are correctly rec-ognized and acted upon.

Bitcoin was launched as a concept in 2008 in a paper proposed by the anonymous writer, or group of writers, Satoshi Nakamoto, who argued that the ability to time-stamp transactions by hashing them into a longer chain of transactions enabled by high-power processing meant that a "network" with "minimal structure" could provide verification for the legitimacy of trans-actions, without having to go through a "third party" such as a "financial institution" or the state (Nakamoto 2008).[4]

The first bitcoin trading began in 2009, but by mid-2013 bitcoin was al-ready estimated to have a value of $964 million, which had risen to $6.16 billion by April 2016.[5] Consequently, bitcoin has become the subject of in-creasing debate among legislators and financial regulators across the globe in recent years.[6] Bitcoin can now be used to buy and sell a wide range of services. Many major retailers, such as Microsoft and Dell, now offer the option to pay with bitcoin online alongside payment in state currencies, and bitcoin can itself be traded for state currencies or other commodities by anyone with internet access with as much ease as other forms of internet-based financial transactions.

For many of its proponents, bitcoin is part of a revolution in currency as utopian as those imagined by Miller and Hart. But with bitcoin the utopian dream is not the reembedding of money in social relations as imagined by Hart but rather the final liberation of money from a particular kind of social embedding, namely, its regulation and ultimate guaranteeing by nation-states or suprastate bodies such as the European Union. Whereas, for Hart, both the state and the "anonymous market" are equally to be opposed to the humanizing effect of personalized money, for some bitcoin enthusiasts it is the anonymous market that, by depersonalizing transactions, finally provides the currency with the capacity to enable the purest form of humanism: absolute individualism. Hart (1986) observed in the days when access to electronic currency was limited to a very small proportion of the world's population that the most common material embodiment of money, the coin, had two sides, which symbolized its Janus-faced character. Coins simultaneously embodied a top-down power of the state and a bottom-up commodity exchange value. One side of the coin cannot exist without being linked to the other, even if we view them as opposites, and even if we prefer the market to the state, or the picture of the queen to that of the lion and the unicorn.[7]

But if the two-sided nature of money is inescapably inscribed into its material nature, then the potential to liberate money from these material forms suggests, to some at least, the possibility to finally liberate its true nature from the other side that compromises its utopian potential. The replacement of these material tokens in exchange raises, in some quarters at least, the possibility of realizing the dream of a technology of exchange that no longer needs the state's backing but can, instead, operate as a pure medium of exchange and the uncorrupted (dis)embodiment of market principles. Hart himself noted that "the rise of . . . plastic credit cards is undermining state control of industrial societies" (1986, 637). Since then, the internet has revolutionized personal consumption and economic transactions in ways that would have been unimaginable in the mid-1980s and has also made possible a vision of currency creation that consciously sets out to achieve what Hart described as an unintended consequence of new technologies of exchange: namely, the undermining of state control of currency circulation and, ultimately, the decoupling of currency from the state, leaving money free to circulate as a pure medium of market exchange.

Such issues are thoroughly questioned in the prehistory of virtual currencies like bitcoin. Enthusiasts who correctly predicted that the technological revolution of the marriage of "computers to telecommunications" (Chaum 1985, 1044; see below) would create a revolution in everyday life debated the extent to which this technological revolution had certain inevitable effects on social relations, and the extent to which the effects of these changes were potentially under conscious human control. In 1985, a year before Hart published "Heads or Tails? Two Sides of the Coin," David Chaum released an article that would go on to have a significant impact on the development of virtual currency: "Security without Identification: Transaction Systems to Make Big Brother Obsolete." The opening lines of Chaum's article identify the potential for future digitalized currency to repersonalize monetary exchanges, identified by Hart twenty years later, but in far more dystopian terms: "Computerization is robbing individuals of the ability to monitor and control the ways information about them is used. Already, public and private sector organizations acquire extensive personal information and exchange it amongst themselves" (1030).

But for Chaum the technology carried a different potential as well. Transactions could be organized electronically in a manner that meant that only the directly relevant elements of a user's identity or transaction history (whether economic or legal) were available to vendors or appropriate authorities. As opposed to the analog forms of all-in-one identity checks, such as drivers' licenses and passports, widespread digitization provided the opportunity for the information aggregated by a person's transaction history to be sliced and diced on a case-by-case basis, preserving anonymity and avoiding the repersonalization of currency so admired by Hart and so feared by libertarians as the outcome of dematerialization. Here the technology has infinitely variable potentials. It can strengthen Big Brother or make him obsolete. The question is what we do with that technology. As Chaum puts it,

> Advances in information technology have always been accompanied by major changes in society: the transition from tribal to larger hierarchical forms, for example, was accompanied by written language, and printing technology helped to foster the emergence of large-scale democracies. Coupling computers with telecommunications creates what has been called the ultimate medium—it is certainly a big step up from paper. One might then ask: To what forms of society could

this new technology lead? The two approaches appear to hold quite different answers. (1985, 1044)

Bitcoin is, in part, an attempt to create a nonstate currency that lives up to Chaum's second vision of anonymized individualism free from domination by big players who may collect illegitimate information on individuals as opposed to merely legitimately recording the chains of their separable transactions in order to verify those transactions' legitimacy (states and major corporations with an interest in manipulating pure markets are the two most obvious candidates who might collect such information; see also Maurer, Nelms, and Swartz 2013). The system works by peer-to-peer electronic verification of chains of anonymized transactions. The longer the chain of transactions that can be verified and agreed to be genuine across the network, then the more likely the transactions are to be genuine and to not involve double spending or fraud. Indeed, once the network and the chains of transactions reach a certain size, then, statistically, it is allegedly virtually impossible that they might be subject to an attack that retrospectively alters the historical chain of transactions that gives bitcoins their value. As such, bitcoin is claimed by its advocates to be a more secure store of economic value than state currency—which relies on trust in that state and trust in that state's good (market-oriented) intentions. As we have seen in recent years, this trust cannot be taken for granted, and neither can we rely on the state to act in the best interests of the market or humanity (the latter being, in this view, strictly reducible to the former). As such, the algorithms that underpin bitcoin value are more reliable than the trust in the state that underpins fiat currency value. In Cyprus in 2013, for example, the rush from the euro to bitcoin in response to the European Central Bank's move to impose a levy on Cypriot bank accounts in order to restore financial stability is taken by some enthusiasts as the first sign of a shift in consciousness in which the state is no longer automatically seen as the best final guarantor of financial value.[8] Such a revolution in state-free value has been made possible only by the technological innovations brought in by the internet and the wide availability of the high-processing-power computer systems that underpin bitcoin mining (the process of maintaining blockchains of transactions that is rewarded with the issuing of bitcoins). But, unlike those anthropologists whose work implies that particular forms of materialization or dematerialization might inevitably lead to particular forms of social change, many of the activist libertarians at the heart of bitcoin development are keenly aware of the dangers of the technology moving in other directions.[9]

Despite bitcoin's novelty, the bitcoin community is already split between moderates, such as those gathered around the Bitcoin Foundation, which is engaged in discussions with financial regulatory authorities in the United States, and those who believe that the radical antistate potential of bitcoin is in danger of being diluted. For example, in 2013 a consortium of well-known bitcoin developers came together under the moniker "unsystem" to organize crowdfunding for a "dark wallet" that would electronically store users' bitcoins on the "dark web" and would bundle and splice multiple bitcoin transactions in a manner that would make tracing individual transactions and linking them to individual transactors next to impossible. The rationale for this is explained by Cody Wilson, the project manager for DarkWallet: "If Bitcoin represents anything to us, it's the ability to forbid the government. . . . DarkWallet is your way of locking out the State."[10] Wilson is perhaps most famous to the general public as the developer of the 3-D printable gun, a project that was largely funded via bitcoin after conventional funding became hard to secure. Wilson justified it on the grounds that "this is about enabling individuals to create their own sovereign space. . . . The government will increasingly be on the sidelines, saying 'hey, wait'. . . . It's about creating the new order in the crumbling shell of the old order."[11]

The promotional crowdsourcing video for Dark Wallet takes the message even further:

> It's the end of empire. . . . The United States imagines the power to regulate the world's first great digital currency—bitcoin . . . to provide a framework for its existence . . . a technology that questions all previous frameworks fitted for its straitjacket. Helping the United States is a group of lobbyists and corporations calling themselves the foundation. The mission's a performance: to both agree with and maintain an independence from regulatory power. But you can't have it both ways. . . . Help us make this implementation a line in the sand. Bitcoin is what they fear it is. A way to leave. To make a choice.[12]

Here we see the desire to escape the state coupled with the sense that the technology provides the potential, but not the certainty, of achieving that escape. This kind of bitcoin activism might be broadly conceived of as a variety of right-wing libertarianism with a strong belief in unfettered markets. One recent survey found that 37 percent of bitcoin users self-identified as libertarians or anarcho-capitalists (by contrast, 2 percent of the general population of the United States self-identify as libertarian). Among those surveyed, the most commonly expressed fear for the future of the currency was "regulatory/legal intervention."[13] It is not always as simple as that, however. Bill Maurer observes, "It's very easy for me to slam it, and say this is really stupid libertarian mumbo-jumbo. . . . But I'm starting to see, particularly among some of the younger folks who are involved in Bitcoin, reconfiguration and rewritings of ideologies into new configurations that I certainly was not prepared for" (Tooker and Maurer 2015, 341). Wilson, for example, in an interview with former Fox News host Glenn Beck, declared that he was torn between left-wing and right-wing anarchism and encouraged Beck to read Michel Foucault's *Discipline and Punish* if he wanted to understand why Romney versus Obama was irrelevant in the context of a political system that wants to exert greater surveillance and control over the individual.[14]

Bitcoin advocacy is, however, often associated more unproblematically with a right-wing pro-market libertarianism, as in the writings of Julia Tourianski, a contributor to the Ludvig von Mises Institute of Canada, who describes herself as "a promoter of anti-state mentality . . . in a love-affair with private property, the free-market." Her manifesto, "The Declaration of Bitcoin's Independence," has been widely circulated and is worth citing at length:

> We have been cyclically betrayed, lied to, stolen from, extorted from, taxed, monopolized, spied on, inspected, assessed, authorized, registered, deceived, and reformed. . . . And then there was bitcoin.
>
> But we are in an age of appropriation, and nothing is immune. Today bitcoin is not only volatile in its value, but in its very essence. Bitcoin is in the crucial stages of development. Its code can evolve in several directions. It's under threat from those who don't understand it; it's under threat from those who do understand it, but fear it. The crusade to absorb bitcoin into the seams of the State has begun. There is a conscious effort to co-opt. The goal is to swallow bitcoin, process it, integrate it, devolve it, and keep it stagnant in the gears of a failed operating system. Bitcoin's potential is being hijacked. They have their own idea of what they want bitcoin to be.
>
> Do not underestimate DNA; nothing is born completely neutral. Follow the protocol: it has anarchistic implications. Bitcoin is inherently anti-establishment, anti-system, and anti-state. Bitcoin undermines governments and disrupts institutions because bitcoin is fundamentally humanitarian. . . . The blockchain is free speech. . . . Bitcoin is not supposed to work within our current mechanisms. Bitcoin needs not entities of authority to acknowledge it, incorporate it, regulate it, and tax it.

Bitcoin means to channel economic power directly through the individual. The voices of the people who are working to preserve the purity of bitcoin's ethos are being drowned out. Bitcoin is not just a currency, a commodity, or a convenience. Just like the internet gave information back to the people, Bitcoin will give financial freedom back to the people. . . . Bitcoin will allow us to shape the world without having to ask for permission. We declare bitcoin's independence. Bitcoin is sovereignty. Bitcoin is renaissance. Bitcoin is ours. Bitcoin is.[15]

A mixture of hubris and anxiety haunts the lines of Tourianski's manifesto. On the one hand, there are the assertions that the technology itself has fundamental and irreversible implications (the DNA means it cannot be neutral; the protocol has inherently anarchist, antistate implications), while, on the other hand, there is the fear that incorporation into the system that bitcoin is allegedly inherently destructive of has now gone so far that the voices of those who wish to preserve bitcoin's "purity" are already being "drowned out." Like Chaum nearly thirty years earlier, she is keen to stress that the code "can evolve in several directions." Such ambiguities are echoed by many others today, such as one contributor to unsystem's web forum who writes, "In the past months I have slowly come to understand how vulnerable Bitcoin actually is, not because of it as a technology [sic], but because of the humans interacting with it."[16]

Tolai Tabu: Imprisoned Capital Waiting to Be "Unlocked"?

If bitcoin's escape from the need for material tokens of exchange is what gives it a particular utopian free-market potential, in the second case, Tolai tabu, it is its specific form of materiality that gives it, in the eyes of some of its would-be users, the potential to act as a spur for the development of capitalist relations in the East New Britain Province of Papua New Guinea (PNG). Many would consider PNG the birthplace of gift/commodity theorizing in anthropology. It is the problem of value transformation in the era of colonial entanglements in PNG that provided the context for the starkest theoretical depiction of this contrast, Gregory's (1982) *Gifts and Commodities*, a book that was a major influence on perhaps the most widely influential work of British social anthropology of the past three decades, Marilyn Strathern's (1988) *The Gender of the Gift: Problems with Women and Problems with Society in Melanesia*.

In most of these depictions, money's origin as a technology for commodity exchange is largely assumed. The only question is whether or not it will "hold its value" by remaining a commodity, as Strathern (1975) put it in *No Money on Our Skins: Hagen Migrants in Port Moresby* (an early pioneering study of money in Melanesia), or whether it will be incorporated into gift-exchange cycles.

This is a perspective that stresses social construction of the kind of core value (the "essence," as Tourianski would put it) that currency has. The physical material nature of the exchange item (in this case money) is largely irrelevant or secondary to the way its value status changes as it passes from one exchange sphere to another (in Strathern's [1975] typology from town to village or in Gregory's [1982] typology from the commodity economy to the gift economy). Gregory (1982) does draw attention to the ways in which the divisibility of paper money and coins can encourage a particular way of quantifying value, whereas the ranking of some shell valuables by size encourages a way of measuring competing values on a hierarchical scale associated with competitive gift-exchange networks. But the underlying message is clear. The value embedded in the object is largely extrinsic to the object itself but is the consequence of the social relations within which the object is embedded at that particular moment. Most of these discussions tend to start from an assumption that these objects originate in one sphere of exchange or another and can then be transformed if they are moved into a context that values them differently.

Tolai tabu is an exchange object that has always complicated such starting points. On the one hand, it would appear to be a gift-like Melanesian exchange item par excellence, marking and making relationships between persons linked by blood and reciprocal interdependence. Yet, on the other hand, unlike the *kula*[17] valuables of the Trobriands, for example, it has always simultaneously been used as a technology to enable short-term exchanges, such as buying food or betel nut from strangers at marketplaces—in other words, it acts, on occasion, as money. In part, this capacity is attributed to the material nature of tabu (see T. Epstein 1968). Unlike the kinds of shell valuables mentioned by Gregory, tabu is quantifiable, divisible, and anonymous, being made up of hundreds of small nassa shells strung together on strips of rattan cane. The origin and history of circulation for any piece of tabu is consequently almost impossible to trace. It can easily be subdivided into smaller units by twisting the cane and snapping a smaller length off. There has long been a counting system for tabu in which the value of a particular item on the marketplace could be calculated in terms of the number of *pokono* (sometimes translated as "fathoms") of tabu.[18] Its particular material form has also made tabu more easily interchangeable with state currency than other such media of exchange. Unlike many other forms of customary shell wealth in the region, tabu is now commonly bought with state currency, and there is a shifting exchange rate between tabu and PNG kina that is largely dependent on the fluctuations of supply and demand.

Although tabu has long circulated as both gift and commodity and, owing to its material nature, has been relatively easily interchangeable with the state currency, there is an enduring, although often hidden, controversy over the extent to which the nature of tabu is threatened by monetization. This is not necessarily a concern with tabu's interchangeability with money per se—tabu has been interchangeable with state currency since the early days of German colonialism in the 1880s—but with the extent and nature of that exchange in recent years.[19] In the years since PNG's independence in 1975, a small but significant national elite has emerged that is able to buy tabu shells in bulk with Australian and US dollars. This trend has turned the creation of a free market in tabu shells into a problem, at least from the perspective of many grassroots villagers, who see in it a tendency for the so-called Big Shots to entrench their new economic superiority. This is the case even in the sphere of customary ritual that is ideally supposed to stress an equivalence in which even those who emerge as "Big Men" are still tied by networks of obligation to those whom they have to convince to accept their leadership (see A. Epstein 1992, 108; Martin 2013, 125). Today, from a grassroots perspective at least, the money power of the Big Shots enables them to shortcut such ties (Martin 2013, 126–128).

In the remainder of this article, I discuss one particular attempt to utilize the convertibility of tabu into money, namely, attempts by the regional government to explore the possibility of establishing a tabu bank in the mid-2000s. This was, in large part, conceived of as an attempt to spur business development in the province by releasing the value that was currently "trapped" in tabu by making it even easier to convert, thus turning it into capital that could be invested. Tabu's particular material form, enabling large-scale two-way convertibility with the state currency, meant that this potential value could be more easily accessed than in other cases, provided the political will was there to make it happen. For example, the *Post Courier* on November 16, 1999, quotes the province's deputy governor, Leon Dion, as saying that "people should be allowed to use their traditional money for trading purposes due to the rapid drop in the value of the kina" and that "only one quarter of the US$2.2 million worth of *tabu* amongst Tolai was in circulation . . . while the other three quarters of it is stored away in rolls or wheels by the elder clansmen in their storage houses." In this he echoed Bryan's concerns about the value locked up and blocked from circulating by the cross of gold 103 years earlier. Dion went on to argue that the establishment of a "customary wealth bank would help to mobilize and control the *tabu* currency."[20]

Around this time rhetoric abounded about PNG facing a major financial crisis that was not expected to resolve itself. The impact of the devaluation of the kina on grassroots villagers was emphasized. In February 2002 Dion opened the Balanataman Tabu exchange, operated by the Balanataman local-level government. Speaking at the launch, the owner of Matikotop Enterprises, Michael Kava, whose business had been instrumental in organizing the project, announced that he hoped "to assist people to transform their traditional wealth into modern PNG currency. . . . If their tradition money is taken into consideration Tolai families were relatively well off."[21] At around the same time Sir Ronald ToVue, one of Dion's predecessors, told a meeting at Navuneram village that "the country is facing a serious financial crisis and the only way for the locals to survive is by using traditional money."[22]

These approaches did not receive universal approval, however. The director of the National Cultural Commission, Jacob Simet, argued that tabu's "ceremonial and ritual value" meant that it could not "function as an alternative to kina." He said, "They seem to think that if people can't get access to the kina then they should turn to *tabu*, and that's something from the word go, something totally wrong with that. . . . They use the term mobilization and standardization. . . . So this is where my fear is" (Simet, quoted in Radio Australia 2002).

The East New Britain provincial government commissioned a report from the Australian development consultants Assai Consult that discussed the possibility of increasing the convertibility of tabu to money for development processes. It was submitted to the provincial government in July 2002. Most provincial government leaders responded with enthusiasm to this report, but from conversations that I had with Simet around this time, it was clear that his skepticism had, if anything, hardened: "People are short of money these days. At the moment it's hard to exchange large amounts of tabu for money. If one could exchange large amounts, the tendency would be for the grassroots to cash in their tabu for money, as they always need money. People like me could hold on to our tabu, as I would never need to do this. I can always get money" (pers. comm., March 15, 2003).

Simet explained to me that in light of the already visible trend for tabu holdings to be concentrated in the hands of the new economic elite, he feared that custom would be fatally damaged by the intensification of that trend that such a ready two-way conversion might entail. From the perspective of would-be economic developers, the process of releasing value locked in tabu stocks rotting away in old men's houses might be attractive. However, for Simet the concern was that a situation in which grassroots people cashed in their stocks of tabu to deal with short-term economic crises, such as paying school fees, would mark the end of tabu's vital role in re-creating enduring ties of reciprocal obligation at customary rituals. "Big Shots" might continue to arrive at customary events to distribute tabu, but the potential for this concentration of tabu ownership to consolidate a two-tier custom in which those without money power were excluded entirely from a leading role was in danger of damaging the noneconomic values of reciprocal interdependence that were as important to tabu as its economic potential. Like money for Hart, tabu for Simet had two sides, and in prioritizing one side of the polarity for a short-term economic fix, the provincial government risked defacing or debasing the more important opposite side of the value embedded within it.[23] One could even argue that, like Tourianski, Simet saw the "essence" of his exchange technology as being at risk. Unlike Tourianski, however, he feared its depersonalizing commodification while she feared its depersonalizing decommodification.

Simet's views, although not so common among his fellow elite members, were more widely held by grassroots villagers. One evening I had a conversation with ToAtun, a grassroots villager who expressed a similar fear. In the previous days, the provincial government's tabu bank plans had been all over the local radio, and many of the biggest proponents of the scheme had been present at a *minamai* (mortuary rite) for a well-known local leader. That evening, the villager raised the scheme with me and expressed his contempt for those proposing it. He agreed with Simet that if tabu were to be more readily transferable into money, that would intensify its consolidation in the hands of "Big Shots." In addition, he raised the fear that it would incentivize young men with criminal intent to begin stealing tabu to convert it into kina, something that was, at the time, not a particular concern. The former PNG prime minister, Sir Rabbie Namaliu, had made a speech at the minamai in which he spoke of the importance of strengthening custom. This had been regarded by some as inappropriately political for such an event. My grassroots informant told me that evening that all those "Big Shots" were hypocrites: "Look at Rabbie Namaliu and that lot making speeches about how we need to strengthen custom, etc., and then they're all backing something like this that will kill custom" (pers. comm., March 22, 2003).

The fears around the future of tabu have some interesting parallels with the fears expressed by some over the future of bitcoin. In both cases there is the fear of state intervention messing with the essence of the true value of the technology of exchange. With bitcoin the fear is that the state wishes to regulate it in a manner that will destroy its potential to make truly anonymous market transactions—the potential that, for its proponents, would make it a truly human medium of exchange. With tabu the fear is that the state will destroy its nonmonetary value and ultimately depersonalize it by overemphasizing its ability to be used in commercial transactions and completing its transformation into a pastiche object incapable of marking and making other kinds of valuable relationships. Of course there are differences. For some bitcoin enthusiasts, the new technology marks the possibility for a complete transformation of old forms of political embeddedness (the ultimate reliance of currency on the state as its guarantor). By contrast, those who wish to unlock the economic potential of tabu have to be careful to defend themselves against the claims of people such as Simet and ToAtun that their revolution will destroy the customary context within which tabu gained and created a particular type of value. After all, if tabu has no customary value at all, it is hard to see why anyone would want it instead of state money. For this reason the revolution needs to be couched as a partial revolution that does not threaten tabu's status as a currency that has two sides. As one news report put it, "The government believes the promotion and mobilization of customary wealth would give shell money more value among the people and raise their purchasing power while preserving the culture,"[24] as opposed to bitcoin, whose sole purpose, in the eyes of its most zealous advocates at least, is to finally rid the world of the negative polarity, the state, which has held money back from finally expressing the potential for exchange to create individual sovereigns.

Conclusion

In both of these cases, it is the particular form of the (im)materiality of the medium of exchange that gives that medium the particular potentials that it has. The code and the immateriality of bitcoin are what gives it the radically revolutionary potential claimed by some of its supporters. The particular anonymity and divisibility of tabu are part of what has made it circulate as both gift and commodity in East New Britain for over a century, and part of what made the sudden emergence of a widespread trade in tabu for cash possible in the years following independence. Yet in neither case is potential necessarily equated with an inevitable unfolding of the DNA of the technology. Conscious human intervention remains a vital component in determining which potentials are realized. As with the legal control of human reproductive substances described by Marit Melhuus in this volume, while the materiality of the substances is central to their potential effects, deliberate intervention by humans through legal mechanisms remains central to how the (literal) DNA of these substances develops its potential.[25] Both tabu and bitcoin demonstrate the importance that particular material or immaterial forms may have in shaping the limits of what kinds of exchange are possible, but they do not determine their form, any more than European bank notes had a magical power to force the Tiv and others to exchange old lives for new sixty years ago. As James Ferguson observes in another context, "With social, as with any other sort of technology, it is not the machines or the mechanisms that decide what they will be used to do" (2009, 183). It is not only bitcoin but all such social technologies that remain vulnerable to the humans they are forced to interact with.

A distinction between the social (or the political) and the technological (or the material), such as that drawn by Ferguson, is never absolute, but to leap from the acknowledgment of this to a position where any drawing of such a distinction is declared obsolete misses the point of the performative power of such distinctions. Political anxiety over the extent to which the transformative potential of specific (im)material manifestations of money is inherent in the material, or is subject to conscious human social intervention that relies on such contested distinctions, remains as important today as in the 1890s. The battle over how to draw such distinctions remains a fundamental part of how politics is configured, and that is a battle in which decisions that can only be made by humans continue to be central.

NOTES

1. "The End of an Epoch," *Economist*, September 26, 1931.

2. Edmund Conway, "Abandoning the Gold Standard Was a Seminal Moment and One We're Now All Paying For," *Telegraph*, August 13, 2011.

3. Of course, the extent to which these items are "immaterial" can be questioned, as indeed can the very utility or universality of a distinction between "material" and "immaterial" (see Harvey, Krohn-Hansen, and Nustad, this volume). Credit cards are physical entities, and online currencies depend on a very material infrastructure of computers and telecommunications (e.g., Maurer, Nelms, and Swartz 2013, 262). Nonetheless, they are experienced as lacking the material character of an actual item of currency, surrendered by one transactor to another, that marked other forms of currency. They are widely contrasted with those forms of currency on that basis.

4. A good basic introduction to the fundamentals of how bitcoin works is provided at https://bitcoin.org/en/how-it-works (accessed April 22, 2017).

5. Jeff Cox, "Bitcoin Bonanza: Cyprus Crisis Boosts Digital Dollars," CNBC, March 27, 2013, http://www.cnbc.com/id/100597242; and John Lanchester, "When Bitcoin Grows Up," *London Review of Books*, April 21, 2016.

6. Daniel Roberts, "Yes, Regulation Is Coming to Bitcoin," *Fortune*, March 24, 2015, http://fortune.com/2015/03/24/bitcoin-regulated-exchanges-winklevoss-coinbase/.

7. Gregory (1996, 211), despite a number of clear differences with Hart, also argues that "we will never succeed in eliminating material standards of money" and that this helps to condition struggles between subalterns and state-backed elites. This is precisely one of the assumptions that libertarian bitcoin enthusiasts hope that their new technology can call into question.

8. Cox, "Bitcoin Bonanza."

9. John Lanchester provides a good overview of the technological basis for the development of bitcoin and its similarities to and differences from other forms of money. Lanchester, "When Bitcoin Grows Up."

10. Quoted in Andy Greenberg, "Dark Wallet Aims to Be the Anarchist's Bitcoin App of Choice," *Forbes*, October 31, 2013, http://www.forbes.com/sites/andygreenberg/2013/10/31/darkwallet-aims-to-be-the-anarchists-bitcoin-app-of-choice/#6aa6f7514cca.

11. Quoted in Andy Greenberg, "Meet the 'Liberator': Test-Firing the World's First Fully 3-D Printable Gun," *Forbes*, May 5, 2013, http://www.forbes.com/sites/andygreenberg/2013/05/05/meet-the-liberator-test-firing - the-worlds-first-fully-3d-printed-gun/2/#e2e7f23329e5.

12. Defense Distributed, "Dark Wallet," 2013, video, https://www.youtube.com/watch?v=Ou07Q6Cf_yc, October 31 2013, 2 minutes 52 seconds.

13. Tyler Durden, "The Demographics of Bitcoin," *Zero Hedge*, March 3, 2013, http://www.zerohedge.com/news/2013-03-10/demographics-bitcoin.

14. Cody Wilson, "Make Your Own Gun with a 3D Printer," January 18, 2013, video, https://www.youtube.com/watch?v=iwkX8sWSxNQ; interview with Glenn Beck, originally published January 17, 2013, theblaze.com, republished January 18, 2013, https://www.youtube.com/watch?v=iwkX8sWSxNQ.

15. Julia Tourianski, "The Declaration of Bitcoin's Independence," *Bitcoin Magazine*, May 14, 2014, https://bitcoinmagazine.com/articles/declaration-bitcoins -independence-1400096375.

16. "Download Latest Releases," December 2, 2018, http://libbitcoin.dyne.org/download.html. See also Lanchester, "When Bitcoin Grows Up," for a discussion of fears in the bitcoin community that the currency and the technology underpinning it are in the process of being incorporated not only by the state but by the other potential enemy of liberty identified by Chaum, namely, large corporations and financial institutions such as banks.

17. The *kula* is a customary exchange network found in the Trobriand Islands of Papua New Guinea. The study of the kula by Malinowski (1922) is one of the foundational texts of economic anthropology as a subdiscipline.

18. A *pokono* is equivalent to approximately two adult male arm lengths of tabu.

19. There is a long history of ethnographic literature dealing with the relationship between Tolai tabu and state currencies (e.g., T. Epstein 1968; A. Epstein 1969;

Salisbury 1970; A. Epstein 1992, 108; Errington and Gewertz 1995; Foster 1998; Martin 2013).

20. "East New Britain Province May Approve Traditional Shell Money as Legal Tender," *Post Courier*, November 16, 1999.

21. Quoted in "First Tolai Shell Money Exchange Launched," *National* (Port Moresby), February 13, 2002.

22. Quoted in Liz Thompson, "Shelling Out: Official Currency Is Challenged in Papua New Guinea," *New Internationalist*, no. 320 (January–February 2000), https://newint.org/features/2000/01/05/update.

23. Simet, like Hart, has a background in economic anthropology, having completed a PhD in anthropology on the subject of tabu circulation at the Australian National University in 1991 (see Simet 1991).

24. Quoted in "Jack Metta Looks at Traditional Money or Tabu in East New Britain," *Post Courier*, November 19, 2001.

25. Although, as Penny Harvey (this volume) observes, "An appeal to the vitality of the nonorganic runs . . . counter to established understandings of the DNA molecule as the basis of all living cells."

REFERENCES

Bloch, Maurice, and Jonathan Parry. 1989. Introduction to *Money and the Morality of Exchange*, edited by Maurice Bloch and Jonathan Parry, 1–32. Cambridge: Cambridge University Press.

Bohannan, Paul. 1959. "The Impact of Money on an African Subsistence Economy." *Journal of Economic History* 19, no. 4: 491–503.

Chaum, David. 1985. "Security without Identification: Transaction Systems to Make Big Brother Obsolete." *Communications of the ACM* 28, no. 10: 1030–1044.

Epstein, Arnold Leonard. 1969. *Matupit: Land, Politics and Change among the Tolai of New Britain*. Canberra: Australian National University Press.

Epstein, Arnold Leonard. 1992. *In the Midst of Life: Affect and Ideation in the World of the Tolai*. Berkeley: University of California Press.

Epstein, Trude Scarlett. 1968. *Capitalism, Primitive and Modern: Some Aspects of Tolai Economic Growth*. Manchester: Manchester University Press.

Errington, Frederick, and Deborah Gewertz. 1995. *Articulating Change in the "Last Unknown."* Boulder, CO: Westview.

Ferguson, James. 2009. "The Uses of Neoliberalism." *Antipode* 41, no. 1: 166–184.

Foster, Robert. 1998. "Your Money, Our Money, the Government's Money: Finance and Fetishism in Melanesia." In *Border Fetishisms: Material Objects in Unstable Places*, edited by Patricia Spyer, 60–90. New York: Routledge.

Foucault, Michel. (1975) 1995. *Discipline and Punish: The Birth of the Prison*. New York. Vintage Books.

Gregory, Christopher. 1982. *Gifts and Commodities*. London: Academic Press.

Gregory, Christopher. 1996. "Cowries and Conquest: Towards a Subalternate Quality Theory of Money." *Comparative Studies in Society and History* 38, no. 2: 195–217.

Gregory, Christopher. 1997. *Savage Money: The Anthropology and Politics of Commodity Exchange*. Amsterdam: Harwood.

Guyer, Jane. 2004. *Marginal Gains: Monetary Transactions in Atlantic Africa*. Chicago: University of Chicago Press.

Hart, Keith. 1986. "Heads or Tails? Two Sides of the Coin." *Man* 21, no. 4: 637–656.

Hart, Keith. n.d. *The Memory Bank: A New Commonwealth—Ver 5.0*. Draft version of published book. Accessed June 1, 2016. http://thememorybank.co.uk/book/.

Kazin, Michael. 2006. *A Godly Hero: The Life of William Jennings Bryan*. New York: Alfred A Knopf.

Kopytoff, Igor. 1986. "The Cultural Biography of Things: Commoditization as Process." In *The Social Life of Things: Commodities in Cultural Perspective*, edited by Arjun Appadurai, 64–94. Cambridge: Cambridge University Press.

Malinowski, Bronislaw. 1922. *Argonauts of the Western Pacific*. London. Routledge.

Martin, Keir. 2013. *The Death of the Big Men and the Rise of the Big Shots: Custom and Conflict in East New Britain*. New York: Berghahn Books.

Maurer, Bill. 2006. "The Anthropology of Money." *Annual Review of Anthropology* 35: 15–36.

Maurer, Bill, Taylor Nelms, and Lana Swartz. 2013. "When Perhaps the Real Problem Is Money Itself: The Practical Materiality of Bitcoin." *Social Semiotics* 23, no. 2: 261–277.

Miller, Daniel. 1997. *Capitalism: An Ethnographic Approach*. Oxford: Berg.

Nakamoto, Satoshi. 2008. "Bitcoin: A Peer-to-Peer Electronic Cash System." Unpublished manuscript. PDF file. http:/bitcoin.org/bitcoin.pdf.

Radio Australia. 2002. "Counting Shells at a New Bank in Papua New Guinea." *Pacific Beat*, Radio Australia, February 27, 2002. Transcript reproduced in S. DeMeulenare, ed., *Articles on Tabu Traditional Shell Currency*. http://www.appropriate-economics.org/asia/png/Articles_on_Tabu_Traditional_Shell_Currency.pdf.

Salisbury, Richard Frank. 1970. *Vunamami: Economic Transformation in a Traditional Society*. Berkeley: University of California Press.

Simet, J. 1991. "Tabu: Analysis of a Tolai Ritual Object." PhD diss. Australian National University, Canberra.

Strathern, Marilyn. 1975. *No Money on Our Skins: Hagen Migrants in Port Moresby*. New Guinea Research Bulletin 61. Canberra: Australian National University.

Strathern, Marilyn. 1988. *The Gender of the Gift: Problems with Women and Problems with Society in Melanesia*. Berkeley: University of California Press.

Tooker, Lauren, and Bill Maurer. 2015. "The Pragmatics of Payment: Adventures in First-Person Economy with Bill Maurer." *Journal of Cultural Economy* 9, no. 3: 337–345.

Williams, Richard. 2010. *Realgning America: McKinley, Bryan, and the Remarkable Election of 1896*. Lawrence: University Press of Kansas.

5. Sperm, Eggs, and Wombs

THE FABRICATION OF VITAL MATTERS
THROUGH LEGISLATIVE ACTS

———

Marit Melhuus

In broad terms, we could say that legislative processes are concerned with the translation of the political into a legal form. Thus, any study of legislation is also ipso facto an engagement with politics, and with the state, insofar as the legislative body is also a political body. My concern is with a specific legislative act—one that explicitly regulates assisted conception, authorizing the use of sperm and eggs and, by implication, wombs, for procreative purposes. The act in question is the Norwegian Biotechnology Act and, more specifically, those provisions that concern sperm and egg donation.[1] Thus, the materiality in focus is the vital substances of humans themselves: eggs and sperm. These substances constitute core elements in procreative practices, signifying the very materiality of human conception. The explicitness of the act necessarily conceals the ethical-political deliberations that underpin it. It is these deliberations that capture the stuff of the legal formulations and their eventual reformulation, refracting the values on which the law was grounded. These turn fundamentally on marriage, parenthood, family, personhood, and rights, and thus the moral fabric of society.

My focus is on the differential treatment of sperm and eggs as detachable (and hence potentially exchangeable) material substances and the ways these bodily substances are conceptually linked to notions of motherhood and fatherhood. By incorporating a temporal dimension, I show how, within the discursive formation of a legal-political discourse, the nature of these material substances shifts over time. Where sperm and eggs were earlier configured as fundamentally different by nature, more recently sperm and eggs have been reconfigured as equal in some essentially natural aspect. These shifts have implications not only for understandings of the materials in question but also for the procreative acts in which they are inscribed. There is, here, an issue of state-produced or state-authorized acts of kinship with regard to those acts produced or authorized by other orders (Lambek 2013, 251), and the way such orders coalesce or are even displaced.

By focusing on these particular materials and the discursive shifts that occur, it becomes evident that they cannot, meaningfully, be approached separately. They are mutually implicated. The material properties of eggs, sperm, and wombs are folded into the political just as the political is folded into these material substances. This chapter attempts to show how "forms of life and politics are affected and shaped through engagements with, and uses of, specific materials" (Harvey, Krohn-Hansen, and Nustad, this volume) by tracing the regulations on third-party gamete donation and exploring the way the material substances of sperm and eggs become politically available. They do so not as stable facts; rather, they are variously mobilized to articulate particular legal-political agendas, potentially reconfiguring fundamental notions of kinship.

In Law

In Norway there has been a certain reticence toward reproductive technologies and the potentialities these technologies represent. This restraint has been articulated through an unambiguous attitude against "meddling with nature" (*tukle med naturen*). "Meddling with nature" refers not only to any interference with the natural act of conception but also, concomitantly, to the moral framework within which conception should take place. Notions of gender, the institution of marriage, and the categories of motherhood and fatherhood are implicit in this framework. This reserved attitude was made amply evident in the various legislative processes leading up to the codification of the application of biotechnology in Norway, now integrated into the Biotechnology Act. This act is based on a cautionary principle that is explicitly iterated and subsumed under an overarching concern for ethics. Two overriding issues are articulated regarding the aim of the legislation: to secure the best interests of the child and to safeguard the interests of society by hindering selective breeding and the commercialization of reproduction.

In what follows, I examine aspects of the Norwegian Biotechnology Act to draw out the ways in which sperm, eggs, and wombs have become subjects of law, reflecting shifting sociopolitical concerns regarding procreation, marriage, parenthood, and gender—in effect, kinship and filiation. In this particular case, eggs, sperm, and wombs are all matters of kinship—and are variously performed, depending on the context. My interest is in the way these matters appear in a legal context, how they are put to work, so to speak. More specifically, my focus is on third-party gamete (sperm and egg) donation. These have been—and, to a certain degree (in the case of egg donation), still are—contested practices. In fact, there is no consensus—either in Parliament or among the public at large—regarding the application of biotechnology in medicine. In Norway sperm donation is legal but only from a known donor. Egg donation is prohibited, as is surrogacy.

As is apparent, my focus is not on the materiality of the law per se but rather on the way law—or, more precisely, a legislative process—engages with vital matters, producing particular categories and relations. This production occurs through the processes (paper trails, debates, and voting) leading up to the codification of a legal act. While the act itself (as a legal document) emerges as unequivocal, in its aim of clarity and singularity it simultaneously conceals not only the endeavors that have been invested to assemble the final outcome but also the practices that the law impels. The Norwegian Biotechnology Act has been the continued focus of a contested biopolitics, with revisions occurring with each shift in government.[2] Such revisions (and the media debates surrounding them) reveal the underlying values and sociocultural processes that are mobilized to change the law and, not least, the appeal these may have to the public at large. In this particular case, there are two things that draw my attention.

One has to do with the differential inscription of sperm and eggs, and the way this difference is challenged by an egalitarian principle. This move is a deliberate effort to reframe the prohibition of egg donation as gender discrimination. The other has to do with sperm donation and the transition from an unknown to a known donor. In 2003 the prevailing anonymity clause was repealed, and known donors became the prescribed norm. This move made explicit the significance of biogenetic connectedness for a child's identity. Both instances turn on notions of maternity and paternity. My focus is on the legal fabrication of vital matters and, more specifically, on the relations that condense these material forms.[3] In other words, I look at how the law materializes vivid reifications and how the material moves the law. In this context, imagination is significant.

I have argued elsewhere that this legislation articulates legislators' efforts to make sense of a world that is both real (in the sense of actual) and imagined, and that social imagination is embedded in the processes that propel the law. There is no doubt that imagination has played a significant part in the codification of the Norwegian Biotechnology Act. Imagining what reproductive technologies might potentially entail (for such fundamental institutions as marriage, family, and, ultimately, society) spurred the will to legislate—and to bring about restrictive legislation (Melhuus 2012). Bruce Kapferer, in pointing to the significance of imagination in conceptualizing the state, comments that "the very reality of the state is in the very character of its imaginary (as a spectre in human consciousness that has, as such, an effect on human action). Such an imaginary of the state is also a materiality, a force (spirit) in the constitution of persons and in the manifold arrangements and their processes of human existence" (2005, viii). I doubt Kapferer had state regulations of biotechnologies in mind, yet this way of conceptualizing the imaginary of the state as a force in the constitution of persons makes sense when dealing with legislative processes that concern the creation of life and the vital materials that constitute that life. It is perhaps this very force that has spurred the legal inscriptions contained in the Biotechnology Act, which point to basic values that have to do with kinship and filiation but also with equality and children's rights.

As a regulatory regime, legislation provides both order and, ideally, a sense of justice. Yet both these elements are subject to continual evaluations, producing potentially alternative modes of ordering based on a recognition of other values that define the factual matters at hand. While legislation is surely a "site in which certain kinship understandings are crystallised" (Edwards 2009, 7; see also Melhuus and Howell 2009), my work indicates that legal attempts to pin kinship down, as it were, are exceedingly difficult. Rather, "kinship escapes laws that attempt to pin it down, that discern and decide according to mutually exclusive choices: biological paternity or not, rights or no rights, one right but not another" (Lambek 2013, 256). This has to do with what Michael Lambek formulates as the superfluity and excess of kinship: "a superfluity of people who can count as kin; an excess in the number of ways kinship can be calculated . . . a surfeit of meaning, feeling and presence" (255). Practices of assisted conception force this superfluity to the fore by making visible not only the discrepancies between what the law prescribes and what people actually want and how they act, but also the tenuous character of the law itself, especially with regard to the materials that are being regulated. The regulation of assisted conception is an effort to stabilize kinship; certain phenomena become reified and essentialized, taking on a truth-value. Facts are produced, but not independently of values. These efforts can be read as "kinship acts," where the state is constituted by "producing and authorizing the means by which people are related to one another as parents, offspring, spouses, siblings and the like" (257).

Fact and Values

Biotechnology has radically changed procreative practices, destabilizing notions of the natural while simultaneously reembedding nature as produced by technological intervention. Third-party gamete donation deals with detachable body parts that can be circulated independently of any whole body. What draws my attention are the ways in which these parts are related to the wholes from which they are potentially detached, that is, how (or even whether) each detached part "remains characterized by the whole of which it once was an integral part" (Pottage 2004, 31), and not least how each whole (for example, male and female reproductive bodies) is differentially apprehended.

Sperm and eggs are human materials that, through conception, can potentially lead to the creation of other humans. Thus, these materials are of a different nature than the concrete and stone discussed by Penny Harvey (this volume). Yet each in its own way is "lively" and deeply embedded in politics.[4] Sperm and eggs are especially evocative as procreative substances because they encompass ideas that draw their force from nature or notions of the natural. As such, these materials are facts of life. But, as we shall see, they are not stable facts. "The nature" of the facts is susceptible to political-rhetorical challenges, thus shifting the very ground from which they draw their potential. Not only are these entities artifacts of the legal procedure itself (Pottage 2004, 25), but they also draw their connotations from spheres external to the legislative process.

Assisted conception is dependent on the availability of sperm, eggs, and wombs. There is an equality between the biogenetic contributions that sperm and eggs make to the human embryo, and this is generally recognized as a fact. They are key components of sexual reproduction, "each containing half of what is necessary to produce new life" (Cobb 2012, 5). Nevertheless, although these materials are, on one level, configured as having the same constitutive role in creating persons and identities, they are also perceived as qualitatively different. The nature of these differences has to do with the physical characteristics of sperm and egg cells[5] and, significantly, also with their gendered properties as constitutive of male and female reproductive bodies. This natural difference between men and women is established through the categories of motherhood and fatherhood.

Marilyn Strathern notes, in her discussion of different routes to kinship knowledge, that in "pre-technology Euro-American systems, motherhood and fatherhood required different kinds of proof to establish the fact of procreation" (1999, 78). Motherhood was established through birth; fatherhood, through presumed coitus with the mother. These different ways of establishing maternity and paternity are captured by two principles that underwrite the deliberations of the Biotechnology Act: *pater est quem numptiae demonstrant* (the so-called *pater est* rule: "the father is he who is married to the mother") and *mater semper certa est* ("the mother is always certain"). The first principle accords true fatherhood through marriage. Recognizing the uncertainty of fatherhood, it stresses the significance of the conjugal tie. The second principle acknowledges that motherhood is always certain, in that it is established through birth. This is perceived as a biological fact. No matter what the conditions of the birth of a child are (whether it is legitimate or not), the mother is always known as she is, by definition, the one who gives birth. These principles have guided the practices that concern the relationships between parents and children, that is, questions of filiation. They rest on what have been perceived as indisputable biological facts: that paternity is always uncertain and that there is no doubt about the identity of the mother. Both of these principles have been challenged (albeit in different ways) by reproductive technologies and associated practices, revealing tensions between notions of social and biological parenthood. In fact, until 1997 Norway did not have a specific legal clause defining motherhood. At that time, as a result of the debates about reproductive technologies and the potential fragmentation of motherhood, the following provision was added to the Children's Act: "The woman who gives birth to the child is considered its mother."[6] This definition of motherhood confirms the prevailing rule of *mater est*. Further, in 2008 Norway passed a gender-neutral marriage act,[7] granting same-sex couples the same rights as heterosexual couples, including the right to assisted conception.

This move created a new agenda for how parenthood should legitimately be determined.

Sperm Donation: A First Attempt at Regulation

Sperm donation in Norway has a longer legal history than egg donation, for obvious reasons. Sperm donation has been practiced since the 1930s (Løvset 1951; Molne 1976), and the first attempt to regulate it was made in 1953, as part of a Nordic effort to coordinate legislation regarding artificial insemination with donor sperm (AID).[8] Egg donation became a reality in the wake of Robert Edwards's pioneering technique of in vitro fertilization (IVF), and the ensuing birth of Louise Brown in 1978.[9] It surfaced on the Norwegian political agenda in 1984, as a result of the first "test-tube baby" made in Norway.[10] This event prompted the politicians to act lest matters get out of hand. In 1987 Parliament passed the Artificial Procreation Act. This act, as mentioned, has since been incorporated into the Biotechnology Act (first passed in 1994; see note 2).

The first attempt to regulate sperm donation did not result in legislation, even though most members of the committee appointed to evaluate the practice recommended regulation. Nevertheless, the effort was significant, not only because sperm donation was on the public agenda for the first time, but also because sperm became visible as a material signifier with respect to particular relations and particular values. Throughout its deliberations the committee took the institution of marriage for granted and upheld the principle of pater est. The discussion for and against AID shifted between biological and psychological arguments, between nature and nurture and the moral connotations these evoke with regard to what is natural, good, and right. Arguments centered, on the one hand, on the institution of marriage (and its purpose), the home, and love, and, on the other hand, on women's natural desire to have children and the significance of male infertility to male identity. The act of lying and the introduction of a third party into a marriage were recurring themes.

To quote the minority: "Our Christian culture rests on the home. Monogamous marriage is the very foundation of our culture. With [artificial] insemination [by donor sperm] a third party is introduced into a relationship between these two, that should be one, and between parents and children. Here one has driven a wedge into the very life principle of the home. . . . It may well be that this is one of those deathblows that our culture cannot tolerate" (Ministry of Justice 1953, 50). Moreover, the minority argued that the "insemination child" (to use their term) would cause marital discord. The husband would be reminded daily of his impotence: "he has by his side a wife whose motherhood is real, while his fatherhood is false" (54). In other words, despite the rule of pater est, true fatherhood is assumed to be biological. Insemination by donor is considered an intervention in a natural process, the consequences of which are unknown. Adoption is put forward as a better alternative because "the adopted child's creation is natural, just as adoption is a natural and familiar practice" (56).

The institution of marriage—and its purpose—is also central to the majority. The argument for legalizing AID rests on an idea that insemination contributes toward realizing "the essence of marriage, which otherwise would not be consummated" (23). Not only does AID make it possible for a woman to become a real mother (in contrast to being a mother by adoption), but it can also allow the husband to overcome feelings of inferiority attributed to his infertility, in that his wife would bear him a child that in the eyes of society would be his own biological child. For both sides, then, sperm donation is perceived in relation to marriage and its purpose. Marriage is at once reified and essentialized as the relevant, natural category within which sperm donation is framed. It is the conjugal relationship that constitutes the whole of which sperm becomes a vital part, whether it is disruptive of it or advantageous to it. Finally, it is noteworthy that the sperm donor is virtually absent from this account. Once the sperm is collected and detached from the provider, its source is rendered invisible. Hence, the sperm appears independent of the whole of which it was once an integral part.[11]

However, perhaps the single most significant argument against permitting a regulated version of AID (at least in hindsight) is that it "conceals the truth and prescribes secrecy about the mutual relations among a series of people . . . and . . . departs from the principle of biological fatherhood" (56). This argument is linked to the assumption that legislation will generate doubt about identity in that the child "will lack true knowledge of its origin and therefore of itself" (55). Although this identity issue was not so prominent at the time, it is precisely this argument that gains prominence in the 1990s: a child's right to know his or her biological origin is viewed as a precondition for knowing who he or she really is. Thus, from arguments that center primarily on marriage (and the relationship between the spouses) and on the meanings of sperm donation for motherhood and fatherhood, the focus shifts to the child and its best interests. Sperm as a biogenetic substance is perceived as vital to identity. Simultaneously, there is a shift in emphasis from parenthood to the separate relationships of mother-child and father-child.

Sperm and Egg Donation

In 1987, under a Labor government, Parliament passed the Artificial Procreation Act. With this act, sperm and egg donation entered the legal realm. The main intention of the act was to ensure that these practices would come under the control and authority of the state, regulated by an ethical framework that would determine what was to be permitted and who was to have access. The act allowed for "artificial procreation" under specific circumstances. It restricted assisted conception to married couples; it permitted AID with anonymous donor sperm; it prohibited egg donation in that fertilized eggs had to be returned to the woman from whom the eggs were taken; and conception outside the body was allowed to occur only with the couple's own egg and sperm. In other words, IVF could not be performed with donor sperm. Fertilized eggs could only be frozen for one year.

The sociopolitical deliberations on which this act was based reflected the main positions with regard to third-party gamete donation and general attitudes toward the developments in reproductive medicine and, for some, the need to curtail these (Odelstingsproposisjon no. 25, 1986–1987). At issue was the question of the extent of manipulation that these technologies entail, especially with regard to IVF. Nevertheless, it is interesting to note that IVF—using the couple's own eggs and sperm—was seen as less problematic than sperm donation (which requires no technological intervention), as the child would be the couple's biological child. To this extent, IVF, despite being a technological intervention, resembles the process of natural conception.

The question of secrecy was explicitly raised with regard to sperm donation; the working group that had prepared the documents (on which the parliamentary document was based) recommended that the anonymity of the donor be revoked. However, despite arguments against secrecy (e.g., third-party intervention in a marriage; the child's potential problems with its identity; the comparison with adopted children's right to know their parents), the principle of anonymity was upheld. Two main reasons were given. One is pragmatic: rescinding the anonymity clause would result in fewer donors, thus endangering the whole procedure. The other is that the child would know its biological identity through its mother (as she gestated it and gave birth). Although the child would not know its biological father, the chances that it would find out about its origins were seen to be minimal, in comparison with an adopted child, as very few people would be privy to the secret.

As far as I have been able to ascertain, it was the pragmatic argument that swayed the vote. However, pertinent to my present focus is the way motherhood was privileged with regard to the biological identity of the child. Knowing who your mother is (where you come from) eclipses knowing who your father is. This highlights how motherhood and fatherhood require different kinds of proof, and how motherhood is rendered unequivocal by the very (f)acts of gestation and birth. In law, this is underscored by the provision that a fertilized egg must be inserted back into the womb of the woman from which it was taken. This prohibition against egg donation was made explicit in a later revision of the law.[12] The framing of these matters would, however, change.[13]

Combined Deliberations on Egg and Sperm

To grasp the explicit differential treatment of sperm and eggs as articulated in the law, it is pertinent to examine how sperm and egg donation have generally been deliberated over in the same breath, as it were. It is the combined discourse of sperm and eggs, the conjoined argument, that is most revealing. As an example, I quote from the Ministry of Health's deliberations as they echo and condense views that have been held more generally and, moreover, have been reiterated since.[14] "There are those who argue that egg donation is in principle not different from sperm donation. . . . This is a view the Ministry rejects. Women and men's reproductive functions are different—seen both from the donor's and the recipient's point of view" (Odelstingsproposisjon no. 25, 1986–1987, 19). The ministry concurs with the working group's proposal:

> In contrast to sperm donation, egg donation requires medical surgery. . . . Donation of an egg has more similarities with transplantation than it has with sperm donation. . . . In contrast to egg donation, sperm donation does not create a situation different from natural reproduction. Donor insemination does not break fundamentally with that which occurs in natural reproduction. Whether conception occurs artificially or naturally, the sperm is something that comes from the outside. This implies that there will always be uncertainty as to who the father of the child is. With natural conception it is not unusual that there is a discrepancy between legal or social paternity and biological

paternity. . . . With natural reproduction the uterus and the egg constitute a natural unity. Conception, pregnancy and birth are a unified process that occurs within the woman. With egg donation this unity is broken. . . . With egg donation physical motherhood is split. . . . There is reason to believe that this lack of clarity will cause uncertainty with regard to the identity of the child." (19)

In a later parliamentary debate, the following is stated: "With regard to the order of nature, egg donation is a significantly larger interference than sperm donation. Egg donation would be a breach of the inviolability and unity of pregnancy." And "we do not know the consequences of introducing a notion of the strange or unknown mother [*fremmed mor*]. The feeling of mother-belonging [*morstilhørighet*] is the most fundamental of human [emotions]." Or in the words of another politician: "It is wrong that the mother of the child should be unknown. Mother-belonging is inviolable. For me this is not a question of gender equality but respect for the order of nature. To permit sperm donation is less problematical than egg donation, first and foremost because sperm is easily available and cannot be regulated by law so that we can prevent a child from having an unknown father."[15]

There are several things that can be gleaned from these excerpts. First and foremost is the insistence on a fundamental difference between egg and sperm donation. This is tied to an idea of the "order of nature," the difference in male and female reproductive functions, and the question of the availability of these two substances. Sperm is, by definition, available (it is "outside" the body), and this form of detachment implies ipso facto paternal uncertainty. Thus, sperm donation does not break with how natural conception is perceived. Eggs, however, are situated differently. Their availability is limited in terms of quantity and restricted in terms of access. Moreover, they are intrinsic to a natural whole that is constituted by the uterus and the eggs. This is then framed in terms of a unified process from conception through gestation to birth, which is inviolable. To disrupt this process would undermine the most fundamental of human emotions, that of belonging to one's mother. Finally, egg donation would split this unity and cause insecurity with regard to the identity of the child (in a way sperm donation would not). In other words, eggs may potentially be detached, but they may not circulate between women. Not only do they pertain to a whole that must not be violated, but this whole is perceived as the unitary process of conception, gestation, and birth, which essentially defines motherhood. Nevertheless, it is important to note that the introduction of a donated egg seems to imply introducing a strange or unknown mother, thus implicitly acknowledging the salience of the egg.

It is also worth noting that in 2003 there was a significant change in the way this issue was framed. Although the qualitative difference between men and women regarding their reproductive roles was upheld, the arguments against egg donation were phrased in cultural and ethical terms. Egg donation was seen to break with "long social and cultural traditions in society that are tied to motherhood and the unity of pregnancy. The Ministry is of the opinion that it is ethically more problematic to distinguish between the genetic and biological/social mother, than it is to [distinguish between] the genetic and social father." In fact, in the ministry's opinion, "the mother who gestates and gives birth to a child has such a strong biological tie to it that she must also be the child's genetic mother" (quoted in Norwegian Biotechnology Advisory Board 2011, 10).[16]

This shift to ethical and sociocultural arguments is significant insofar as it displaces the self-explanatory argument of nature, or what is natural, and hence potentially opens a different space for debate. Even though the cultural-ethical argument upholds an idea of a unitary motherhood, the comparative framing (which, to my mind, implicitly recognizes a certain equality between sperm and eggs) offers, perhaps inadvertently, an argument of gender discrimination. Such an argument shifts the locus of attention from motherhood and fatherhood to equal rights for infertile women and men. I return to this point below.

Rescinding the Anonymity Clause

It was also in 2003 that Norway repealed its anonymity clause with regard to sperm donation and legislated that only known donors could be used. The decision was based on a child's right to know its biogenetic origins. Thus, knowledge of biological relatedness was affirmed as fundamental to a child's identity and its legal right. This view was seen to be in accordance with the UN Convention on the Rights of the Child (UN 1989).[17] The question of origin was tied to identity, and the argument was that access to this knowledge was in the best interests of the child. (This argument finally became established as the ethical position in Parliament and gained an overwhelming majority vote.) As a result, Norway had to establish its own sperm bank with a register of sperm donors that also documents to whom the sperm had been donated. This register ensures that knowledge of the "real" father is lodged with the state and can, on request, be made available to a person over the age of eighteen who was conceived with the use of donor sperm. Sperm thus not only becomes identifiable with the "real" father but also becomes reattached to its source, as it were. Thus, sperm is restored to its proper (natural/biological) origin, mediating a relationship that "in fact" was always there.

To all intents and purposes, anonymous sperm donation collapses social and biological paternity into one father, the assumption being that knowledge of conception is considered a private matter (between the spouses) and not revealed publicly. The legal prescription of a known donor creates a different situation. With this move, biogenetics is the fact that establishes "true" fatherhood, but not necessarily legal fatherhood. Sperm donation with a known donor makes the distinction between *pater* and *genitor* explicit and public. Donor disclosure does not subvert pater est, but it does make evident the potential proof of fatherhood.[18]

Seen from the perspective of the state, it is a matter of getting the facts right: to be able to identify the biological and the social/legal father and, in so doing, remove uncertainty about paternity, while also ascertaining the legal kinship relationship. This is all done in the best interest of the child. However, for the child, the knowledge of this fact is conditional. The child has the right to know who its biogenetic father is, but its parents are not obliged to reveal the facts of conception. So we have a fact, and we have public (state) knowledge of the fact, but not necessarily "personal" knowledge of the same. Rescinding the anonymity clause means there is a legal fabrication of a certain filiation, based on a natural fact, but this "fact" may not necessarily materialize for those involved. The rescinding of donor anonymity is fundamental to the debate insofar as it is a claim about the significance attributed to genetics and biology in establishing filiation and identity. However, this conflation of facts and values is, at the same time, nothing more than a legal potentiality insofar as disclosure remains at the parents' discretion. Facts are dependent on acts.

Mater est? The Egg and the Womb

As I have said, in terms of their biogenetic contributions to the human embryo, there is an equivalence between sperm and eggs. One could assume that, at one level, they are imagined as having the same constitutive role in creating persons and identities. But, as we have seen, this same constitutive property does not necessarily translate into an equal treatment of sperm and eggs, as is evident from the different regulatory regimes that address assisted conception and third-party gamete donation. Whereas a child can de facto have two fathers, it can have only one mother. This is assured through the rule of mater est.

However, in practice the law is not incontrovertible on this score. Women/couples in need of an egg can travel to clinics abroad where such treatments are offered.[19] If conception and pregnancy are achieved, the woman will eventually give birth to a child. According to Norwegian law, she is then the mother of this child. The origin of the egg is effectively erased, even rendered irrelevant. Thus, the value of a unitary motherhood is upheld as a legal fiction. If the legal regulations were driven by a need to establish some kind of certainty in the wake of the potential fragmentation of motherhood that reproductive technologies represent, actual practices undermine these efforts.

The use of egg donation by Norwegian women can be seen as analogous to anonymous sperm donation. Just as anonymous sperm donation (within the terms of pater est) collapses pater and genitor, so egg donation collapses *mater* and *genetrix*. In both cases, the origin of the biogenetic material introduced is concealed, and the attempts of the legislators to get the facts right are subverted/undermined. Donor disclosure mitigates this situation. Gestation and birth are visible "facts" of who the mother really is. But acts distort the facts, and certain acts (e.g., receiving a donated egg) do not map onto the perceived connections between certain parts and imagined wholes. In Lambek's terms we could say that this is an instance where kinship escapes the law, an example of an excess in the number of ways kinship can be calculated.

Gender: Difference and Equality?

There has been—and to a certain extent still is—an entrenched gender difference with regard to third-party gamete donation, for what are seen to be very valuable reasons. These have to do with the understandings of fatherhood and motherhood. The process of procreation (conception, pregnancy, birth) and the ties between children and parents are understood as given by nature. However, whereas a man can have only one biogenetic tie to a child, a woman has both a biogenetic tie and a biological one. This has been framed as the natural difference between men and women.

The substantial difference between eggs and sperm is articulated through the notions of maternity and paternity. Fatherhood is established on different criteria than motherhood. One way to phrase this differential treatment of sperm and eggs is in terms of alienation: eggs are inalienable, whereas sperm is not. Hence, in legal terms sperm and eggs are valued differently. These substances are, as it were, the subjects of inegalitarian practices. Egalitarian principles are not universals, but in Norway such principles have good purchase, and perhaps even more so if the issue is one of gender inequality. It is therefore worth noting that already in 2003 a majority of the comments (*høringsuttalelser*)[20] submitted with regard to the revision of the Biotechnology Act argued that "masculine and feminine gender cells have the same ethical value" and stated that the prohibition on egg donation was a "biased discrimination" (*usaklig forskjellsbehandling*) between infertile men and infertile women" (quoted in Norwegian Biotechnology Advisory Board 2011, 12). The revision of the law in 2003, however, upheld the continued prohibition on egg donation.

In 2011 the Norwegian Biotechnology Advisory Board submitted its statement on egg donation.[21] The majority of the board members considered egg donation to be an extension of other kinds of assisted conception that are legal, accepted, and supported by the current authorities. This was the first time the board had had a majority in favor of permitting egg donation. Moreover, it called for women and men, and sperm and egg cells, to be treated as similarly as possible by the law. The board argued that egg donation does not threaten fundamental values in society, nor does it harm a third party. It also insisted that a distinction between the genetic/biological mother and the social mother is no more problematic than the already established distinction between the social and the biological father.[22] The board thus found that there were no good reasons to uphold the prohibition on egg donation (Norwegian Biotechnology Advisory Board 2011, 1).

In 2015, as a contribution to the current reevaluation of the Biotechnology Act, the same board upheld this majority view, stressing some additional points that were tied to possible discrimination. The majority view was that infertile men and women should be treated equally and that the children born from either egg donation or sperm donation in Norway should have the same right to know their biological origin (which may not be the case with egg donation performed abroad). Finally, the board's majority, presuming that the donated eggs would be fertilized with sperm from the partner, argued that there would be a genetic link with one of the parents. A minority of the board members upheld earlier arguments: that throughout human history the woman who gives birth to a child has been its genetic mother, even though her partner is not necessarily its genetic father. They also argued that legalizing egg donation would further contribute to a technologization and commodification of reproduction and, not least, would remove the barrier to surrogacy (Norwegian Biotechnology Advisory Board 2015, 14).

Surrogacy further visualizes the fragmentation of motherhood, while making highly evident some of the implications of the differential treatment of eggs and sperm, and thus of men and women.[23] Cross-border surrogacy has become an option for many couples in Norway, in particular for male homosexual couples. This is due to Norwegian paternity laws. A man may enter a surrogate contract and obtain legal fatherhood by acknowledging his paternity and also by providing proof through a DNA test. Because Norwegian citizenship is based primarily on jus sanguinis, the child will be granted Norwegian citizenship if the father is Norwegian. A woman entering a surrogacy contract, despite having used her own eggs, has no way to claim the child as hers. Her biogenetic connection is not recognized. The only legal way to transfer motherhood is by adoption. Thus, the minority has a point: permitting egg donation, with a concomitant recognition of the biogenetic contribution of the egg donor to the child's identity, may lower the barrier to surrogacy. Moreover, in the longer term, an argument that male and female infertility should be treated equally may potentially open the way for legal surrogacy in Norway.

Conclusion

This article has been concerned with the translation of the political into a legal form, with a particular focus on the authorization of kinship acts. At issue has been the very question of human conception—and the very materials and relations that this act conjures. I have focused on the particular discursive formations that have generated the legislation on assisted conception and its de facto and potential reformulations. I have traced the regulation of third-party gamete donation to illustrate how a shift in such practices has been constituted through a configuring and reconfiguring of the attributes attached to sperm and eggs. Drawing on the vital substances that ground this act, my thrust has been to indicate how these discursive formations are mediated through the material properties of sperm, eggs, and wombs. These various mediations not only make evident the mutual entanglement of discourse and materiality but also highlight the thwarted legal attempts to pin down kinship.

Early arguments tied to sperm donation were couched in terms of the natural difference between men and women. The pros and cons of the arguments around sperm donation were firmly lodged in the institution of marriage and its purpose and in the significance of family in society. Pater est was the principle that was applied, underscoring the natural fact that paternity is always uncertain. Although the question of secrecy and its implications for the parties involved (especially the child) was not a major issue, as we have seen, this issue became paramount many years later. With the introduction of IVF, egg donation became a possibility, one that Norwegian authorities did not wish to authorize, and motherhood displaced marriage as the nexus around which the debates turned. The egg became explicitly tied to the unity of motherhood (conception, gestation, birth) and hence, it was argued, should not be separated from the woman in which it originated. Such separation would be tantamount to acknowledging that a mother could be "unknown," which was deemed inconceivable. Mater est was upheld, albeit as a legal fiction, as women could always obtain a donated egg abroad.

With the rescinding of the anonymity clause, the biogenetic property of sperm came to the fore. Thus, the right of the child to know its origins resulted in the reconfiguration of sperm as essential to identity, while at the same time restoring its connection to its point of origin. Donor disclosure made explicit the distinction between pater and genitor. Yet, and perhaps paradoxically, eggs (alone) were not granted the same constitutive force, despite their equal contribution to the creation of the embryo. Materially they were still the discursive glue of a unitary motherhood. It took quite a different discursive formation to reconfigure eggs. By granting eggs the same ethical value as sperm, authorities turned the prohibition on egg donation into a matter of gender discrimination. The argument was that infertile men and women should be treated equally, as should children born from either donor sperm or a donor egg: in both cases the child should have a right to know its biogenetic origin.

The regulations pertaining to third-party gamete donation indicate that the material properties of vital matters matter. It is not coincidental which properties are mobilized to articulate a particular legal-political discourse (see Martin, this volume, concerning bitcoin and *tabu*). Thus, the discursive move from the order of nature to one of ethics, and eventually to one of rights, follows a more general discursive trend in society. Nevertheless, recognizing that sperm and eggs have the same value ethically, and the same constitutive value in creating persons, does not displace the difference between men and women when it comes to reproductive capabilities. The fact that the very act of conception is framed in terms of equality does not necessarily upset the privileging of birth. Hence, in legal terms, mater est will prevail, even as the eggs are recognized as potentially other.

The long-term research grounding this chapter has over the years been generously funded, through my participation in several collaborative projects, by the Norwegian Research Council (NRC) and the European Commission. The project "Anthropos and the Material: Challenges to Anthropology" (NRC) and the Department of Anthropology, University of Oslo, have provided a fruitful framework for engaging the material. I want to thank the editors—Penny Harvey, Christian Krohn-Hansen, and Knut Nustad—for pulling this volume coherently together. I also want to thank Kim Miller, the copyeditor, for meticulous reading and incisive queries.

1. Act relating to the Application of Biotechnology in Medicine, etc. (Biotechnology Act), Act 2003-12-05-100.

2. The first regulation of assisted conception was the Artificial Procreation Act, Act 1987-06-12, no. 68. It was incorporated into the Biotechnology Act in 1994, which was revised in 2003 and 2007. At the time of writing (2015), the act is being reevaluated. All translations from Norwegian documents are mine, unless otherwise indicated.

3. I draw freely on Alain Pottage's notion of legal fabrication, which captures a mode of action that draws on the culturally specific layers of a range of techniques while stressing how "in a given social, historical or ethnographic context elements . . . are mobilised by legal techniques of personification and reification" (Pottage 2004, 1).

4. There is another point to be made here. This has to with the stabilizing properties of stone and concrete. Law or legislative processes may also be seen as acts of stabilization—and can be counted on to "fix" things, or hold them in place, as Harvey notes for the materials that concern her. Yet both cases demonstrate the inherent instability of all of these materials. Thus, there is something to be gained by examining and comparing not only the kinds and qualities of assemblages that are mustered to convey stability, but also the forces that drive them.

5. These physical characteristics include visibility, quantity, size, availability, and reproductive qualities. See Cobb (2012) for an overview of the medical history of sperm and eggs; see Martin (1991) for an analysis of the imagery of sperm and eggs in scientific literature, which demonstrates how facts of biology are construed in cultural terms, confirming gender stereotypes.

6. Amendments to the Children's Act, Act 1997-06-13, no. 39, chapter 1A, §2. This provision excludes surrogacy arrangements as a legal practice in Norway, specifying that "an agreement to give birth to a child for another woman is not binding." Note that a man's agreement to let a woman give birth to his child is not even mentioned.

7. Act relating to Changes in the Marriage Law, Child Law, Adoption Law, Biotechnology Law, etc., Act 2008-06-27-53.

8. The government, as part of a Nordic effort, appointed a committee to review and evaluate the need and conditions for artificial insemination by a donor. The committee submitted its report in 1953. See Ministry of Justice 1953, *Innstilling fra inseminasjonskomitéen.*

9. Robert Edwards was recognized for this extraordinary achievement in 2010 when he was awarded the Nobel Prize for medicine.

10. Issues related to biogenetics were already on the agenda in the early 1980s. Theologians and medical experts were involved in extensive ethical debates about new reproductive technologies and prenatal diagnosis, where the status of the fetus was a central concern (Melhuus 2005).

11. On donor insemination, see Daniels and Haimes (1998) and Hargreaves (2006); and on sperm donors, see especially Daniels (1998). One of the few to actually consider the sperm donor was a well-known Norwegian author, Aksel Sandemose. In a polemic account he characterizes sperm donation as an act of homosexuality (Sandemose 1952).

12. Section 2-15 states: "Fertilised eggs cannot be inserted into the uterus of another woman, than the woman from where the egg cells originate." The explicit prohibition was included in 2003. Section 2-18 states: "Donation of an egg or parts of this from one woman to another is prohibited." Both paragraphs are from Act 2003-12-05, no. 100.

13. It is also of interest that at the time only one person was quoted with regard to the differential treatment of sperm and eggs. The Fylkesmann (county governor, an administrative position) of Oslo and Akershus questioned why sperm and eggs were not treated equally (*som likeverdige*).

14. For example, the Norwegian Biotechnology Advisory Board, in its statements on egg donation in 2011 and 2015, reiterates these arguments.

15. All quotations are taken from parliamentary records or Stortingsforhandlinger. See *Stortingstidende,* June 10, 1993, item 1. *Stortingsforhandlinger* session 1992–1993, 4346–4387. The question of a known egg donor is not even contemplated in the debates.

16. Here the Norwegian Biotechnology Advisory Board's (2011) statement on egg donation quotes the document submitted by the Ministry of Health (Odelstings-proposisjon no. 64 [2002–2003]: 61).

17. Article 7, no. 1, states: "The child shall be registered immediately after birth and shall have the right from birth to a name, the right to acquire a nationality and, as far as possible, the right to know and be cared for by his or her parents" (UN 1989).

18. It is important to highlight that Norwegian paternity laws have also been changed, making it easier, among other things, for the parties involved to have pater-nity ascertained. There are three ways paternity can be established: through pater est, through recognition of the child, or through prosecution (with the use of DNA).

19. Single women and lesbian or heterosexual couples may also travel abroad to ob-tain treatments with anonymous sperm. In such cases motherhood is not challenged, whereas fatherhood may be an issue, especially if the woman is single or the couple les-bian. For a heterosexual couple, the situation is different. If they are married, pater est applies. If not, the intended father can recognize the child as his when the child is born.

20. In Norwegian, the term *høringsuttalelser* (consultative statements), in addition to referring to a public hearing, may also refer to written submissions from interested parties to the case being heard.

21. See also Directorate of Health (2011), a commissioned report on the status and development of areas affected by the Biotechnology Act. This report also raised the question of gender discrimination in the context of egg donation. In 2015 the director-ate submitted another commissioned report, an update to the previous one.

22. As in the case of eggs and sperm, political intervention and anxieties underpin Keir Martin's (this volume) argument about bitcoin and *tabu*. Among other things, Martin's concerns turn on the performative power of distinctions. He concludes that politics is configured in the battle over how to draw such distinctions. My analysis of the differential treatment of sperm and eggs could also be phrased in such terms, all the while paying attention to the tensions inherent in the socially potential activation of these distinctions for the materials in exchange.

23. Issues of surrogacy are complicated and beyond the scope of this article. But see Melhuus and Syse (2016) and Melhuus (2012).

REFERENCES

Act 1987-06-12, no. 68 [Artifical Procreation Act]. Oslo: Government of Norway.

Act 1994-08-05, no. 56. Om medisinsk brtuk av bioteknologi (bioteknologiloven) [Act relating to the Application of Biotechnology in Medicine; Biotechnology Act]. Oslo: Government of Norway.

Act 1997-06-13, no. 39. Lov om endringer i lov av 8 April 1981, no. 7 [Amendments to the Children's Act]. Oslo: Government of Norway.

Act 2003-12-05, no. 100. Lov om humanmedisinsk bruk av bioteknologi m.m. (bioteknoloigloven) [Act relating to the Application of Biotechnology in Medicine etc.; Biotechnology Act]. Oslo: Government of Norway.

Act 2008-06-27-53. Lov om endring i ekteskapsloven, barneloven, adopsjonsloven, bioteknologiloven mv (felles ekteskapslov for heterofile og homofile) [Act relating to Changes in the Marriage Law, Child Law, Adoption Law, Biotechnology Law etc.]. Oslo: Government of Norway.

Cobb, Mathew. 2012. "An Amazing 10 Years: The Discovery of Egg and Sperm in the 17th Century." *Reproduction in Domestic Animals* 47, no. 4: 2–6. https://10.1111/j.1439 -0531.2012.02105.x.

Daniels, Ken. 1998. "The Semen Providers." In *Donor Insemination: International Social Science Perspectives*, edited by Ken Daniels and Erica Haimes, 76–104. Cambridge: Cambridge University Press.

Daniels, Ken, and Erica Haimes, eds. 1998. *Donor Insemination: International Social Science Perspectives*. Cambridge: Cambridge University Press.

Directorate of Health. 2011. *Evaluering av bioteknoloigloven: Status og utvikling på fagområdene som reguleres ved loven*. Report 15-1897. Oslo: Directorate of Health.

Directorate of Health. 2015. *Evaluering av bioteknologiloven 2015: Oppdatering om status og utvikling på fagområdene som reguleres av loven*. Report IS-2360. Oslo: Directorate of Health.

Edwards, Jeanette. 2009. "Introduction: The Matter in Kinship." In *European Kinship in the Age of Biotechnology*, edited by Jeanette Edwards and Carles Salazar, 1–18. New York: Berghahn Books.

Hargreaves, Katrina. 2006. "Constructing Families and Kinship through Donor Insemination." *Sociology of Health and Illness* 28, no. 3: 261–283.

Kapferer, Bruce. 2005. Foreword to *State Formation: Anthropological Perspectives*, edited by Christian Krohn-Hansen and Knut Nustad, vii–xi. London: Pluto.

Lambek, Michael. 2013. "Kinship, Modernity, and the Immodern." In *Vital Relations: Modernity and the Persistent Life of Kinship*, edited by Susan McKinnon and Fenella Cannell, 241–260. Santa Fe, NM: School for Advanced Research Advanced Seminar Series.

Løvset, Jørgen. 1951. "Artificial Insemination: The Attitude of Patients in Norway." *Fertility and Sterility* 7, no. 1: 133–136.

Martin, Emily. 1991. "The Egg and the Sperm: How Science Has Constructed a Romance Based on Stereotypical Male-Female Roles." *Signs* 16, no. 3: 485–501.

Melhuus, Marit. 2005. "'Better Safe than Sorry': Legislating Assisted Conception in Norway." In *State Formation: Anthropological Perspectives*, edited by Christian Krohn-Hansen and Knut Nustad, 212–233. London: Pluto.

Melhuus, Marit. 2012. *Problems of Conception: Issues of Law, Biotechnology, Individuals and Kinship*. New York: Berghahn Books.

Melhuus, Marit, and Signe Howell. 2009. "Adoption and Assisted Conception: One Universe of Unnatural Procreation. An Examination of Norwegian Legislation." In *European Kinship in the Age of Biotechnology*, edited by Jeanette Edwards and Carles Salazar, 144–161. New York: Berghahn Books.

Melhuus, Marit, and Aslak Syse. 2016. "Gestational Surrogacy in Norway." In *Handbook of Gestational Surrogacy*, edited by Eric Sills, 217–224. Cambridge: Cambridge University Press.

Ministry of Justice. 1953. *Innstilling fra Inseminasjonslovkomitéen*. Oslo: Ministry of Justice.

Molne, Kåre. 1976. "Donorinseminasjon: En oversikt og et materiale." *Tidsskrift for Den norske lægeforening* 17/18: 982–986.

Norwegian Biotechnology Advisory Board. 2011. *Bioteknologinemdas uttalelse om eggdonasjon*. Oslo: Norwegian Biotechnology Advisory Board.

Norwegian Biotechnology Advisory Board. 2015. *Bioteknologirådets uttalelse om eggdonasjon: Evaluering av bioteknologiloven*. Oslo: Norwegian Biotechnology Advisory Board.

Odelstingsproposisjon No. 25. 1986–1987. Om lov om kunstig befruktning'. Oslo: Ministry of Social Affairs.

Pottage, Alain. 2004. "Introduction: The Fabrication of Persons and Things." In *Law, Anthropology, and the Constitution of the Social: Making Persons and Things*, edited by Alain Pottage and Martha Mundy, 1–39. Cambridge: Cambridge University Press.

Sandemose, Aksel. 1952. "Unnfanget i løgn." *Årstidene* 2: 24–86; 3: 39–53.

Stortingstidende 10.06.1993, Item 1. Stortingsforhandlinger session 1992–1993.

Strathern, Marilyn. 1999. *Property, Substance, and Effect: Anthropological Essays on Persons and Things*. London: Athlone.

UN (United Nations). 1989. Convention on the Rights of the Child (UNCRC). New York: United Nations.

6. Lithic Vitality

HUMAN ENTANGLEMENT WITH
NONORGANIC MATTER

———

Penny Harvey

The Anthropocene is a contentious concept, not least because the magnitude of its implications rests on a simple causal relation between human action and a resulting material imprint. The term may well have been propelled to public visibility by the media (and the lucrative market for crisis narratives), but it also speaks to more complex concerns about shifting relations between human beings and the wider material world. Beyond the claim that human beings have now left indelible geological traces on planet Earth (a mark not made in the 135 million years of dinosaur habitation), the traces are taken to signify the destruction of habitats and atmospheric conditions that sustain not only human life but the life of all the other plants and creatures on which human life depends. In these narratives of irreversible change, geological time is collapsed into a planetary moment, the implications of which seem both inescapable and yet hard to grasp, producing a sense of urgency in some and inertia in others. Nevertheless, the term has political impetus and has been taken up as a call for new modes of attention and responsibility for collective environmental futures.

In anthropology there are many recent initiatives to interrogate how material relations are lived and understood at different scales and in different circumstances. I am particularly concerned in this chapter with how recent discussions of multispecies encounters both recognize and undermine the boundedness of living entities, challenging human exceptionalism and opening up a more comprehensive discussion of the interdependencies of living beings. I am interested in extending this discussion to include consideration of the vitality of nonorganic matter. There are some long-running turf wars to be managed here beyond the foundational modern distinction between the "natural" and the "social" sciences (to which I return below). An appeal to the vitality of the nonorganic runs counter to established understandings of the DNA molecule as the basis of all living cells, and to the exciting research agenda of the anthropologist Eduardo Kohn, who has begun to explore how other-than-human encounters (as Donna Haraway puts it in her endorsement of the book) bring the world into being through semiotic engagement (Kohn 2013). Kohn's interest in the communicative capacities of all living beings opens new spaces for thinking about continuities between human and other-than-human worlds. However, he is explicitly not dealing with the vitality of inorganic matter and plainly states, "I recognize of course that those we call animists may well attribute animacy to all sorts of entities, such as stones, that I would not, according to the framework laid out here, consider living selves" (94). Kohn argues that we should not confuse materiality with vitality, resistance with agency. It is not my purpose here to review Kohn's project or to argue with his reasoning, but I was provoked by Kohn to think more deeply about the vitality of stone and concrete, materials that had caught my attention on road construction projects in Peru. I am interested in the presence and the affective force of these materials, in how it is that stone and concrete do (and do not) assume vitality in human affairs, in ways that are not captured by the framing of animacy. I am not alone in this thought space! Hugh Raffles is currently writing a book about stone in which he moves away from asking what stone "is" to asking what it is that stone can do. This question opens up a world of fascination:

> Stone can endure, it can change, it can harm, it can heal. It can make you rich, it can make you poor, it can become an enemy, a friend, and a teacher. It can carry your memories and your dreams. It can build empires and bury cities. It can reveal the history of the universe. It can open and close the gates of philosophy. It can open and close the doors of Hell. It can change the course of nature. It can change its own nature. It can empty the world of time. (Raffles 2012, 527)[1]

Beyond our mutual fascination with the inherent plurality and the deep temporality of stone, I was particularly captivated by Raffles's formulation of stones as "demanding objects." In the Andes, where my ethnographic research is focused, stones—mountains, rocks, and pebbles—are often treated as demanding energetic forces in ways that I discuss in more detail below. However, it is the unfolding relationship between stone and concrete that informs my current discussion of material vitality.

Stone and concrete are entangled but contrasting materials. Their materiality is complex and processual. It unfolds in different ways through multiple relational encounters. Neither is straightforwardly apprehended as either lively or inert, but the differences and specificities of their relational potential crosscut many of our established dichotomies of material and immaterial, organic and inorganic. In terms of this volume, they offer a particular perspective on the political by the ways in which they conjoin material and social forces, and they have prompted me to think again about how materials themselves might be enrolled in our deliberations of planetary futures.

Marisol de la Cadena (2014) has been more directly critical of Kohn's approach and challenged him to respond to the political implications of denying the existence of Andean "earth beings." Her argument (see also de la Cadena, this volume, 2015) turns on the ethnographic understanding that *bios* and *geos* (biology and geology) are co-constitutive of the Andean *ayllu*, kindred groups that, critically, exist through the entanglement of human and other-than-human forces.[2] The separation between living and nonliving is precisely that made by the mining companies who refuse to engage with the ways in which the specificity of place disrupts the dichotomy of living and nonliving beings. Their offers of compensation and/or relocation respond to the loss of land but not the loss of life. Kohn (2014) in turn acknowledges the value of de la Cadena's intervention and agrees that not every entity in the world is alive in the same way. This focus on discontinuous and often-incommensurable vitalities is a key concern of this chapter.

Material Vitality and Immaterial Forces

In 2007 Tim Ingold wrote an essay titled "Materials against Materiality" in which he argued that the distinction between matter and materiality is not simply unnecessary but problematic, as it reinforces the erroneous modern conceit that "materials" are passive and inert, lacking the lively qualities that scholars who study fetishism, or animism, seek to invoke with their use of the term. He argues that those who deploy the concept of materiality to conjure up the vitality of materials are missing the fundamental point that all materials are lively in their own way rather than simply being the passive objects of our attention—they exist in dynamic relations and have a presence and a force that most people in the world recognize, and it is only we "moderns" who forget this and then have to somehow explain how materials after all seem to be quite active.

Ingold's case is somewhat overstated, given that neither modern science nor modern philosophy has any trouble in assuming the dynamic vitality of matter, and in what follows I pay particular attention to "soft matter," the focus of rheology, that subdiscipline of physics that explores soft solids and material flows.[3] Ingold's criticism of the notion that materials are passive and inert is presumably not directed at chemists and physicists. It resonates more directly with the social effects of the ways in which the modern world is engineered to meet desires for material stability. In this respect Ingold's argument points to the ways in which the modern world might encourage a particular insensitivity to the dynamic energies of materials such as stone and concrete. The implication of Ingold's argument is that a focus on material vitality could be of interest to *social* scientists and not confined to the natural sciences or to the field of animistic (nonscientific) belief. This approach has also been articulated from other perspectives. Jane Bennett, for example, is a political theorist who wrote an influential book entitled *Vibrant Matter: A Political Ecology of Things* (2010) in which she argued for the social importance of thinking in more expansive and ecological terms about material relations. Such thinking, she argued, would open political theory to the agency of matter—fostering ecological awareness and addressing the need for a deeper understanding of the vitality that connects human and nonhuman bodies. The contemporary interest in multispecies ethnography takes a similar approach (see Kirksey and Helmreich 2010; Kirksey 2015). By contrast with the multispecies approach, Bennett includes inorganic matter in her discussion of vital materialism.[4] Contra Ingold, Bennett is a trenchant defender of "materiality" precisely because the term draws attention to a vitality that might otherwise be dismissed or ignored. Her political intention is clearly articulated: "If environmentalism leads to the call for the protection and wise management of an ecosystem that surrounds us, a vital materialism suggests that the task is to engage more strategically with a trenchant materiality that is us as it vies with us in agentic assemblages" (Bennett 2010, 111; see also Braun and Whatmore 2010).

The relations inherent to vital materialism are not necessarily harmonious, and the tensions or frictions (Tsing 2005) between qualities and capacities of being preoccupy anybody who attends to environmental struggles—human or nonhuman (see Tsing 2015; Weston 2017). Indeed, concern with the material politics that arise in spaces of material transformation (especially in contexts of capitalist extraction such as mining, agribusiness, and energy) is central to debates about ontological difference (see de la Cadena, this volume; Nustad, this volume; see also Povinelli 2014; Reinert 2016). The key point here is that the mutually constitutive relationship of human and other-than-human worlds is not under human control, even when human intention appears paramount. In this respect Ingold's argument that all materials have energy and vitality sidesteps the question of material agency, of how materials shape human worlds both in their energetic movements (Bennett 2010) and in their obdurate resistance (Latour 2004). There are issues here concerning the relative significance of human will and material force. However, my interest in this chapter is to move the discussion away from the more general ground of political theory and/or philosophical debate and to look more closely at how material vitality gets caught up in specific political histories.

Erstwhile-neglected materials have been brought to the fore recently in Ann Stoler's edited collection *Imperial Debris: On Ruins and Ruination* (2013) and Gastón Gordillo's monograph *Rubble: The Afterlife of Destruction* (2014). Both authors are concerned to highlight the immaterial dimensions of material vitality in their exploration of the material residues of violence— the ruins and abandoned spaces, the haunted and haunting imaginaries that can assume a visceral presence in people's everyday lives. Walter Benjamin's (1999) focus on ruins alerted many to the potential social force of ruined forms, their potential to speak of past violence and destruction while carrying forward a potent remainder of a previous dream. These more recent studies are attentive to how the ruins do not simply remind people of past violence but mediate the force of that past in the present. Materials can index these forces. For Benjamin it was iron that fascinated, the iron of bridges and railway tracks, and particularly of the arcades. He traced the ways in which iron, as a material, was thus implicated in the emergent world of urban consumption, enabling the architectures of the nineteenth-century city, offering both social promise and critical residue. It is in this spirit that I now turn to explore two materials that have had commensurate force in Andean Peru—stone and concrete.

The Partial Domestication of Inka Stone

The Inka are famous for their stonework, and the masonry of their key ceremonial buildings is the source of much admiration. Stones, sometimes with many angles, were fitted with meticulous precision without mortar or iron tools. The capacity of their structures to withstand earthquakes, and simply to endure over the centuries, speaks of sophisticated hydraulic infrastructures, which were as important as the stonework in ensuring the resilience of the buildings (see Harvey and Knox 2010). Some of the stones are huge, weighing hundreds of tons, often moved over massive distances without wheels. Not all buildings were built to the same finish, and the Inka signature took different forms. From today's perspective their achievements appear miraculous, and scholars continue to work on trying to understand what the Inka engineers knew, how they worked, what these structures can tell us about Inka times, and what they can teach us about how to confront the material challenges of building in the Andes today.

Inka stonework offers a clear example of the material politics of state form. For a start, the constructions display Inka capacity to mobilize a workforce of many thousands. The structures also index practices of domination that went beyond the capacity to make people transport and transform stone from throughout the empire in order to create the material structures that glorified Inka power and prowess—their palaces, temples, agricultural terraces, and fortresses. These constructions did not merely symbolize the power of the Inka; they also enacted it. Throughout the Andean region, many different ethnic groups actively engaged the life-giving force of the land (its stone, its water, its soil) and the sky (the sun, the rain, the celestial bodies). The land and the sky (the upper and lower orders of the universe) were the sources of identity (origin) and of productive capacity (ongoing life). Conquered groups were integrated into the Inka kindreds as subordinated wife givers. The integration came with guarantees of life, land, and livelihood— but it also required subordination within an encompassing Inka cosmology, which was manifest in the requirement of sacrificial offerings (including the sending of young women to serve the Inka in the imperial capital). Acts of integration included the transportation of local rocks, or *huacas*, revered as the sacred sources of life in specific places, which were effectively held hostage as they were folded into the wider imperial scale of the capital city. The Inka thus dominated conquered groups through a material logic of incorporation and differentiation (which worked through many complex forms of kinship, sacrifice, and ritual and through administrative structures that gathered tribute for the maintenance of both the religious complex and the imperial army; see, for example, Gose 1996, 2000; Zuidema 1964).

Beyond these feats of territorial integration, the Inka were also specialists in the integration of "living rock" in procedures that art historian Carolyn Dean (2010) has described as "grafting" as opposed to building. Dean shows how certain significant Inka buildings were clearly rooted in the earth, like plants. This procedure reflects the huge importance that the Inka placed on ensuring ongoing relations between the earth and the sky. Theirs was a dualist cosmology of hierarchical complementarity deployed to embrace the whole universe and center it on the sacred city of the Cusco, and ultimately in the body of the Inka ruler—the source of all creativity, and of life itself. Dean's analysis of Inka grafting techniques suggests that the stone-working procedures, which she refers to as "nibbling," were a way of partially domesticating the stone. This partial domestication acknowledged the hubris inherent in the ambition to control the forces of the environment through the construction of a structure that could be seen to appropriate these forces to serve human ends. The buildings were thus not simply monuments to Inka power; they also acknowledged the continuity between that power and the power of other-than-human forces—particularly the power of a sentient environment that registered and responded to human engagement. However, the Inka were themselves not simply human. They ruled as divine beings who channeled the creative force of the universe to make human life possible. Such channeling was not without risk. Material engagements with the sentient forces of the universe were always unpredictable, and it mattered that these forces remained beyond the control of humankind. Engagement with the forces of the environment was then, and is still today, hedged with considerable ritual precaution. Dean's suggestion is that the grafting of worked stone onto living rock served to domesticate the stone, in the sense that it created a tangible and enduring relation between the stone and the site of human activity. At the same time, the grafting crucially did not dislodge the stone from the earth, thus enabling the channeling of telluric forces directly into these hugely significant ceremonial spaces.

Concrete and Its Fascination

The capacity to enact state power through the construction of monumental stone structures has long since disappeared. When I began ethnographic work on the state in the 1990s, concrete was the material that was bursting onto the scene in rural Peru, and concrete has now become the key material used for the demarcation and ordering of public space. Discussions surrounding the aesthetics of state power prompted me to think more carefully about the specific material potency of concrete (Harvey 2010). As concrete began to appear in the Peruvian countryside, there was little or no sense of an unwelcome intrusion. On the contrary, when people referred approvingly to buildings constructed from "noble materials," they were not talking about marble tiles and oak paneling but concrete. These deliberations took me well beyond the confines of rural Peru, to explore the cultural history of this ubiquitous material.

Adrian Forty's work *Concrete and Culture: A Material History* (2012) opened a new avenue of inquiry. Forty was less interested in the nobility of concrete than in its "mongrel" qualities, its capacity to exceed categorical classification. Concrete is a composite material, made from the mixing of cement, water, and aggregates, which are typically sand and crushed stone. The strength of the material depends on the ratio of cement to water and on the type of aggregate used. Add steel and you have the reinforced concrete that can support high-rise towers or expansive roof spans. The material has historical roots in both vernacular building practices and processes of scientific experimentation and analysis. In Roman times people already knew how to make concrete by mixing crushed limestone with sand and water. Chandra Mukerji (2009) explains how these techniques were supposedly lost after the fall of the Roman Empire. However, the knowledge had been transmitted in the practice of artisans who knew that the addition of volcanic sands enhanced the capacity of concrete to set in water. This knowledge of how to make hydraulic cement was clearly used in the construction of the Canal du Midi in southwestern France in the seventeenth century. However, these artisanal skills were not recognized, and cement was repeatedly "discovered" in the eighteenth century (Taussig 2004, 160). Portland cement was patented in England in 1824 and by the mid-nineteenth century dominated the market, displacing most local cement production.

Portland cement is an extremely stable and standardized material. Its commodification enabled the widespread use of concrete that we find across the world today, and yet its composite makeup results in a material that is never fully standardized and always open to experimentation and modification. Concrete takes the shape and the surface texture of the molds in which it is cast. It sets hard, but it can be worked as "soft matter," and its plasticity has been at the heart of its fascination for both artists and architects. We are thus dealing with a material that has the potential to produce highly standardized forms but that is also accessible to vernacular use and modification. It is an entirely synthetic material, but the aggregates intrinsic to its composition carry a degree of uncertainty associated with the unconformity of soft matter. In short, in concrete we have an intriguing material. It furnishes the spaces where people routinely engage state officials—in municipal buildings, schools and hospitals, and so on. It paves highways and fashions office blocks. It also enables experimentation and artistic expression. The

Sydney Opera House is, for many, an opera in concrete, its surfaces and the shell-like domes a monumental and deeply controversial achievement of design and engineering that emerged from a fascination with the qualities and potentialities of concrete (Jones 2006).

And what of its vitality? Concrete is not animate, in the sense that there is no suggestion that concrete forms carry or channel the vitality of other-than-human being, as was the case with the *huacas* or origin forces described in the previous section on Inka stonework. Nevertheless, it has an intrinsic vitality. It is a material that has to be assembled; it has the strength of stone but is more malleable; it is a synthetic but lacks perfectibility: "defects in it are inescapable, indeed essential—for the steel in reinforced concrete to work, the concrete has to crack, however microscopically. This is a material whose success rests upon an imperfection" (Forty 2012, 52).

Material Politics

Cement is also a global commodity, and the cement trade is big business. Commenting on the geopolitics of concrete, Forty notes, "The German cement company Heidelberg, for example, one of four large cement producers that between them account for a quarter of the world's cement production, operates a fleet of over 900 ships to move cement around the world to take advantage of local spikes in price. The trade relies upon the absolute uniformity and consistency of a bag of ordinary Portland cement, wherever in the world one buys it" (2012, 101).

But the politics of concrete differs from that of cement. People trade cement to make concrete, and it is the desire to build with concrete that sustains the cement trade and its capital circulations. Concrete famously became a key medium of the Cold War. In the postwar competition between East and West to rebuild and transform society in ways that enacted specific political ideologies, concrete demonstrated flexibility not just in its malleable form but in its symbolic and ideological resonance. In both the East and the West, concrete facilitated the provision of mass housing, standardized structures, *and* creative singularity and always demonstrated the capacity for innovation and accelerated change.[5] Today the staggering rate of urbanization in China rests on a spectacular investment in concrete, in new buildings, roads, power plants, and dams.[6]

However, there are other relational dynamics in play that open concrete to the political in a way that takes us beyond the ownership and distribution of cement, and beyond the symbolic resonances of standardized form.

Another way of approaching the politics of concrete is to think further about the intrinsic multiplicity of this material and the ways in which its mongrel qualities and its processual form blur the distinction between natural and social worlds. The emergent quality of this material preoccupied the engineers working on the road construction projects that were the focus of the ethnographic research that Hannah Knox and I conducted in Peru in 2005–2006 (Harvey and Knox 2015). Once again the specific nature of material vitality was in question. Fully aware of the processual dynamics of concrete, the engineers needed to understand how the aggregates would react with the cement, and how the emergent concrete would withstand the pressure of vehicles, the extreme climatic conditions of the high Andes, and the seismic movements of the terrain. The objective of producing a stable road surface required endless testing as the engineers got to know their materials. They focused initially on the aggregates, collecting samples, sorting and classifying, and conducting tests that allowed them to specify the properties and capacities of the materials available to them. Mixing the aggregate with the cement and water was another stage in which particular attention was paid to the strengths and weaknesses of concrete in relation to water. One of the particularities of concrete as a building material derives from the chemical reaction produced by mixing cement and water, which effects an irreversible process of gradual hardening. Indeed, as mentioned above, being able to set hard in water is what makes cement indispensable to many construction projects. Exposure to water is typically beneficial to concrete. However, our "noble/mongrel" material is also vulnerable to water because water transports aggressive chemicals (acids, sulfates, chlorides) that can destroy it, and water can react adversely with particular aggregates. The engineers thus test the concrete for porosity, flexibility, and resilience in an effort to ensure that the process of hardening produces stable material forms. Their methods of knowing concrete involve sampling and modeling, retesting, and further sampling and modeling. These are standard scientific procedures of close observation and informed projection through design. When the engineers are satisfied that they have an optimum mix, the proportions are translated into the algorithms that direct the machines that produce the concrete in situ. At this point the rhythm of work takes on an urgency as the concrete mixers deliver the concrete to the site where it will set. Workers have to be totally prepared and ready to channel the concrete in the short time that it remains liquid and pliable. Once the concrete has set, errors are hard to correct. Concrete is, in this respect, an "evental" material. The mixing and setting process produces a form that is both finished and yet open-ended as, once set, the concrete continues to react to its new material environment.

Engineers are highly aware of this duality, and in the field laboratories they look for evidence of how the material will emerge and endure. Each new job brings new challenges. The engineers cannot know the concrete in advance, and so they have to get to know the aggregates and the qualities of the water. The need to understand the aggregates brings its own problems because it is, on the whole, difficult to get a secure sense of where they will come from. This mode of uncertainty derives from the social properties of the aggregates, which, on large construction projects, are typically sourced locally. The cement may be delivered in a relatively standard form in ready-packed sacks, but the stone, the sand, and the gravel have to be excavated and brought to the construction site from nearby quarries or riverbeds. Getting to know how the materials will relate to each other is part of an analytic process that can begin only once the materials are safely impounded on the construction site. In some projects materials are extracted without dissension, but more usually it is a protracted process. Materials such as sand and gravel are both legally and socially volatile because they are often owned in different ways by different individuals and institutions. In Peru the central state owns the riverbed, the provincial municipality has the right to extract materials for construction projects, and local people can also extract small quantities of these materials for personal construction use.[7] Small riverside communities often find their agricultural lands eaten away by rivers that do not hold their course owing, in part, to unauthorized extraction upstream. But it is not always possible to determine the exact cause of flooding, or to be certain why heavy rains cause flooding in some areas and not others. The extraction of materials from riverbeds is thus always a sensitive issue, especially when the construction project is of a certain scale. As a result, engineering companies tend to source aggregates as they go along, and access to local sources is negotiated via the client—frequently the state itself in some guise or other. The result is that the aggregates are rarely consistent throughout a major project, and the field laboratories remain active for the duration of a large project, constantly testing and attending to the changing material relations in play.

But these materials have social qualities that exceed legal notions of ownership and responsibility. Andean people today are still very attentive to the vitality of stone in ways that demonstrate continuities with Inka understandings of material vitality. Many large rocks are thought to channel the energetic life-giving forces of the earth, and even small stones are sometimes engaged as commensurate with the larger rock formations of which they are still part. In the Cusco region of southern Peru where I carried out extensive fieldwork in the 1980s, peasant farmers engaged particular mountains or large rock foundations as sentient beings who should always be treated with respect and care. Libations were regularly made to these lithic beings in the course of everyday life, when people sat to chew coca, or on occasions when alcohol or *chicha* (corn beer) was served in the course of any ritual or social event. In larger and more dramatic ritual events, such as the pilgrimage to the shrine of the Señor de Qoyllor Rit'i, mountains, large rocks, and small stones all played and still play a central role. This popular shrine to a miraculous Christ figure has two central foci: the large rock on which the figure of the Christ appeared and around which the church building was constructed, and the glacier of the Ausangate mountain, which is equally revered. People go to great efforts to enter the church and get as close as possible to the rock, and key figures (the *ukuku*, or bear dancers) climb up onto the glacier to place and subsequently retrieve a cross in a wider ritual process that oscillates between the mountain and the Christ figure, both encompassing something of the other as the Christ is etched on the rock, and the cross placed lovingly onto the mountain.[8] By contrast to these dramatic lithic sites, pilgrims also play with stones, using them as miniatures in personal moments of ritual play, building tiny houses or corrals of animals. Catherine Allen (2016) stresses that the stone miniatures (*illa*) are not simply representations of things desired. Unlike the manufactured miniatures (*alasitas*) offered for sale these days at the pilgrimage site, the small stones differ in their materiality for they are of the mountain—they are the mountain, and it is the productive potentiality of the mountain being that pilgrims seek to engage in their games.

Furthermore, in a vibratory environment (this is a seismic and volcanic zone), rock is on the move. Landslides and subsidence routinely destroy even the most carefully laid surface. In one small town where I lived for many years, people showed me small stones they had found "wandering" alongside the roads. To find such a stone is an unusual but fortunate occurrence. They serve as amulets and promise protection.[9] It is perhaps surprising then that concrete is never expected to move in this way, despite the aggregates that are integral to its formation. On the contrary, concrete is expected to hold things in place. Its nobility resides in its capacity to withstand environmental forces. It is superior to and more resilient than adobe (sunbaked bricks); it carries its own force; it is modern and reliable. But of course there are many occasions when it does not withstand the violent movements of the earth or is invaded by frosts and floodwaters. Where such movements occur, interest in the possibility of a resurgent environment is never far away. Deaths on road construction projects were always attributed to an unwelcome disturbance of the land, for which the only appropriate response is a sacrificial offering, a replacement of energies that is seized by the earth, if not offered freely. People desire concrete for its stabilizing properties, but they are also aware that, like the grafted Inka stone, asphalt concrete only partially "domesticates" the forces of the Earth. Vitality remains rooted in the Earth, but concrete can become an intermediary, modern but still entangled in extended relations with other-than-human being, evental and processual, the outcome of both industrial process and artisanal craft.

Soft Matter

These tensions between the evental and the processual dimensions of concrete are characteristics that have long fascinated artists and scientists. In 2009 the sculptor Anish Kapoor staged an exhibition at the Royal Academy of Arts in London, presenting himself as an artist of "soft matter." Kapoor was working primarily with wax in this exhibit, but he also worked with concrete, equating the two in a wider effort to explore the frontier zones of order and chaos, systemic form and random distribution. His work was staged as an invasion of the classical building, the seventeenth-century London mansion. In one room he set up cannons to fire wax at the walls; elsewhere, he drove a massive "train" of wax slowly through the central galleries, scraping through the doorways and leaving marks and traces of these movements on the gilded interiors. The exhibition communicated his fascination with the ways in which malleable, soft matter could continually change its form and the form of the space in which it was being exhibited. He also displayed a work entitled *Greyman Cries, Shaman Dies, Billowing Smoke, Beauty Evoked*. This work was produced in situ by a concrete printer, referred to as the Identity Engine, a reference to Charles Babbage's early computer, the Difference Engine. Babbage was interested in the capacities of machines to reliably repeat. The concrete printer works in the following way: "Data is entered into the Identity Engine in a regular and ordered form then the artist, the engine, the operators and various concrete mixes are allowed to take part in constrained random walks" (Lowe 2009, 43). However, soft matter resists reliable replication. "Although a relatively simple machine, the many variables in play when digital data enters the physical world prevent predictable repetition" (43). The printer produces similar but not identical forms. The forces of fluid emergence that Kapoor was exploring are those of unconformity and entropy, forms that are constrained but not determined by the materials, the programmers, and the operators.

The catalog for the exhibit includes a short essay on soft matter by the historian of science Simon Schaffer, in which he discusses how soft matter has long fascinated scientists because of how material forms change under everyday conditions and in mundane surroundings, in ways that cannot easily be predicted simply by analyzing either internal structure or external influence. Schaffer's essay elaborates historical understandings of how unpredictable formations have been assumed to offer evidence of pattern in what might otherwise be seen as meaningless data. His essay is followed by an apophenic appendix. "Apophenia" is "the tendency to see patterns in meaningless data" (Schaffer 2009, 175). Soft matter can produce such forms and can also suggest possibilities of meaning that may point to a more ordered and less chaotic reality, which nevertheless remains elusive.[10] The appendix comprises a compilation of strange and wonderful objects and materials that include a reference to complex lead forms that are created by pouring molten metal into cold water. In many places, including rural Peru, it is widely believed that these forms may hold clues to future events. In Peru on the first of August, the people I lived with used to cast small pieces of lead into glasses of water and look for a recognizable pattern. There may be no such pattern, but the first of August is the day when the force of the Earth (*Pacha*) is celebrated. Small domestic gatherings draw close families together to eat and drink, and make libations to the earth and to the mountains. People also engage in play with miniatures, similar to the games played at the pilgrimage shrine described above. Objects are crafted out of clay, a motorbike or a loudspeaker, a cow or a sheep made from the earth and committed to the earth in the hope of connecting to a generative energy that is never fully under human control or accessible to human comprehension (Harvey 2001).

Lithic Vitality

The vitality of inorganic matter is a paradoxical formulation that I have tried to keep at the heart of this exploration of stone and concrete. As stated at the outset, I make no claim for the sentience of either stone or concrete as materials. However, a sense of material vitality, and an awareness of the unpredictability of material processes, is what I have attempted to keep in view, as a mode of vitality that neither assumes nor precludes animism. Geological imaginaries and the ways in which "the deeply inhuman forces of the earth and the cosmos" might become integral to human politics, as discussed by Nigel Clark (2013, 49), is the topic that I have been more interested in exploring. As Clark suggests, "The challenge of the geo-political is not only about the way we negotiate our relationship with each other and with our environments, but also about how we collectively deal with the interface between what is and what is not negotiable" (49). It is perhaps ironic that this sense of an emergent and ultimately unpredictable dimension to material "life" can emerge through the consideration of a synthetic material such as concrete. At the same time, this material is perhaps a crucial entry point for human contemplation of how the material traces of our ingenuity shape our futures in ways that we can address only through an attentiveness to that which lies beyond the realms of human control, and how we thus might need to imagine a politics that embraces entities we cannot expect to fully understand.

The Inka worked with an awareness of stone as living matter, a force that they sought to channel to sustain human life and to support their imperial expansion. For the engineers and the artists, concrete, while not alive, is certainly "lively": it is appreciated as an active force, a force that combines the unpredictability of form with the promise of stability. The desire for concrete that is so tangible in the Andean region is linked to this sense of both potency and stability, and engineers deploy their expertise to manage the diverse internal and external relations of concrete in order to produce the intended outcomes. The artist, by contrast, constrains the materials in particular ways in order to better appreciate their fluidity and unconformity.

Ingold (2007) asks us to take materials seriously, to think about materials as life forces, transforming and transformational, and he argues that there is no need to deploy terms like "materiality" or, worse still, to invoke the spirit of matter. We simply need to recognize the intrinsic vitality of materials. The mongrel qualities of concrete disrupt this argument and call forth a potential politics that draws attention to divergent vitalities and conflicting notions of how the evental and the processual might be addressed. The lithic vitality of concrete comes in and out of view in different relational configurations that cannot necessarily be known in advance. The key point in this material is that these configurations are simultaneously internal (to the emerging material structure) and external (configured in terms of the very human intervention in the processes of composition and decomposition). Thinking with stone and concrete brings together physical properties with material biographies and affective forces that may leak from a material to an object without firmly residing in either. Anthropos and the material are thus folded together in the dynamic morphologies of matter.

1. The original paper on which this chapter is based was presented at a workshop organized by John Law at the Centre for Research on Socio-Cultural Change in 2014—an event at which Raffles also presented some of his initial work on stones. Our conversation encouraged and enthused me to keep thinking with these materials in the ways I have developed here.

2. Thomas Abercrombie (2016) also draws on ethnographic and historical accounts of how Andean miners attribute "human semiotic practices" (84) to mountains, among other things. Abercrombie, like Kohn, draws on Peircian semiotics, but unlike Kohn he questions the assumption that the attribution of the qualities of persons to "things" is necessarily best understood as animism. Rather, as with de la Cadena's argument, he draws attention to the fact that mountains are always "concrete places" (90) that are constitutive of people's lives, and not general beliefs projected onto an external world.

3. See also Strang (2014) for a critique of Ingold's argument that focuses on the specific materiality of water. In this chapter my interest in soft matter and flow, and in the dynamic energy of materials, connects with Strang's position. I also acknowledge here the support of Durham's Institute of Advanced Study, where I held a fellowship in the autumn semester of 2015. The possibilities afforded by that fellowship to engage others working on volcanic magma, and more generally on rheology, greatly advanced my understandings of how contemporary physics and chemistry address the energetic force of matter. As director of the institute, Veronica Strang is a key contributor to developing ways of thinking across the natural and the social sciences—not least on the issue of material flows.

4. A notable exception in the multispecies literature is the work by Hugo Reinert (2016) that explores what he terms the "geologic conviviality" of human-stone relations in Finnmark in northern Norway.

5. See Fehérváry (2013) for a discussion of the resonances surrounding how concrete fashioned domestic space in Hungary from the 1950s to the 1990s.

6. A recent article in the *Washington Post* supports the claim that China used more cement between 2011 and 2013 than the United States used in the entire twentieth century. Anna Swanson, "How China Used More Cement in 3 Years Than the U.S. Did in the Entire 20th Century," *Washington Post*, March 24, 2015.

7. The ethnographic research from which this example is drawn was carried out with Deborah Poole from 2010 to 2013 on a project entitled *Experimental States*. See Harvey and Poole (2012).

8. I made several visits to this sanctuary in the 1980s when I was doing fieldwork in the region. Michael Sallnow (1987) published one of the most detailed accounts of this pilgrimage site, but there are many subsequent ethnographic accounts and films.

9. Allen (1997) also reports the movements of such stones in another region of the Andes.

10. Contemporary experiments in finding patterns in the vast accumulations of big data perhaps offer a provocative analogy.

Abercrombie, Thomas. 2016. "The Iterated Mountain: Things as Signs in Potosí." *Journal of Latin American and Caribbean Anthropology* 21, no. 1: 83–108.

Allen, Catherine. 1997. "When Pebbles Move Mountains: Iconicity and Symbolism in Quechua Ritual." In *Creating Context in Andean Cultures*, edited by Rosaleen Howard-Malverde, 73–84. Oxford: Oxford University Press.

Allen, Catherine. 2016. "The Living Ones: Miniatures and Animation in the Andes." *Journal of Anthropological Research* 72, no.4: 416–441.

Benjamin, Walter. 1999. *The Arcades Project*. Translated by Howard Eiland and Kevin McLaughlin. Cambridge, MA: Harvard University Press.

Bennett, Jane. 2010. *Vibrant Matter: A Political Ecology of Things*. Durham, NC: Duke University Press.

Braun, Bruce, and Sarah Whatmore, eds. 2010. *Political Matter: Technoscience, Democracy, and Public Life*. Minneapolis: University of Minnesota Press.

Clark, Nigel. 2013. "Geopolitics at the Threshold." *Political Geography* 37, no. 3: 48–50.

Dean, Carolyn. 2010. *A Culture of Stone: Inka Perspectives on Rock*. Durham, NC: Duke University Press.

de la Cadena, Marisol. 2014. "Runa: Human but Not Only." *HAU: Journal of Ethnographic Theory* 4, no. 2: 253–259.

de la Cadena, Marisol. 2015. *Earth Beings: Ecologies of Practice across Andean Worlds*. Durham, NC: Duke University Press.

Fehérváry, Krisztina. 2013. *Politics in Color and Concrete: Socialist Materialities and the Middle Class in Hungary*. Bloomington: Indiana University Press.

Forty, Adrian. 2012. *Concrete and Culture: A Material History*. London: Reaktion Books.

Gordillo, Gastón. 2014. *Rubble: The Afterlife of Destruction*. Durham, NC: Duke University Press.

Gose, Peter. 1996. "Oracles, Mummies, and Political Representation in the Inka State." *Ethnohistory* 43, no. 1: 1–33.

Gose, Peter. 2000. "The State as a Chosen Woman: Brideservice and the Feeding of Tributaries in the Inka Empire." *American Anthropologist* 102, no. 1: 84–97.

Harvey, Penelope. 2001. "Landscape and Commerce: Creating Contexts for the Exercise of Power." In *Contested Landscapes: Movement, Exile and Place*, edited by Barbara Bender and Margot Winer, 197–210. Oxford: Berg.

Harvey, Penelope. 2010. "Cementing Relations: The Materiality of Roads and Public Spaces in Provincial Peru." *Social Analysis* 54, no. 2: 28–46.

Harvey, Penelope, and Hannah Knox. 2010. "Abstraction, Materiality and the 'Science of the Concrete' in Engineering Practice." In *Material Powers: Cultural Studies, History and the Material Turn*, edited by Tony Bennett and Patrick Joyce, 124–141. London: Routledge.

Harvey, Penelope, and Hannah Knox. 2015. *Roads: An Anthropology of Infrastructure and Expertise*. Ithaca, NY: Cornell University Press.

Harvey, Penelope, and Deborah Poole, eds. 2012. "Estados experimentales: Presentación." *Anthropologica/Año* 30, no. 30: 77–82.

Ingold, Tim. 2007. "Materials against Materiality." *Archaeological Dialogues* 14, no. 1: 1–16.

Jones, Peter. 2006. *Ove Arup: Masterbuilder of the Twentieth Century*. New Haven, CT: Yale University Press.

Kirksey, Eben. 2015. *Emergent Ecologies*. Durham, NC: Duke University Press.

Kirksey, Eben, and Stefan Helmreich. 2010. "The Emergence of Multispecies Ethnography." *Cultural Anthropology* 25, no. 4: 545–576.

Kohn, Eduardo. 2013. *How Forests Think: Toward an Anthropology beyond the Human*. Berkeley: University of California Press.

Kohn, Eduardo. 2014. "Further Thoughts on Sylvan Thinking." *HAU: Journal of Ethnographic Theory* 4, no. 2: 275–288.

Latour, Bruno. 2004. *Politics of Nature*. Cambridge, MA: Harvard University Press.

Lowe, Adam. 2009. "An Identity Engine." In *Unconformity and Entropy*, edited by Anish Kapoor, Adam Lowe, and Simon Schaffer, 43–49. Madrid: Turner.

Mukerji, Chandra. 2009. *Impossible Engineering: Technology and Territoriality on the Canal du Midi*. Princeton, NJ: Princeton University Press.

Povinelli, Elizabeth. 2014. "Geontologies of the Otherwise." In "Fieldsights— Theorizing the Contemporary," special section, *Cultural Anthropology* online, January 13. http://www.culanth.org/fieldsights/465-geontologies-of-the-otherwise.

Raffles, Hugh. 2012. "Twenty-Five Years Is a Long Time." *Cultural Anthropology* 27, no. 3: 526–534.

Reinert, Hugo. 2016. "About a Stone: Some Notes on Geologic Conviviality." *Environmental Humanities* 8, no. 1: 95–117.

Sallnow, Michael. 1987. *Pilgrims of the Andes: Regional Cults in Cusco*. Washington, DC: Smithsonian Institution Press.

Shaffer, Simon. 2009. "Soft Matters." In *Unconformity and Entropy*, edited by Anish Kapoor, Adam Lowe, and Simon Schaffer, 163–175. Madrid: Turner.

Stoler, Ann. 2013. *Imperial Debris: On Ruins and Ruination*. Durham, NC: Duke University Press.

Strang, Veronica. 2014. "Fluid Consistencies: Material Relationality in Human Engagements with Nature." *Archaeological Dialogues* 21, no. 12: 133–150.

Taussig, Michael. 2004. *My Cocaine Museum*. Chicago: University of Chicago Press.

Tsing, Anna. 2005. *Friction: An Ethnography of Global Connection*. Princeton, NJ: Princeton University Press.

Tsing, Anna. 2015. *The Mushroom at the End of the World: On the Possibility of Life in Capitalist Ruins*. Princeton, NJ: Princeton University Press.

Weston, Kath. 2017. *Animate Planet: Making Visceral Sense of Living in a High-Tech Ecologically Damaged World*. Durham, NC: Duke University Press.

Zuidema, Tom. 1964. *The Ceque System of Cuzco: The Social Organization of the Capital of the Inca*. Translated by Eva M. Hooykaas. Archives Internationales d'Ethnographie 50. Leiden: Brill.

7. Traces of Pasts and Imaginings of Futures in St Lucia, South Africa

Knut G. Nustad

St Lucia, situated on the east coast of KwaZulu-Natal, is a landscape inscribed with the material traces of past uses. But these traces, rather than merely serving as memories of the past, are part of competing historicities, conflictual contemporary realities, and highly contested and ambivalent futures. Serving as hunting grounds for the colony of Natal in the nineteenth century, the area was, in the twentieth century, transformed into one of South Africa's most important sites for industrial agriculture and sugarcane production, as well as industrial forestry. As a reaction to these transformations of the landscape, there emerged, as in many other parts of the world, an ideal of nature as separate from human transformation and in need of protection. The Greater St Lucia Wetland Park, later renamed the iSimangaliso Wetland Park, became South Africa's first UNESCO world heritage site in 1999. But rather than marking the end point of a long trajectory of different uses, the creation of the park opened up and made visible past conflicts and contestations.

At the heart of these contestations are conflicting understandings of both what the landscape *is* and how its material potential should be exploited. The chapter begins with an instructive debate between social scientists, who explain landscapes as the result of humans ascribing their cultural values and meanings to them, and conservationists, who argue that landscapes such as

St Lucia have an intrinsic value, independent of human perceptions of them. This debate foreshadows the contemporary debates over material potentials and agency discussed in the introduction to this volume. Both positions, I will argue, are problematic, and the landscape should rather be understood as the material excesses of past uses.

Constructing Wilderness

St Lucia as a wilderness area emerged when its disappearance seemed imminent: in the final days of apartheid, the Richards Bay Minerals company received a concession for strip-mining the costal sand dunes of St Lucia. This would have drastically changed the area. With the volatile political situation, the entire future of St Lucia seemed undetermined. It was clear that political change would involve some form of change in landownership, and both the mining company and conservationists tried to persuade representatives of the black population to back their version of St Lucia—as industrial mining and with it job creation in the mines; or as a nature conservation area that, it was promised, would bring in tourists, generate revenue, and also create jobs.

In the end the Campaign to Save St Lucia, a mobilization of conservation groups and individuals, managed to force through an environmental impact assessment (EIA), the largest undertaken to that date in South Africa. Work on the EIA commenced in 1989 and was published in 1993. The EIA concluded that mining could be undertaken on condition that it was strictly regulated. But, in what was seen as an important victory for the emergent environmental movement in South Africa, after massive mobilization Parliament decided to impose a ban on all mining of the sand dunes in 1996. The UNESCO world heritage site was declared in 1999 (see Nustad 2015 for a detailed account of the process).

Social Construction versus Intrinsic Value

One chapter of the EIA, written by J. Butler Adam and M. J. Haynes, is titled "St Lucia: The Sense(s) of the Place" (1993). The debates evoked by that chapter make for interesting reading and provide a window into the debates that underpin the very real material struggle over the natures of St Lucia.

Being a product of their time, Butler Adam and Haynes adopted a straightforward yet sophisticated social constructivist approach to "sense of place," which itself highlighted both the complexities and problems inherent to such an approach. Opposition to mining, they argued, stems largely from the sense that many people have of St Lucia as a unique wilderness area, as a special place, as a sacrosanct environment. Such senses of place, they wrote, "derive from a complex combination of romantic notions of wilderness, rooted in traditions of Western civilisation, from culture, religion and from individual cognition and environmental awareness" (1993, 696). They also argued that the national and local press had been formative in establishing the image of St Lucia as a wilderness place and, in a comment that was to receive much criticism from conservation circles, pointed out that this "'dominant' image is one which is held by the current electorate in South Africa, i.e. the literate White public" (696).

Their argument is familiar to anyone who has encountered social constructivist accounts of places. Contemporary ideas of a sense of place, in Butler Adam and Haynes's view, stem from the Roman notion of a genius loci: just as every person born possesses a spirit, so do significant places. In contemporary use, however, the term "spirit of place" has shifted in meaning and come to connote the feelings invoked in us by specific places. This shift, they hold, involves more than a secularization of the term:

> It points out to the common realization, as well to the scientific knowledge, that the "sense" or "spirit" of place is not something "behind" the place, making it what it is, nor simply something imaginary, in our heads or hearts, but rather a product which has an intermediate locus. The product is what we call our sense of place: its locus is half-way (although it sometimes shifts one way or the other) between what is there, on the ground, and what we have made of that "reality" in our heads. (699)

The chapter ends with a response section with responses and comments from key institutions and individuals. One commentator from the Zululand Environmental Alliance wrote, "The methodology of this report is based on the relativist assumption that St Lucia has no intrinsic value and that the value attributed to it depends purely on human perception" (in Butler Adam and Haynes 1993, 726), to which the authors responded, "That is correct. The validity of the concept of 'intrinsic value' is debatable. Our philosophical stance recognises that 'value' cannot exist in a vacuum as it is always relative to human judgment. By and large, and particularly with respect to sense of place, value is relative to perception" (726).

A second commentator from the same organization began by saying, "It is natural in human nature to abhor the destruction of a natural environment such as St Lucia," and then continued, "This report falls exclusively into the nurture side of the nature/nurture debate and exposes the narrowness of its assumption. Because of this, it fails to comprehend the instinctive, deep-rooted feelings of the people who recognize encroachment upon natural areas that will finally be destroyed by man. The report fails to convey the interdependence of humans and environments" (in Butler Adam and Haynes 1993, 728).

The Natal Parks Board argued along the same lines that the "spiritual power of unspoiled natural areas, and the psychological benefit and sense of well-being gained therefrom, should not be understood simply as 'based on romance rather than reality'" (in Butler Adam and Haynes 1993, 723). Further driving home the point that St Lucia has intrinsic value and that any mention of perceptions undermine this are comments such as "the realisation by a large number of people that St Lucia's natural environment is of great intrinsic value can only be ignored at peril" (Zululand Environmental Alliance, fifth commentator, in Butler Adam and Heynes 1993, 730).

Reality Absolutism

Butler Adam and Haynes's overall response to these criticisms was to evoke the duality of social constructions: "We recognise that 'sense of place' is by definition relative to the perceptions of people and that these perceptions vary. Perceptions are often grounded in 'objective reality,' but not necessarily so. We furthermore do not assume 'intrinsic value' as it is highly debatable (we would argue that all 'value' is defined in human terms) and cannot account for the fact that perceptions are heterogeneous" (728). In other words, they argue that an objective reality exists independently of human perceptions and relations, and that differences in values and senses of place result from different perceptions.

Most of the statements made by the conservationists make sense when they are located in a specific historical context of human-environment relations. The conservationists commenting on Butler Adam and Haynes's report avoid a dualist ontology in that they insist that the *inherent* value of the environment is what makes it important. The commentators explicitly criticize Butler Adam and Haynes for seeing wilderness as a meaning ascribed to an experience of an intermediate level, between what is there on the ground and what we imagine in our minds (our mental images). Wilderness, they insist, exists objectively and in the world. It is real. The conservationists commenting on the EIA object to the social scientists' model, which assumes that meaning is mapped onto landscapes, and insist, as does Tim Ingold (2000), that meaning is located *in* environments.

This confrontation between the conservationist insistence on one true nature and the social science insistence on multiple interpretations is not accidental. It foreshadows later debates, in the social sciences, about a "one-world world" and about multiplicity and critiques of representationism (Law 2015; see also Crawford 1993; Bennett 2008; Viveiros de Castro 2015). Social constructivist theories were indeed meant to show the fallacies of the kinds of accounts put forward by the conservationists here. As we have seen, the commentators insist on one externally given objective nature, and they are authoritative and highly emotional in their prescription for human relationships to this nature, especially when nature takes the form of wilderness.

"Wilderness" is variously defined by the conservationists commenting on the chapter, but at the core of the concept is "nature" undisturbed by humans. In arguing that this nature is constructed, however, social constructivist theories create problems of their own: by insisting that interpretations are multiple, they inevitably reinforce the singularity and objectivity of that which is represented, and create a dichotomy between humans as representing and nonhumans as represented.

Interestingly, the opposition to the social constructivism evident in the comments ends up imposing a very similar dichotomy between nature and society, even if they argue for "the interdependence of humans and environments," in the words of one of the commentators cited above. The responses, while positing a fundamental unity between humans and environments, also argue that there is only one correct way of being in environments, only one sanctioned human-environment relation, only one way of dwelling.

The theoretical underpinnings evident in these comments therefore avoid the dualist ontology of social constructivism by replacing it with what we might call a *reality absolutism*: nature exists as an entity independently of human engagements, and there is only one true way of relating to nature—with respect, care, awe, and noninterference. The problem, I would argue, is that this notion of one objectively existing reality, one nature, *itself* hides a dualist ontology: the idea that something called nature exists independently of humans. Nature, then, is seen in these texts as existing outside a human-environment relationship, in the sense that only one human-environment relationship is acknowledged. Other people's ways of being in their environment, of dwelling, are, in this reality, seen not as acceptable but as abhorrent, wrong, and destructive. And when nature is separated from human-environment relations, history disappears as well.

In their reply to the social scientists who drafted the EIA, most conservationists thus employed a straightforward definition of wilderness as nature untouched by humans. But those who did acknowledge previous human settlements as part of the environment seemed to wish to freeze human-environment relations in a timeless precolonial past. The best example here is Ian Player, a longtime advocate of conservation and a key figure in the opposition to mining. He argued that the authors of the EIA had failed to understand "the spiritual role and power of St Lucia, as a symbol of unity in the shaping of the new South Africa, a merging of African and European appreciation of wild lands" (Player 1993, 6). This is a misconstruction, at best. St Lucia has been anything but a symbol of unity: rather, human-environment relations there have been characterized by increasing elite control of access to natural resources, both animal resources and land.

But what makes Player's account subtler than a flat denial of past human involvement in wilderness is that he seeks to project back in time a present-day conservationist relationship between people and environments. He writes:

> Since the 1500s the lake has been known to Portuguese and European as well as Arab and Chinese explorers. The black people knew it as Cwebeni throughout Zululand and Maputaland. The older generation of blacks knew it as Cwebeni las Entlengeni (The lagoon of rafts). It was recognised by hunters throughout the Western world as *the* place to hunt hippo and elephant. Countless books and articles were written by the early hunters—Baldwin, Drummond, Ludlow, to mention a few. In the twentieth century it was to become known as a fishermen's paradise and in the most recent decade, ornithologists and visitors interested in other aspects of natural history are growing in number. Sir Peter Scott the British ornithologist and artist, and Prof. Raymond Cowles the zoologist from UCLA, and Professor Day of UCT were pioneers of this trend in the 1950s and 60s. (Player 1993, 6)

This seems at first glance a strange justification for a wilderness area—what is recounted here is a long history of human involvement with environments. But Player is also selective in the kinds of relationships he mentions. Apart from the area "being known by blacks," his history of human-environment interactions is a history of elite European access to these resources. His use of the term "natural history" and academic titles is telling in this respect. No mention is made of how Africans used these resources and how such uses gradually became restricted.

Material Traces

To move beyond such a view, one needs to try to map out the multiple histories of the landscape. One way of doing this, as Gastón R. Gordillo (2014) has recently suggested, is to look at material traces and the ways in which they are made to perform different pasts, which in turn implies different futures. Gordillo examines rubble, and the ways rubble is sometimes reified as ruins to celebrate colonial and imperial pasts.

When I first began fieldwork in St Lucia in 2007, traces of past uses of the landscape were everywhere, first and foremost in the many burnt-out roots of pines. The pines had been planted during the 1950s when St Lucia was turned into a forest plantation. Their burnt-out state told a story of ruination, in more senses than one. Tour guides explained to visitors that with the proclamation of the park, nature was in the process of restoring itself. The human transformation of the landscape—felling alien trees and burning roots—was part of this restoration.

But this transformation of the landscape could also be seen as a double negation—a negation of a first negation: the industrial transformation of the landscape (Gordillo 2014, 120). This is a different form of double negation than that pointed to by Theodor Adorno, where the negation of the negation "proves that the negation was not negative enough" (Gordillo 2014, 119). However, it is also similar in that "to negate a negation does not bring about its reversal" (119). Removing the rubble of industrial transformation does not restore St Lucia to a precolonial natural state but rather creates something new.

Today the traces are beginning to fade. And in the same way that these material traces of past human industrial use are fading, so are stories and traces of other people's use of the landscape. While the early nineteenth-century populations who shaped the landscape are acknowledged in official histories, the fact that people were living in what now constitutes the core of the park up until they were forcibly removed in the 1950s is not part of the story presented to visitors. These people were removed to make place for the landscape that is now being negated, and their story is likewise caught up in the negation. In one version of the past, as well as in one possible future of St Lucia (St Lucia as wilderness), humans are not seen as belonging.

So what stories do these traces tell? They tell a history of long human involvement with landscape, plants, and animals. Zululand, and especially the St Lucia area, was an important hunting ground for the colony of Natal. As Player points out, St Lucia was seen as *the* place to hunt hippos and elephants. At first, however, this had little to do with sports hunting and recreation. Between 1856 and 1906, 800,000 kilograms of ivory was shipped out of Natal, much of it from hunting expeditions in the St Lucia area (Merrett 1991). The trade in animal goods created networks of African and European hunters that supplied a global market (MacKenzie 1988). By the time the nineteenth century drew to a close, all animals made part of this relationship around large settlements such as Durban had been exterminated, and expeditions had to travel farther afield into Zululand (Ballard 1981; McCracken 2008).

In response to this situation, colonial elites promoted preservation policies, which led to the establishment of reserves (Brooks 2000). To explain the establishment of reserves, one needs to look further than the promotion of wilderness values: as game disappeared, colonial elites took steps to restrict access to animals to people like themselves. Colonial administrators in Zululand, most of whom were sport hunters, imposed laws to protect those animals they saw as important for hunting, and they took steps to have other animals exterminated. Animals were categorized into different classes: those that were not protected and could be hunted without restriction, those that could not be hunted during a closed season, and royal game, the animals traditionally hunted by white hunters, such as elephants, rhinos, and hippos (McCracken 2008). These could be hunted only with a permit issued by the governor.

These restrictions were bitterly resented by many Africans, who now found their hunting practices labeled as poaching. Not only did the law restrict their access to animals, but the resulting increase in wild animals led to outbreaks of the wasting sickness *nagana* (from the tsetse fly), which killed their cattle. Despite intense lobbying by the Society for the Protection of the Fauna of the Empire, a powerful organization consisting of former hunters, Natal authorities decided to try to eradicate wild animals near human settlements. But at the same time it was decided to set aside four game reserves in those areas most affected by nagana, where consequently no people were living. St Lucia was one of these areas (Brooks 2000, 2001).

Another threat to wild animals arose in the form of capitalist agriculture at the beginning of the twentieth century (Nustad 2011, 2015). Recognizing that the St Lucia area was extremely fertile, the government in Pretoria decided to invest in sugarcane production. But first the swamps along the Mfuluzi River had to be drained. As a result of these interventions, silt washed down the river and clogged up the estuary mouth, which was seen as a disaster by the many sport fishers who had begun to use the area. To solve this problem, the river was channelized and its outlet moved so that the agricultural waste emptied directly into the Indian Ocean (Copley 2009).

This transformation of the landscape led, as it had in England in the previous century, to the idealization of an undisturbed nature in South Africa that predated human interference. As David Bunn points out:

"Nature," in South Africa, becomes significantly problematized at a time when agriculture is modernizing, when it is reducing the eco-environment to an exchange value and hastening the destruction of sharecropping and the smallholder's sustained utilization of resources. . . . [T]here was a critical point at which modernizing agrarian capitalism in Natal visibly began to destroy the "natural" environment fast becoming a valued tourist commodity amongst the white population, and it is not surprising to find a compensatory logic in which value comes increasingly to reside in those landscape features that appear to predate these effects. (1996, 43)

This is one of the origins of wilderness values in St Lucia. But it was probably the realization that the reserves could generate revenues as tourist destinations that saved them. A pamphlet produced in 1934 to market the reserves as tourist destinations clearly demonstrates a distinction between nature and modern society: "To escape from the restraint of towns and the monotonous daily routine to which most of us are confined, and to be immersed for a brief moment in wild nature, exercises that revitalising influence which is becoming so increasingly necessary to modern man, for in wild nature alone can be found the antidote to the soul-destroying effects of this mechanical age" (quoted in Brooks 2001, 414).

From the 1960s, environmental ideas and ideals became part of public and policy discourse in Europe and North America, but also in South Africa. An enactment of nature as the opposite of industrialization, as something external to humans and an object for preservation, also shaped St Lucia. The Dukuduku forest part of the park, which I return to below, emerged as an object of conservation at this time.

In 1966 government plans to build a dam on the Hluhluwe River at Hluhluwe to control periodic flooding led to the first public protest cast in a recognizably modern conservationist form. The Commission of Inquiry into the Alleged Threat to Animal and Plant Life in St Lucia Lake, later known as the Kriel Commission of 1966, argued that the Dukuduku forest was the "type of forest that is portrayed in the earliest descriptions, drawings and paintings of Natal" (Kriel 1966, 100). In 1977 the Natal Parks Board and the Department of Forestry decided to jointly manage the eastern shores of the park, and in 1986 St Lucia was declared a wetland of international importance under the Ramsar Convention. In 1992 all of the eastern shores were transferred to the Natal Parks Board, and in 1999 the St Lucia Wetland Park, later renamed the Isimangaliso Wetland Park, was listed as South Africa's first world heritage site.

Contemporary Double Negations

When this long history of human use is negated by establishing a park, other stories are silenced as well. Just as white industrial capital had transformed the area, so did the many black smallholders living there (see Nustad 2015 and Sundnes 2013b for a full account). Little is known about them, but archival research shows that people were forcibly removed in the 1930s to make way for forestry operations and again (much better documented) in the 1950s when what today constitutes the core of the park was planted with pines (Sundnes 2013b).

Human settlement became even more problematic for those who wanted to create St Lucia as a natural area in the 1990s. From a conservation point of view, the fact that a huge number of poor people had settled in the Dukuduku forest part of the park was seen as a disaster. Today most of the forest has been cleared for small-scale agriculture. But it is highly problematic to accuse the inhabitants of Dukuduku of having invaded the forest, as the press and the authorities have repeatedly done. Its population as it appears today is diverse and consists of a mix of people who claim that their ancestors lived in these forests and people who moved into the area later. One should therefore be careful of imagining this population as a single cohort of people that can be called the "Dukuduku community" or of trying to claim that they all inhabit the same nature. Some speak of the land as ancestral land, theirs by right of birth, and others speak of it as an area where land is plentiful and productive.

In 1998 a group of forest dwellers contacted the Association for Rural Advancement, a nongovernmental land rights organization based in Pietermaritzburg, and asked for help filing a claim for the land under the South African Land Restitution Program. A claim that covered the whole of Duku-

duku, many surrounding farms, and a substantial part of the park was subsequently filed with the regional land claims commissioner. After ten years
of struggle and opposition from the park, and from neighbors and people
living in the forest who feared they would be left out of a restitution plan, the
court finally awarded them the claim in 2003, but from that decision to an
actual transfer of ownership is a long way (Nustad 2015).

I became involved in the process through the Association for Rural
Advancement and a joint research project examining property forms, land
claims, and conservation (Nustad 2015). Together with the claimants, we
planned a survey to establish existing resource uses and property relations.
This was highly desired by some people living in the forest, but also opposed
by groups who saw any outside intervention as a threat. Given their history
with outside authorities, this did not come as a surprise (see Nustad 2005
for a description of similar processes). We did, however, initiate a round of
interviews and, later, a number of workshops outside the forest, in which the
claimants, representatives of the association, and I participated.

In these meetings people told us how St Lucia provided them with different types of resources, including those from marine sources, indigenous trees,
and wild animals. They emphasized how good it was to live there. The fertile
soil made it possible to live off the land; they did not have to go to shops, as
one elderly woman put it. The land between the two big rivers running into
the estuary was especially fertile. In addition, there was grass and fruit to collect and antelopes to hunt.

It is over access to these resources, however, that conflict arose. People living in Dukuduku gave numerous examples of conflicts with park employees.
Merely being found on park land would elicit allegations of poaching. One old
man recounted how, when he was young, they had made boats for catching fish
and had set snares for hunting animals. With the establishment of the park, old
hunting practices were treated as poaching. When asked who controlled access
to natural resources today, several groups responded that it should rightfully
be them and the other people who live in the forest, but that in reality the park
denies people the right to access these resources. One group complained that
if they tried to use the resources that they saw as rightfully theirs, they would
be arrested. Permits to fish and collect grass to use for weaving mats had to be
bought from the park, but this group, and all other groups on separate occasions, held that they were denied these permits because they lived in Dukuduku and that this was done to punish them for living in the forest.

Many people living in Dukuduku compared their use of the forest with
what white people had done to St Lucia and the wetlands. They had also

cleared the forest for their own use. In a public meeting in November 2009, one man said, "Let me tell you something, my brother, you cannot say, 'I am protecting a tree, the tree is better.' Give me an example of a place where buildings were erected without removal of trees. Right here in St Lucia when they were building their offices, did they not remove trees there? How much more then from a person who is growing crops in the fields?"

Others pointed to the managed nature of the park and were nonplussed by being accused of interfering in nature. Phrases such as "government cattle" were widely used for the wild animals, and there was a clear perception that park authorities had introduced species that had not been there before and managed these as well. As Gordillo (2014) pointed out with references to ruins and heritage, creating these "natural" landscapes takes a lot of interference.

Timelessness as Negation

Negating the negation of industrial transformation requires careful management. It is not enough merely to remove the traces of industrial transformation. Continued management is needed to create a version of the landscape that visitors recognize as wilderness. Thus, not all ideas of the human are abolished from these areas. Landscapes shaped by what are perceived as premodern humans are often placed on the nature side of a nature-society divide.

In this denial of any contemporary human presence in the wilderness, and corresponding portrayal of a different kind of human presence as part of a precolonial past, there is a conception of nature as timeless. As Shirley Brooks argues concerning the nearby Hluhluwe-Umfolozi Park, "There are at least two senses in which the cultural category of 'nature' carries with it a hidden time dimension. First, natural spaces are often seen as timeless, outside of time, or located in pre-history, before the beginning of recorded time. To call a particular landscape 'natural' is often to deprive it of its historical context—effectively to remove it from society" (2000, 64).

When I first met one of the people responsible for the management of the park, he stated that people had always been an integral part of the landscape in St Lucia. The dunes, he explained, are some six thousand years old, and at the time they were formed, people were definitely living there. This meant, he continued, that the landscape had been formed by people's past uses of resources, mining, cattle grazing, and so on.

However, it soon became clear that this acknowledgment of human presence, and the ways it had shaped what we now think of as nature, was limited to the past. He went on to explain: the fact that people formed the landscape does not mean that you can have people living in the park now, because one cannot tell people to live without cars, chain saws, television, and electricity.

I asked him about the use of fire: huge areas of the park had been burned recently, and the newspaper issued by the park seemed to explain this as a natural process. The park manager explained fire as mainly set by humans in the past, used by pastoralists to create grazing for their cattle. Today fire was used by the park management to provide grazing for animals that had been reintroduced into the park.

He also explained how he saw the work of the park as mimicking the presence of a preindustrial society, creating the effects and impacts on the environment that these long-gone peoples and their cattle had once created. The park was, in other words, using science and ecological knowledge to create the effect of the presence of a now-absent element: premodern human society.

This is a fascinating endeavor: the use of one specific set of human-environment relations, that of a scientific, ecological human intervention in nature, to mimic another set of human-environment relations—an absent one, that of an unspecified, premodern, and preindustrial *anthropos*. Thus, wilderness, in this instance, is achieved by trying to re-create a specific past.

Material Excess

Wilderness in St Lucia is, as we have seen, created as the negation of industrial transformation. A similar, although on the face of it totally opposing process, took place in Dukuduku. The people who now inhabit the forest are accused of destroying it, or turning wilderness into agricultural land. But some of the inhabitants of the forest insist that this is not the case. They are negating their own experience of industrial transformations.

An elderly man explained that when he grew up in the forest in the 1950s, much of it had been cleared by people for grazing. From around 1950, the government had tried to move them out of the forest to make way for forestry plantations but had not succeeded until the early 1970s. It was at that time, he said, that the forest started to grow back, covering what had been their grazing grounds.

His story is corroborated by a series of photographs analyzed by Frode Sundnes (2013b). The photographs, taken in 1937, 1969, and 1975, tell a story of an expanding forest. G. F. Van Wyk and colleagues (1996) conclude from these photographs that the forest expanded by some 336 hectares between 1937 and 1988. The expansion, they explain, resulted from the absence of "disturbances" such as fire and large animals. That Van Wyk and colleagues label the sudden absence of people as the cessation of "disturbances" is an example of an ontology based on a duality of pure nature and disruptive human societies. The historically situated human-environment relations apparent in the histories of the people I spoke to in Dukuduku are repressed, made invisible by this version of nature.

The removal of people and elephants from the forest created room for bush and trees. The forest grew thick and dense. Instead of human habitation destroying wilderness, the all-too-common tale of industrialization, here wilderness values replaced the human use of resources. As a result of apartheid's forced removals, undisturbed nature emerged. But, as should now be apparent, this undisturbed nature was in fact very much the result of a long history of humans, animals, and environments interacting, and also a result of forced removals and apartheid policies. In the reserve itself, this nature is continued: a landscape populated by animals and emptied of people. What is physically re-created here, then, is the nature of romanticism, on the margin of the social—an unsullied, pure nature defined in opposition to humanity (Franklin 2001). This raises the question of who is doing the "ruining" in the first place: whether the inhabitants of Dukuduku are "ruining the forest" or whether the forest itself is a product of colonial wreckage and ruination (Stoler 2013).

Conclusion

When the fate of St Lucia seemed undecided and volatile, and when two possible futures seemed to be emerging, St Lucia either as a mining town or as a conservation area, the question of what the land was became much more than an academic exercise. The predominant social theories of the time, variations of social constructivism that argued that different human groups imbued the external world with their own cultural meanings, were seen by the conservation lobby as an attempt to deconstruct the inherent value of landscapes such as St Lucia. In a sense, this debate between conservationists and social scientists foreshadowed later social science debates about perspectivism, multiplicity, and ontology. Then, as now, the debate was about where to locate multiplicity: in human perceptions or in an external world.

I have argued that less focus on social constructions versus inherent value, and more on the material manifestations of past practices in the landscape, would help to highlight the various and multiple competing historical trajectories of the landscape. The burnt-out roots of pines in the park remind us that this region has a long history of human use and contestation, but also that these roots form part of different realities. They were planted as a way of making unused land productive, and they are now destroyed as aliens in a wilderness.

The invasion of the Dukuduku forest since the 1980s by squatters, who have cleared it for agricultural use, has been lamented as one of the worst ecological catastrophes in modern South Africa. But as we have seen, the forest that was destroyed, itself now a symbol of a wild indigenous forest, achieved its present form because people had been forcibly removed from their grazing grounds in the 1950s. And in the park careful management is needed to re-create materially an idea of a timeless wilderness that itself emerged as a reaction to the industrial transformation of landscapes. This would suggest that one path beyond the impasse of debates such as that between the social scientist and the conservationist—and beyond the contemporary stalemate between the so-called ontological turn and its critics—is to pay attention to the material traces of landscapes, as well as to the political economies embedded in them.

REFERENCES

Ballard, Charles. 1981. "The Role of Trade and Hunter-Traders in the Political-Economy of Natal and Zululand, 1824–1880." *African Economic History* 10: 3–21.

Bennett, Tom. 2008. "'Officials' and 'Living' Customary Law: Dilemmas of Description and Recognition." In *Land, Power and Customs: Controversies Generated by South Africa's Communal Land Rights Act*, edited by Aninka Claassens and Ben Cousins, 138–153. Cape Town: University of Cape Town Press.

Brooks, Shirley. 2000. "Re-reading the Hluhluwe-Umfolozi Game Reserve: Constructions of a 'Natural' Space." *Transformation* 44: 63–79.

Brooks, Shirley. 2001. "Changing Nature: A Critical Historical Geography of the Umfolozi and Hluhluwe Game Reserves, 1887 to 1947." PhD diss., Queen's University, Kingston, Canada.

Bunn, David. 1996. "Comparative Barbarism: Game Reserves, Sugar Plantations, and the Modernization of South African Landscape." In *Text, Theory, Space: Land, Literature and History in South Africa and Australia*, edited by Kate Darian-Smith, Liz Gunner, and Sarah Nuttall, 37–52. London: Routledge.

Butler Adam, J., and M. J. Haynes. 1993. "St Lucia: The Sense(s) of the Place." In *Environmental Impact Assessment, Eastern Shores of Lake St Lucia, Kingsa/Tojan Lease Area*, 695–734. Pretoria: Council for Scientific and Industrial Research.

Copley, Gail J. 2009. "Shifts in Environmental Policy Making Discourses: The Management of the St Lucia Estuary Mouth." Master's thesis, University of KwaZulu-Natal, Durban.

Crawford, Hugh T. 1993. "An Interview with Bruno Latour." *Configurations* 1, no. 2: 247–268.

Franklin, Adrian. 2001. "Neo-Darwinian Leisures, the Body and Nature: Hunting and Angling in Modernity." *Body and Society* 7, no. 4: 57–76.

Gordillo, Gastón R. 2014. *Rubble: The Afterlife of Destruction.* Durham, NC: Duke University Press.

Ingold, Tim. 2000. *The Perception of the Environment: Essays in Livelihood, Dwelling and Skill.* London: Routledge.

Kriel, J. P. 1966. *Report of the Commission of Inquiry into the Alleged Threat to Animal and Plant Life in St Lucia Lake, 1964–1966.* Pretoria: Government Printer.

Law, John. 2015. "What's Wrong with a One-World World?" *Distinction: Journal of Social Theory* 16, no. 1: 126–139.

MacKenzie, John MacDonald. 1988. *The Empire of Nature: Hunting, Conservation and British Imperialism.* Manchester: Manchester University Press.

McCracken, Donald P. 2008. *Saving the Zululand Wilderness: An Early Struggle for Nature Conservation.* Auckland Park: Jacana Media.

Merrett, Patricia L. 1991. Introduction to *Hunting Journal, 1852–1856: In the Zulu Kingdom and the Tsonga Regions,* by Robert Briggs Struthers, edited by Patricia L. Merrett and Ronald Butcher, 11–59. Durban: Killie Campbell Africana Library.

Nustad, Knut G. 2005. "State Formation through Development in Post-apartheid South Africa." In *State Formation: Anthropological Perspectives,* edited by Christian Krohn-Hansen, and Knut G. Nustad, 79–95. London: Pluto.

Nustad, Knut G. 2011. "Performing Natures and Land in the iSimangaliso Wetland Park, South Africa." *Ethnos* 76, no. 1: 88–108.

Nustad, Knut G. 2015. *Creating Africas: Struggles over Nature, Conservation and Land.* Crises in World Politics. London: Hurst.

Player, Ian. 1993. "Additional Comments." In *Environmental Impact Assessment, Eastern Shores of Lake St Lucia, Kingsa/Tojan Lease Area,* 1–10. Pretoria: Council for Scientific and Industrial Research.

Stoler, Ann Laura. 2013. Introduction to *Imperial Debris: On Ruins and Ruination,* edited by Ann Laura Stoler, 1–35. Durham, NC: Duke University Press.

Sundnes, Frode. 2013a. "The Past in the Present: Struggles over Land and Community in Relation to the Dukuduku Claim for Land Restitution, South Africa." *Forum for Development Studies* 40, no. 1: 69–86.

Sundnes, Frode. 2013b. "Scrubs and Squatters: The Coming of the Dukuduku Forest, an Indigenous Forest in KwaZulu-Natal, South Africa." *Environmental History* 18, no. 2: 277–308.

Van Wyk, G. F., D. A. Everard, J. J. Midgley, and I. G. Gordon. 1996. "Classification and Dynamics of a Southern African Subtropical Coastal Lowland Forest." *South African Journal of Botany* 62, no. 3: 133–142.

Viveiros de Castro, Eduardo. 2015. "Who Is Afraid of the Ontological Wolf? Some Comments on an Ongoing Anthropological Debate." *Cambridge Anthropology* 33, no. 1: 2–17.

PART III

Material Uncertainties and Heterogeneous Knowledge Practices

———

8. Matters That Matter

AIR AND ATMOSPHERE AS MATERIAL POLITICS IN SOUTH AFRICA

———

Rune Flikke

There have been a number of conceptions of and approaches to modernity since the term entered the social sciences. One of the more intriguing is Peter Sloterdijk's ([2002] 2009b, 10) suggestion that we received the final push into modernity at six o'clock in the evening on April 22, 1915, when the first chlorine gas canisters were opened and discharged on French and Canadian troops at the Ypres front. Though Sloterdijk (2009a, 45) was well aware that the preoccupation with unbreathable spaces was expressed through the notion of miasma, the novelty of his argument was that the gas attacks of World War I were to become the turning point in the formation of a new Western ontology. We could no longer take for granted that the air we were breathing was life-sustaining, which turned it into a vital object for political control: wars are won or lost based on the capacity to conquer the respiratory potential of hostile people and climates. I believe Sloterdijk has a strong case. For this reason it is striking that Tim Ingold (2010) has argued that until recently little has been published in the social sciences on our air dependency and the influence of air and atmospheres on human lifeworlds. In this chapter I discuss this through two interrelated yet historically and culturally distinct cases.

The first is a historical case that ties air as an object of material politics back to the colonial contact zone, where efforts to control the air settlers were breathing resulted in landscape alterations, instigated to secure a home in an alien, threatening environment. Building on previous work (Flikke 2016b), I argue that Victorian settlers in Africa experienced air and atmosphere as a problematic aspect of African otherness, where both conceptions of climate and people were obstacles to be dealt with through a politic of "air-conditioning" (Sloterdijk [2002] 2009b). For the Victorian settler communities, breathing the tropical air was a question of destiny, which made it existentially too important to breathe without air-conditioning (see Sloterdijk [1998] 2014, 961–967).

The second case is a contemporary ethnographic account of Zulu Zionism—a part of the African Independent Churches—in an African township in the vicinity of Durban, South Africa. Here I show how Zionists consider the air to be of vital importance for health and disease. I track the imagery this case reveals back to precolonial Zulu and southern Bantu conceptions and practices, and suggest that certain contemporary healing practices can be traced back to settler efforts to govern the air and the effects these practices had on native lives.

Victorian Air-Conditioning

The Victorian epidemiological model relied heavily on notions of the quality of the air, atmosphere, and climate. In Britain it ascended to prominence in the 1840s through the work of a group known as the Ultra-Sanitarians and Edwin Chadwick, a lawyer who made a career within the British central government and had the top post on the General Board of Health. For the Ultra-Sanitarians, epidemics were the product of miasma caused by accumulated dirt and decomposing matter. In this model the physical causes of European epidemics were spatially distributed, and mostly located in towns and cities where dirt and organic matter accumulated and decomposed. The putrefaction caused the noxious air, and this was the primary source of contagion.

This conception of epidemics and health constituted an epidemiology, though it was not built on the germ theory developed by the German physician and microbiologist Robert Koch, who, through his studies of cholera in Alexandria and Calcutta in 1883 and 1884, had discovered bacteria as the causative agent of cholera and, later, tuberculosis. All fevers, often indiscriminately referred to as "malaria" or "cholera," were thus conceived to be different manifestations of the same problem—miasma. Chadwick defended this position as late as 1877, when, in his opening speech to the public health section of the Social Science Congress, he claimed that it was heretical to assert that the causative agent of cholera could be imported. He argued that the cholera epidemics in India could not be the same as those experienced in Great Britain. Cholera was a local phenomenon attached to local atmospheres. This view was decisive in the argument against introducing a quarantine, ensuring that the rich, who were not affected by the cholera outbreak, could continue to profit from trade. Chadwick was the primary advocate of a hodgepodge of ideas that from the 1830s became known as the Sanitarian Ideal (Pelling 1978).

The Sanitarian Ideal had two implications. First, because cholera had been designated as an aspect of local atmospheres and hence noncontagious, it would affect only those predisposed to it because of their immoral conduct. Second, there was a strong political message, as the Sanitarian Ideal viewed epidemics as preventable through legislation and public health engineering aimed at controlling the quality of air and water. Because the Victorian medical gaze naturally focused on the sources of miasma, Chadwick's concern was to outline the structural hindrances to the improvement of public health (see Chadwick [1842] 1965). As a consequence, the roles of medical doctors became limited, while those of people working in public health policy and engineering became more central. This related directly to the three main objectives of this form of medicine, which Michel Foucault (2000, 142–151) referred to as "urban medicine." The first concern was to analyze the city and locate zones of congestion and disorder; the second was to gain control of the circulation of water and air; and the third was to ensure that public health officials properly managed different elements such as drinking fountains, sewers, and churchyards. Though based on a faulty understanding of the disease vector, these efforts to condition the air greatly reduced the urban mortality rate.

The invisibility of the poor—referred to as "the great unwashed" by Edward George Bulwer-Lytton in his 1830 novel *Paul Clifford*—was a great source of fear, for the poor and dirty were, in a very real sense, disease (see Stallybrass and White 1986, 135). The poor were controlled through architectural visibility as the city streets were widened so the wind could carry away miasma. In this way diseases were also controlled. Following this line of thought, in which disease was an aspect of the local air and atmosphere, and the poor—as dirty—were a source of miasma, we can see how the Victorian conflation of air and disease physically opened up British cities. Architectural refashioning allowed the polluting air to be "blown away." At the same time, engineering addressed the public health hazard associated with dirt.

In what has been called the Roe-Chadwick scheme, Chadwick teamed up with the engineer John Roe and drafted plans to create a network of sewerage and water pipes below the public streets. This was a successful way of ameliorating the stenches caused by decaying organic material and the miasma causing the epidemics. The tree-lined boulevards that emerged in Paris at the time were similarly constructed as aeration corridors to direct air currents away from the urban population (see Foucault 2000, 148). At the same time, the removal of architectural barriers addressed what remained Chadwick's primary concern, namely, poor drainage and ventilation owing to streets that were "very narrow, and houses . . . built so much behind each other that the entrance to a great many of the dwellings is by passage, lane, or alley, either a steep ascent or descent, where, from a proper want of receptacles and sewers, filth is allowed to accumulate and there necessarily is a constant emanation of fœtid effluvia" ([1842] 1965, 94).

The "open cities," in other words, ensured that the conditioned citizens, as good role models and observers, monitored the laboring classes, and the open spaces also made policing easier. Thus, the disease-inducing immoral behavior of the poor would be restricted, and, at the same time, the streets would be cleaner, better ventilated, and free of miasma. Breathable public environments were created. As such, political efforts to control and purify the air not only became well established but were also a well-known success as, for the first time, the populations of European cities grew without an influx of people from the countryside.

In southern Africa the climate and the social context were, needless to say, vastly different from those in Great Britain, yet the dangers of the air were also manifest, although they played out in a different manner.

African Atmospheres and Settler Policies

My material is from King William's Town in South Africa's Eastern Cape province in 1876, toward the end of Chadwick's restructuring of the British urban landscape. The town is situated on the frontier where the nine Xhosa wars took place, which destabilized the region between 1779 and 1879. The mid-1870s were characterized by drought and epidemics that surfaced in the aftermath of the wars and the Great Cattle Killing of 1856–1857 (Peires 1989). This occurred during the craze of the great mineral discoveries, which resulted in an acute labor shortage and ever more pressure on the African population through the introduction of new taxes and other policies that forced more African males into the labor market. Perhaps because of these tumultuous times, the area became the birthplace of the African Independent Churches. I will only briefly introduce the case since I have elsewhere described in more detail how the sanitation hysteria emerged in King William's Town (Flikke 2014, 2016b).

During the early months of 1876, King William's Town was plagued by a "sanitation syndrome" (see Laidler and Gelfand 1971, 362), followed by efforts to sanitize the air to prevent miasma and address the epidemics that plagued the area in the wake of nearly a century of wars and social unrest. After being reduced to a heap of ruins during the war of 1847–1848, King William's Town had been rebuilt, and part of the town, referred to as the "Pensioner's Village," was set aside as a retirement village for pensioners from overseas (Laidler and Gelfand 1971, 295) because the town was considered to have one of the "finest climates in the world" (see Flikke 2016b).

After several heated meetings and numerous passionate letters to the editor of the *Cape Mercury*, the town council promoted the planting of eucalyptus trees because of the trees' "deodorizing" and thus sanitizing qualities. This, I suggest, was a colonial strategy to deal with stenches, which—as an indication of miasma—were seen as the cause of the epidemics that ravaged European settlements all over colonial Africa.

Several ecological as well as demographic changes resulted from this sanitary restructuring of the town. First, the landscape started changing in different ways than in Australia and Tasmania, where eucalyptus trees tended to be underrated by the English settlers and replaced with oaks and pines. While this change in the South African landscape has been ascribed to aesthetic and economic concerns (see Witt 2005), I argue that there is a need to place greater analytic emphasis on the air and atmosphere in order to understand these divergent attitudes among the expatriate English (Flikke 2016b). As with the Victorian view of the poor as "the great unwashed," the conflation of air and disease resulted in a number of pass laws that aimed to control the movement of the "deranged" and the native populations, since their bodies were associated with dirt and hence were considered producers of miasma (Flikke 2003a, 2003b). This can be seen as a precursor to the introduction of the first segregationist laws, implemented in Cape Town after a brief appearance of the plague in January 1901 (Swanson 1977).

The common characteristic of these two efforts to control African movements and proximity to white lives was that segregation was rationalized as a necessary public health initiative. In the case of King William's Town, still in the grips of Galenic medicine, which dominated the Victorian era with its acute belief in the dangers associated with breathing miasma, political efforts to control the air were at the core of these early efforts to police racial and climatic otherness.

The Transformation of Air in Material Politics

Though it is true, as Gaston Bachelard once quipped, that "air is a very thin matter" ([1943] 1988, 8), it is worth pondering why the atmosphere, until recently, has attracted so little attention in social theory. This lack of attention is evident even though we know that weather and climate are central to the human experience and exert a strong impact on social organization. As mentioned in the introduction, Sloterdijk saw the chlorine gas attacks during World War I as the final push into modernity as, once and for all, it robbed us of a taken-for-granted attitude toward the air we were breathing. We also know that religions all over the world closely relate air and wind to notions of spirits.

Ingold (2005; 2011, pt. 3), a prominent social theorist, has pondered why weather has been so understudied. The reason for this lack of analytic investigation, he argues, is that since René Descartes the Western world has increasingly conceived of life as existing on the external surface of the globe, thus turning humans into "exhabitants" who are composites of body and mind, residing in a world of matter and a world of ideas, respectively (see Ingold 2011, 96, 116). This occurred alongside developments in which vision gained prominence over the other senses (Urry 1990), and the relationship between an observing subject and an observed object became increasingly disconnected. As Foucault ([1973] 1994) famously argued, the medical gaze fixed the location of the body in space, increasingly policing and hence solidifying the boundaries of the body (see Harris, Robb, and Tarlow 2013).

In this world of increasingly separate and labeled objects and subjects, the ground under our feet has become the source of stability and the material subsistence for life, while the atmosphere has retreated to become a passive backdrop through which mobility and olfactory, visual, and auditory perceptions occur. In this modernist understanding of nature, the surface of the landscape marks the limits of materiality, and the air is, for the most part, conceived of as immaterial, the opposite of solidity (Harris, Robb, and Tarlow 2013); an empty space that allows the "important" interaction to occur—namely, that between human agents and material objects (see Ingold 2005, 103). In short, we have an ontology that places surface before medium.

Unless the air is heavily polluted, filled with uncanny smells or stenches, it recedes to the background of our consciousness as well as our theorizing (see Choy 2011; 2012, 125).

Ingold (2011, 116) suggested we follow the lead of James J. Gibson (1979) and turn this ontology on its head, understanding the world as comprising earthly substances and an aerial medium in which we are immersed. However, Ingold departed from Gibson's view of the world as "furnished" with objects, arguing that we instead need to resort to Martin Heidegger's vision of an emerging world of growth and motion that cannot be described by nouns (117–125). Rather than taking the landscape as the surface on which human activities are played out, we should view weather and the earth's atmosphere as the central medium in which most human actions occur and seek to capture it through verbs. In Ingold's account, the earth is "neither an object in space nor a space for objects. . . . [T]he earth is 'earthing'" (114). This reversal creates a world where human life, rather than being founded on a solid, stable earth, emerges as spun on "a fragile ephemeral raft" (Ingold 2005, 103) that ties the human experience closer to fluidity, flux, transformations, and transience.

As we all know, air is the foundation of our existence. Without air we cannot live, and without breathing there is no life. In line with Ingold's argument, we could therefore agree with Robert Chapigny that "air is breathing rather than what a body breathes" (in Bachelard [1943] 1988, ix). Air, with its "lightness" and "thinness," is the essence of life that enables movement. On clear days we do not see the air, but we can feel it touch the surface of our skin; we can be aware of it when we see clouds pass over the horizon; we notice it when we study birds that soar, rising effortlessly on its currents. With air, Bachelard says, "Movement takes precedence over matter" ([1943] 1988, 8). For Friedrich Nietzsche, this openness and motion and the unbounded nature of air constituted the very substance of human freedom (see Bachelard [1943] 1988, 136; Nietzsche [1883–1889] 1961).

The rapidly growing literature on climate change has, in a similar vein, pointed out that weather and the atmosphere cross-culturally have tended to be viewed as the sphere of gods and the divine, outside the realm of human intervention (Donner 2007). Hence, the fluctuating and unruly atmosphere tends to surface as a source of uncertainty that needs to be regulated and controlled to create a needed sense of predictability. Mike Hulme (2015) has suggested that the climate, understood as certain atmospheric conditions typical of a given region, is one such metaphor that embeds the air and atmosphere in human projects; these projects create a sense of stability and consistency, carving out spaces for meaningful human action and interaction. This fleeting nature of air makes it somewhat resistant to a stringent language of "science," yet it is potent as a metaphor; metaphors of height, depth, falling, and soaring are dream symbols par excellence. Dreams of flight are therefore joyful dreams of youthful lightness, freedom, endless possibilities, upliftment, and growth (see, for example, Bachelard [1943] 1988, 33–35).

In Flikke (2016a) I argue that local winds entered into the ritual activities of the Zionist congregation where I worked in South Africa, thereby transforming the air and atmosphere into a metaphysical, stabilizing space. Here I will argue that local engagements with winds enabled constructive processes of subjectification in otherwise-dire living circumstances.

Winds Embodied: Contemporary Zulu Zionist Air-Conditioning

During my fieldwork in a Zulu Zionist congregation in an African township outside Durban, the main activity I witnessed was ritual healing. The majority of the cases were afflictions associated with black urban life that were a legacy of the racist policies of apartheid South Africa (see Flikke 2016a, 2006). One reoccurring ailment was respiratory problems, often understood as coming from problematic winds that did not respect the body boundaries of the afflicted. These winds did not blow around the person but were often described as stabbing sensations (*isibhobho*) that opened them up and blew through them, filling them with disease or "good luck," all according to the matters the winds carried with them.

The story of one informant, Thandi, drew my attention to the significance of air and atmosphere for well-being among my respondents (see Flikke 2016a, 2007). I will briefly describe the case here. During my first proper interview with Thandi, she responded to my presence with excessive yawning, belching (isibhobho), and hiccups. These, she said, were internal winds, *umoya*, a term used to depict wind, air, and spirits (see Flikke 2016a). During that interview Thandi told me about oneiric dreams that, she said, were warnings of an impending violent attack on her and her family. The attack, which aimed to harvest her body parts as ingredients in a potent strengthening medicine (*umuthi*), had taken place a few months before we met. Thandi was treated by Themba, the prophet and founder of the Zionist congregation she attended, and through his treatment she recovered quickly as she went through several ritual processes accompanied by bodily experiences with winds that penetrated her body and filled her with spirit. These processes drew on a rich cultural arsenal of imagery and bodily relations to the weather-world (Ingold 2010) to reshape her relation to the external social world. Her experiences indicated that the winds she encountered were healing, yet wild, unruly, and problematic (Flikke 2016a).

Thandi's account brings together polluting winds and stabbing pains as her upper body was opened and filled with wind. The fact that Thandi's experience of the stabbing took the form of wind blowing through her open body suggests a strong connection between wind, stabbing pains, and the upper chest, which needs to be understood in a historical context. The hole she experienced in her chest is well known and has been described in ethnographic studies since the mid-nineteenth century (see Flikke 2016a).

There are long-standing traditions in southern Bantu thought that perceive winds as sources of both disease and health. The missionary Alfred T. Bryant noted that, for the Zulu, the common cold (*umkuhlane*) was brought by the winds. Certain winds were therefore threats to health and were to be avoided when possible (see Bryant [1909] 1983, 17). The stabbing nature of Thandi's encounter with winds was an experience of being compromised and opened up by spiritual forces, effectively merging her fate with the qualities of the surrounding material world, including those carried by the winds.

Air, Environmental Pollution, and Disease

In Zulu cosmology, all substances have metaphysical qualities. As we move through the landscape, some of our substances are shed and left behind, whereas others are picked up (see Ngubane 1977, 24–29.). These are the tracks (*umkhondo*) that dogs scent while hunting. When people or livestock cross tracks left by unsavory humans or animals, such as hyenas or certain snakes associated with pollution, they are exposed to defiling forces that will eventually make them sick unless they are properly strengthened (see Beinart and Brown 2013, 210–214). These tracks become particularly troublesome in large cities, plagued as they are by pollution and an abundance of people. Substances can also float in the air as "threads" that connect people and places (see Ingold 2011, 121). In this case they are spoken of as *imimoya*, the plural of the word used for wind and spirit—*umoya*. They can be inhaled, and if these aerial threads are defiling (*imimoya emibi*), they will pollute (Ngubane 1977, 24–29). The imimoya emibi carried by the wind were still perceived as a source of environmental pollution and a problem associated with urbanization when I conducted my fieldwork. The then well-known *inyanga* (herbalist) and leader of the Traditional Healers Association Mr. Sazi Mhlongo expressed his—and the organization's—concern about the spread of Zulu healing practices to urban street corners. In an interview about umuthi street vendors in Durban, printed in the *Natal Witness* on November 7, 1995, he is reported to have said, "They are not traditional healers, and they should be arrested for treating people on the streets where the wind blows everything onto those herbs." Even the healing herbal remedies (umuthi) can be infused with the dirt of the cities and transformed from a health-giving remedy to a carrier of illness, misfortune, and "bad luck" (*umnyama*) or "darkness" (see Flikke 2006). Once polluted, the muthi generates illness and suffering for the users instead of healing. Hence, people I encountered in Themba's congregation would at times sneak out at night to be ritually cleansed at marketplaces, crossroads, and busy thoroughfares, where the pollution was shed and picked up and carried away by strangers who passed through during the day.

Winds also carry odors, creating perceptible threads that connect people and places in ways that cut across time and place (see Flikke 2014). As Eileen Jensen Krige ([1936] 1950) noted, the presence of witches and their evil deeds cannot be seen, only sensed, "in the air." The Zulu "witch finders," she wrote, "smelled out" the witches. As the witch finder danced toward the suspects, he "examine[d] them by means of his olfactory sense" (225), thus following the threads in the air left behind by the evildoers. The perception of witchcraft, as a substance of a negative, forceful, and dark appearance, therefore has certain olfactory qualities.

This finds a parallel in Khoisan notions of both wind and witchcraft (see Low 2007). Bryant (1949, 109) also discussed the attention paid to odors brought by the wind, referring to an elderly woman obviously bothered by the smell from a new steam train moving some seven miles away. She described the scent, not noticeable to Bryant, as suffocating (*bopile*). Although Bryant did not situate this discussion in the context of contagion and disease, I think the overall ethnographic evidence suggests that the acute awareness of olfactory signs is best understood in the context of Bantu notions of health and disease. Within this ontology, in which air and wind disperse "good luck" and "bad luck" to those exposed, the urge to control the air and atmosphere will naturally be different than in those ontologies that conceive them predominantly as empty space.

Although the winds were a potential carrier of illness and suffering, my informants mostly engaged them as a positive force since they were experienced within a carefully staged ritual context. A central ingredient in all ritual proceedings was the incense *imphepho* (*Helichrysum miconiaefolium*), a perennial that gives off a sweet smell when burned. This is the plant of the ancestors and was always circulated among the ritual participants, who would be enveloped in the smoke and would breathe in the health-giving protective smoke. Interestingly, the root of this word (*phepho*) is also used in the word for a hurricane or gale (*isiphepho*), which strengthens the connections between air and the politics of health.

In the following section, I draw attention to places where the boundaries between the surface of the ground and the atmosphere were blurred and the invisible atmosphere was made sensorily present. During my fieldwork these locations emerged as vitalizing zones with a ritual significance. They were windy places that anchored Thandi to a world of well-being, where the wind (umoya) filled her with spirit (umoya) and provided an evanescent foothold in a world that cut through time and space. After the attack made her lose her footing in the world, oneiric encounters with winds and water reestablished a sense of belonging and purpose that was aerial at its core yet strong enough to put her back on her feet in the same social environment in which she was attacked—perpetually plagued, as it were, by violence, poverty, and suffering.

Religion and Frictions between the Material and Aerial

As "creatures of the air," birds have a long-standing significance in Zulu ritual practice (see Flikke 2016a). In the ritual known as *amalathi*,[1] conducted to set up a bridge of communication with the ancestral spirits of the afflicted, chickens are slaughtered, enveloped in imphepho (smoke). Themba explained the ritual to me: "The fowls—actually, in the traditional setup of African people, they represent the spirits. Because each time a person has to slaughter a goat, a fowl, he has to address the spirits through the fowls: 'Today I'm bringing you this offering. Please, so and so, take care of me.'" This resonates with the role played by birds in postcolonial Zulu practice (Callaway [1868] 1970, 130; Flikke 2016a). The birds belong to the air, just like the spirits, and the spirits communicate with the living through bird talk. Birds soar on the thermals that arise as the winds interact with the rolling hills so characteristic of KwaZulu-Natal. Consequently, birds straddle the gap created through the interaction between the invisible winds and the surfaces of the landscape; their very habitat—the intersection between the landscape and the atmosphere—reveals the power of the invisible winds. When birds soar on the currents, they are, in fact, making manifest the connections between surface and medium, revealing that the atmosphere is not empty space but a surface in the world that can provide vital insights in cultural analyses.

I also suggest that mountains are spiritually important because of their exposure to winds. Unprotected landscapes such as mountaintops and coastlines are open spaces, spaces of contact and predation, places where things become visible (Bachelard [1943] 1988, 136). These places are favored sites for Zulu Zionist ritual proceedings. Having spent many nights on mountaintops with Zionist informants, I have vivid memories of how we were gradually exposed to the wind on gusty nights as we climbed the hill toward the cairn at the highest peak in the area, or on the beaches, facing the winds blowing in from the Indian Ocean, whose powerful waves are sought out by surfers from all over the world. The winds at these locations interacted with the surroundings; they grabbed hold of our bodies, and we responded by bending over, flexing muscles to withstand their force. On these occasions, the bodies of the afflicted take shape from their will to resist the power of the wind. The force and lightness of the wind (umoya) shape the force of the spirit (umoya).[2] Not only are wind and spirit signified by the same word; they are the same. The afflicted moving in this ritual landscape are physically challenged to rise, stand, and not fall again, while they are also filled by the lightness of the air (spirit) (Bachelard [1943] 1988, 156). The wind not only forced us to respond physically but also spoke to us as it whistled over the top, carrying sounds from afar and, at times, drowning out the voices of those standing nearby.

To understand the significance of these whistling sounds, it is important to look more closely at the association between the spiritual power of *abalozi*, the head of the diviner, and "whispering winds." Abalozi is also a form of divination where the *isangoma* (traditional healer) sits in the *umsamo*, the place where the ritual artifacts of a household are stored, and interprets the whistling sounds (the voices of the spirits) coming from the sacred area in the thatching at the back of the hut, known as *ikhothamo*.[3] There was thus great significance in the howling sounds as the wind blew around huts and the corners of houses—it was the same voice of the spirits that emerged when the wind mingled with the landscape as it blew through valleys, whistling as it grabbed hold of caves and caverns, filling the hollows of the ground with sounds. The Zionists, then, sought communion with their ancestral spirits at places exposed to winds. The ancestors, spoken of as *abaphansi* ("those down below") in this context, were often associated with ritual places such as canyons, waterfalls, and caves—all permeable openings to the ancestral world below. These are places that come alive with sound when the winds grab hold of the crevices of the landscape, filling these locations with the audible and haptic presence of the ancestral spirits.

Conclusion: Air as the Object of Material Politics

In this chapter I used Sloterdijk's work on atmospheres to approach the colonial contact zone in southern Africa. I suggested that the massive landscape alterations that started during the 1870s could, in part, be explained as a result of public health policies that connected tropical atmospheres to epidemic diseases as an aspect of places. Though the concern with air disappeared from view around the turn of the twentieth century, these atmospheric concerns have contemporary socioeconomic consequences. Precolonial South Africa had a forest cover of less than 1 percent, yet now the country is a leader in the contemporary global pulp industry, largely owing to the appeal of imported eucalyptus (see Carrere and Lohmann 1996, 198; Flikke 2016b).

At the same time as the inhabitants of King William's Town planted eucalyptus to combat diseases, the first African secessions from the mission churches occurred in the same area, laying the foundation for the Zulu Zionist movement. Though I have not directly related the two cases in this chapter, my ethnographic material indicates that the ritual practices of the Zulu Zionists can be recast as a contemporary material politic of air that resonates with the Victorian landscape transformations. The rituals open up "breathing spaces" as a prerequisite for a good, healthy life in the midst of disease, poverty, and existential insecurity. These two cases are well-researched aspects of South African society yet have thus far not been analyzed in relation to our atmosphere dependency. Through Ingold's work I argued that this is due to a retreat of air and atmosphere in Western culture that also influenced social theory in ways that have prevented us from seeing how alternative engagements with air and atmospheres have influenced social dynamics. This suggests that we should question our own sensory access to the world as part of a long social history that has opened but one of many possible experiences with air and atmospheres.

My discussion underscores that we embody atmospheres and that phenomenologically tuned analyses could benefit from taking our "being-in-the air" (Sloterdijk 2009b, 48) as a starting point for analysis. This will help us show how air, as a fluid, unstable, and continuously fluctuating medium, has the ability to traverse cultural domains and instigate major social processes, only to retreat into a religious and metaphysical sphere that is largely left unrelated to material politics, concerned as it often is with the concrete and more tangible (see Ingold 2011; Choy 2012).

Since air is not external to subjects but part of the self—our setting in relation to the world, as we embody atmospheres at the same time as we produce them—I suggest it is of vital importance to reconnect air and atmosphere with social and individual well-being. The atmosphere is folded into us, and our activities are folded into the atmosphere in ways that challenge our neglect of air as a significant analytic space. This repositioning can be a useful theoretical contribution to the burgeoning studies of climate change, the Anthropocene (Choy and Zee 2015), and late industrialism (Fortun 2012; Shapiro 2015). These studies clearly show that air, which the Nobel laureate Elias Canetti in 1936 called "our last common property" ([1976] 1987, 13), yet again surfaces as a central aspect of global processes that distribute disease and misfortune (Zee 2015). Air ties individual bodies directly to global processes, bridging the social, temporal, and conceptual scales needed to sufficiently address the challenges facing the global community today (Eriksen 2016).

NOTES

1. *Ilathi* literally means "altar" and refers to a ceremony Zulu Zionists stage for their ancestral spirits (see Flikke 1994).

2. The KiKongo term *moyo*, translated as "soul" or "life force" by John M. Janzen (1978, 179n7), was used in the same context as breath (175) and dizziness (177).

3. For more on the significance of the ikhothamo, see Berglund (1989, 104–110) and Flikke (1994).

REFERENCES

Bachelard, Gaston. (1943) 1988. *Air and Dreams: An Essay on the Imagination of Movement*. Translated by Edith R. Farrell and Frederick Farrell. Dallas: Dallas Institute Publications.

Beinart, William, and Karen Brown. 2013. *African Local Knowledge and Livestock Health: Diseases and Treatments in South Africa*. Woodbridge, UK: James Curry.

Berglund, Axel-Ivar. 1989. *Zulu Thought Patterns and Symbolism*. London: C. Hurst.

Bryant, Alfred T. (1909) 1983. *Zulu Medicine and Medicine-Men*. Cape Town: Centaur.

Bryant, Alfred T. 1949. *The Zulu People: As They Were before the White Man Came*. Pietermaritzburg: Shuter and Shooter.

Callaway, Henry. (1868) 1970. *The Religious System of the Amazulus*. Africana Collectanea 35. Facsimile, Pietermaritzburg: Davis and Sons.

Canetti, Elias. (1976) 1987. *The Conscience of Words*. Translated by J. Neugroschel. London: Picador.

Carrere, Ricardo, and Larry Lohmann. 1996. *Pulping the South: Industrial Tree Planta-tions and the World Paper Economy*. London: Zed Books.

Chadwick, Edwin. (1842) 1965. *Report on the Sanitary Condition of the Labouring Population of Great Britain*. Edited with an introduction by Michael W. Flinn. Edinburgh: Edinburgh University Press.

Choy, Timothy. 2011. *Ecologies of Comparison: An Ethnography of Endangerment in Hong Kong*. Durham, NC: Duke University Press.

Choy, Timothy. 2012. "Air's Substantiations." In *Lively Capital: Biotechnologies, Ethics, and Governance in Global Markets*, edited by Kaushik Sunder Rajan, 121–154. Durham, NC: Duke University Press.

Choy, Timothy, and Jerry Zee. 2015. "Condition—Suspension." *Cultural Anthropology* 30, no. 2: 210–223.

Donner, Simon E. 2007. "Domain of the Gods: An Editorial Essay." *Climatic Change* 85, nos. 3–4: 231–236.

Eriksen, Thomas Hylland. 2018. "Scales of Environmental Engagement in an Industrial Town: Glocal Perspectives from Gladstone, Queensland." *Ethnos* 83, no. 3: 423–439.

Flikke, Rune. 1994. "The Past in the Present: A Semiotic Exploration of Urban Zulu Zionism in Durban, South Africa." PhD diss., University of Oslo, Norway.

Flikke, Rune. 2003a. "Offentlig Helse som Rasisme: Epidemier og Biopolitikk i Sør-Afrika." *Norsk Antropologisk Tidsskrift* 14, nos. 2–3: 70–83.

Flikke, Rune. 2003b. "Public Health and the Development of Racial Segregation in South Africa." *Bulletin of the Royal Institute for Inter-faith Studies* 5, no. 1: 5–23.

Flikke, Rune. 2006. "Embodying the Occult: Religious Experiences and Ritual Practices in Urban Zulu Zionism." In *The Power of the Occult in Modern Africa: Continuity and Innovation in the Renewal of African Cosmologies*, edited by James Kiernan, 206–232. Berlin: Lit.

Flikke, Rune. 2007. "Thandis Historie: Når Tid, Sted og Kropp Møtes." *Norsk Antropologisk Tidsskrift* 18, nos. 3–4: 296–307.

Flikke, Rune. 2014. "Smell of Decay, Scent of Progress: Eucalyptus as a Public Health Actor in Victorian South Africa." In *Wreckage and Recovery: Exploring the Nature of Nature*, 16–35. AURA Working Papers 2. Højbjerg, Denmark: Department of Culture and Society, Aarhus University. http://anthropocene.au.dk/fileadmin /Anthropocene/Workingpapers/AURA_workingpaperVol2.pdf.

Flikke, Rune. 2016a. "Enwinding Social Theory: Wind and Weather in Zulu Zionist Sensorial Experience." *Social Analysis* 60, no. 3: 95–111.

Flikke, Rune. 2016b. "South African Eucalypts: On the Aerial Roots of the Colonial Contact Zones." *Geoforum* 76: 20–27.

Fortun, Kim. 2012. "Ethnography in Late Industrialism." *Cultural Anthropology* 27, no. 3: 446–464.

Foucault, Michel. (1973) 1994. *The Birth of the Clinic: An Archaeology of Medical Perception*. Translated by A. M. Sheridan Smith. New York: Vintage Books.

Foucault, Michel. 2000. "The Birth of Social Medicine." In *Power*, edited by James D. Faubion, 134–156. New York: New Press.

Gibson, James J. 1979. *The Ecological Approach to Visual Perception*. Boston: Houghton and Mifflin.

Harris, Oliver J. T., John Robb, and Sarah Tarlow. 2013. "The Body in the Age of Knowledge." In *The Body in History: Europe from the Palaeolithic to the Future*, edited by John Robb and Oliver J. T. Harris, 164–195. New York: Cambridge University Press.

Hulme, Mike. 2015. "Better Weather? The Cultivation of the Sky." *Cultural Anthropology* 30, no. 2: 236–244.

Ingold, Tim. 2005. "The Eye of the Storm: Visual Perception and the Weather." *Visual Studies* 20, no. 2: 97–104.

Ingold, Tim. 2010. "Footprints through the Weather-World: Walking, Breathing, Knowing." Supplement, *Journal of the Royal Anthropological Institute* 16, no. S1: S121–S139.

Ingold, Tim. 2011. *Being Alive: Essays on Movement, Knowledge and Description*. London: Routledge.

Janzen, John M. 1978. *The Quest for Therapy: Medical Pluralism in Lower Zaire*. Berkeley: University of California Press.

Krige, Eileen Jensen. (1936) 1950. *The Social System of the Zulus*. Pietermaritzburg: Shuter and Shooter.

Laidler, Percy Ward, and Michael Gelfand. 1971. *South Africa: Its Medical History, 1652–1898*. Cape Town: C. Struik.

Low, Chris. 2007. "Khoisan Wind: Hunting and Healing." *Journal of the Royal Anthropological Institute*, n.s., 13, no. 1: 71–90.

Ngubane, Harriet. 1977. *Body and Mind in Zulu Medicine: An Ethnography of Health and Disease in Nyuswa-Zulu Thought and Practice*. London: Academic Press.

Nietzsche, Friedrich. (1883–1889) 1961. *Thus Spoke Zarathustra*. Translated by Josefine Nauckhoff and Adrian del Caro. Edited by Karl Ameriks. New York: Penguin.

Peires, Jeffrey B. 1989. *The Dead Will Arise: Nongqawuse and the Great Xhosa Cattle-Killing Movement of 1856-7*. Johannesburg: Ravan.

Pelling, Margaret. 1978. *Cholera, Fever, and English Medicine, 1825–1865*. Oxford: Oxford University Press.

Shapiro, Nicholas. 2015. "Attuning to the Chemosphere: Domestic Formaldehyde, Bodily Reasoning, and the Chemical Sublime." *Cultural Anthropology* 30, no. 3: 368–393.

Sloterdijk, Peter. 2009a. "Airquakes." *Environment and Planning D: Society and Space* 27, no. 1: 47–57.

Sloterdijk, Peter. (2002) 2009b. *Terror from the Air*. Translated by Amy Patton and Steve Corcoran. Los Angeles: Semiotext(e).

Sloterdijk, Peter. (1998) 2014. *Spheres*. Vol. 2, *Globes: Macrospherology*. Translated by Wieland Hoban. Los Angeles: Semiotext(e).

Stallybrass, Peter, and Allon White. 1986. *The Politics and Poetics of Transgression*. London: Methuen and Co. Ltd.

Swanson, Maynard W. 1977. "The Sanitation Syndrome: Bubonic Plague and Urban Native Policy in the Cape Colony, 1900–1909." *Journal of African History* 18, no. 3: 387–410.

Urry, John. 1990. *The Tourist Gaze: Leisure and Travel in Contemporary Societies.* London: Sage.

Witt, Harald. 2005. "'Clothing the Once Bare Brown Hills of Natal': The Origin and Development of Wattle Growing in Natal, 1860–1960." *South African Historical Journal* 53, no. 1: 99–122.

Zee, Jerry. 2015. "Breathing in the City: Beijing and the Architecture of Air." In "Weather," special issue, *Scapegoat: Architecture, Landscape, Political Economy* 8 (Winter/Spring): 46–56.

9. The Ghost at the Banquet

CEREMONY, COMMUNITY, AND INDUSTRIAL

GROWTH IN WEST NORWAY

———

Marianne Elisabeth Lien and John Law

The Construction Site

It's a cool April morning in West Norway. Down by the fjord there are large patches of snow on the ground. After several days of cleaning roe, feeding fry, and monitoring oxygen in freshwater tanks, we are beginning to get a feel for the daily routines. The fish farm, a salmon hatchery with its sheds and pipes, outdoor tanks and water filters, our current field site, is by now familiar. Inside the buildings are offices, workshops, changing facilities, and a lunchroom. Outside, there is a giant construction site, with cranes, trucks, and cement mixers. The startling noise from high-pressure drills intermittently disrupts conversation. Men wearing hard hats and overalls with a construction company's logo are moving about. The hatchery, which has been running since the 1980s, is about to expand.

You can see this as you arrive, for next to the existing sheds the slope of a hillside has been dug out, and part of the seafront has been filled in. A huge new building is going to dwarf all the existing facilities. The footings are in place, and the concrete floors and walkways one level up are partially built, with scaffold railings to stop people falling off. There is some pipework installed too. But, most conspicuously, as you approach the premises from the winding narrow road leading down to the fjord, you see several rows of very large cylindrical fiberglass tanks. Four meters high? Six or seven meters in diameter? Our notes don't record their dimensions, but they are far,

far larger than any of the tanks in the existing buildings. Soon the number of salmon smolt produced is going to increase—to double, perhaps treble. Most of these tanks are standing empty. But even though they are open to the elements—the roof of the building is not yet in place—two of them have been filled with water. As we shall soon discover, this will be a special day. The first tank in this new building is going to receive its first salmon. And this, it turns out, is an occasion to be marked. It's all very informal, but in a quiet way this afternoon has been set aside. Most unusually, work everywhere will come to a halt. Everyone who works at the hatchery will gather to watch as the first salmon are washed down a long pipe into that first tank in the huge new building. It will be a moment of celebration; modest but, even so, an out-of-the-ordinary, impromptu *ceremony*.[1]

Many share an inclination, one that has been refined within anthropology, to see rituals as moments of condensation; to see the macrocosm echoed, reaffirmed, reproduced, or enacted in a more or less structured moment. The anthropological literature also tells us that ceremonies may reassert wholes, create hierarchies, or affirm egalitarianisms, divisions, significant forms, appropriate subjectivities, beginnings, transitions, or endings.[2] No wonder, then, that anthropologists pay attention when ceremonies, or rituals, appear to unfold. Science and technology studies (STS) joins anthropology in attending, inter alia, to the enactment of materials, fleshy bodies, extended networks, forms of alterity, the ordering of nature-culture binaries, transnational commodity chains, and conditions of work (see, e.g., Harvey and Knox 2014). The general lesson is thus that, like rituals, ceremonies are moments of condensation. Rituals are assemblages that work by shaping and conjuring the worlds we inhabit. In this way, they are not only reflexive or representational but performative too, a point recently taken up by Bruce Kapferer in his analysis of "the event." Revisiting the Manchester school and the extended-case method (situational analysis) proposed by Max Gluckman, Kapferer (2010, 2) argues for a focus on the event as an alternative to a notion of society. For Gluckman (e.g., 1958), the events of interest were atypical, the moments that broke the apparent calm or routine of everyday life.

In this chapter we examine one such atypical event, which we will refer to as a ceremony. Surely, the ceremony performed (and reflected) particular contexts, and we start by considering these. But then we make a second and different move. Instead of asking what worlds (or contexts) it performed, we ask about the gaps that it laid bare. Our question, then, is, what were the absences made apparent by the unfolding ceremony? What can we say about its *manifest absences* (Law 2004, 84)? What were the metaphorical ghosts present at the banquet?[3]

Our argument is first that what is commonly black-boxed as "capitalist expansion" relies on the successful stitching together or assembling of heterogeneous elements. In the present context, the endless list of these elements includes water, fertilized eggs, financial capital, concrete, able-bodied workers, feed pellets, pumping and filtration systems, municipal support, and biomass.[4] It is also, however, similarly dependent on specific modes of *separation*, or *detachment*. The argument is not new. Classic analyses of the plantation as the cradle of capitalist industrial production remind us how it is precisely through processes of social detachment that slaves, for example, could become a readily available workforce in an ever-expanding imperial trade (Mintz 1985).[5] Anna Tsing (2012, 507) develops this idea in her analysis of scalability as the feature of design that enables something to expand (or multiply, as in the expanding salmon tanks) without simultaneously changing the relations between the elements in the assemblage. Hence, scalability is not a feature of "a thing itself" but the outcome of heterogeneous sets of relations. This requires attention to material relations, which are active constituents in the making and arrangement of the firm as a political and economic collective (Law and Lien 2014). But, as Tsing (2012) says, "making projects scalable takes a lot of work," and the necessary separation, or detachment, can be difficult to achieve in practice.

This is because, as Tsing (2013) notes, capitalist commodity value is created through tapping and transforming noncapitalist social relations. Commodification of all aspects of the human and nonhuman labor forces that inhabit salmon farms, both within and beyond the tanks, may be the vision of financial investors but can never be fully achieved in practice. Thus, capitalism relies on noncapitalist relations to accomplish its goals, and salmon farming is no exception. Another way of saying this is simply to note that the so-called social and the economic are deeply entangled and are jointly embedded and performed in relation to materials (lively and otherwise) that invariable break, fail, implode, or simply die (Callon 1998; see also Law and Lien 2013; Lien 2015). Hence, scalable expansion is also uncertain. This is our second point. And sometimes, as we shall see, it calls for the finely tuned sense of local cultural codes and values, deeply embedded in the habitus of a local owner.

Third, we challenge the assumption that there is a naturally occurring distinction between macro and micro, or big and small. In doing so, we make what seems like a trivial point for STS-inclined readers, but one that is easily lost when the focus is on capitalist expansion. Rather than assuming that "big" exists in the order of things, we argue that size is a relational effect (Law 2000). To understand the mechanisms of the dramatic expansion of salmon aquaculture across the globe and in countries such as Norway, we therefore attend ethnographically to specific moments when scales and sizes are performed. And focusing on scalability as a process rather than a premise, we pay attention to how separations and attachments are enacted as well, contributing to or facilitating scalable projects.

To summarize: if ceremonies (or events) are moments of condensation and enactment, conjuring and momentarily reasserting multiple contexts, then they are interesting both for what they make manifest and for what they leave out. They are also interesting for the multiple scales and sizes they enact. Hence, we invite the reader to join us in paying ethnographic attention to what may seem to be a rather modest ceremony. Through this exercise we also show how ethnographic analysis may mobilize gaps and absences to speak to pressing political concerns, partly by disrupting the established notions of scale that set the terms for articulating the political. Our concern has to do with capitalist growth in salmon farming as it is performed through national aquaculture policy, on an industrial site on the west coast of Norway, and as environmental effects, in Norway and elsewhere.

During our fieldwork, growth and expansion appeared in many different forms: the expanding firm, the markets for seafood, the use of Norwegian waters for aquaculture installations, the salmon that put on weight, the number of permanent jobs for salmon farm workers, the number of sea lice and other parasites that feed on salmon, the number of forms that had to be filled in, the legal regulations to which they refer, the prevalence of fish diseases, the extending and intensifying supply chains for pelleted fish feed, the volume of feed required, the burgeoning fishing industry in Peru that provisions those supply chains, and many more (see also Law and Lien 2014; Lien 2015). Sometimes these found their way into our field notes as comments on recent changes, such as when experienced operation managers said, for instance, "I would never have imagined that the pens could be more than that size over there, but look what we have now," or when they told us about their own careers, saying, "When I first began, we thought 20,000 fish in a pen was a lot, now we have 120,000." Sometimes we noticed expansion as graphic figures, tables, and numbers, posted by the Directorate for Fisheries or environmental nongovernmental organizations. But, most days, such references did not find their way into our field notes at all. Our ethnographic involvement on the fish farm alerted us instead to quite different concerns:

how well the salmon are doing today, how much to feed each pen, how to fasten the ropes securely so that the netting stays in place, how to collect dead fish in the most efficient manner, now with a different tank in place. Day-to-day concerns such as these were what we tripped over as we worked on the farm (see Law and Lien 2014; Lien 2015). The ecological impact of salmon farming on relations elsewhere was hardly ever mentioned. Except for the biweekly visits by feed-delivery vessels, we sometimes felt as if the salmon farming operation existed on its own, autonomous and detached from the rest of the world, as if all its challenges, and their solutions, were right there, below our feet. The content of fish feed, for example, was a topic that most salmon workers knew very little about. Hence, Peruvian anchovies and Brazilian soy are largely absent in our field notes, as are the global inequalities implied in transnational trade. If such elements emerged in our ethnographies at all, it is because we moved beyond the farm to mobilize a broad spectrum of fragmented and more or less easily available sources (though in some areas—for instance, the composition of feed—these were difficult to find). And yet without these—without Peruvian anchovies and Brazilian soy and an industrial infrastructure for creating feed pellets and transcontinental shipping—the recent expansion in the salmon industry would not have been possible.

In other words, the gaps and the manifest absences to which we attend were, indeed, absences for us as ethnographers just as much as they were for our interlocutors. This chapter thus attempts to move beyond the unspoken boundaries of what mattered to our informants, and thus came to matter to us while we were in the field. To some extent, it is also an attempt to move beyond the boundaries of what matters for policy makers. So how are these separations—these invisibilities—achieved in practice? How does the industry's reliance on feed deliveries, for example, remain tacit and unarticulated? To address this question, we begin by briefly visiting the futures enacted by the Norwegian Ministry of Trade, Industry and Fisheries.

The Future Is Blue

Salmon farming has spearheaded the expansion of aquaculture worldwide. And when it comes to salmon, the Norwegian salmon farming industry has taken the lead. The official figures and numbers tell a story of exponential growth in production since the mid-1970s. Figure 9.1 shows the annual increase in the tons of farmed salmon slaughtered in Norway since 1976. Figure 9.2 comes from a white paper by the Norwegian Ministry of Trade,

Industry and Fisheries. It tells us that the value created by Norwegian aquaculture grew more than tenfold between 1995 and 2012, far outpacing any other economic sector. Table 9.1 compares the growth of production in major salmon-producing countries.

The numbers tell us that world production of farmed Atlantic salmon grew from 1.2 million tons in 2005 to 2.3 million tons in 2015, and that more than half of the 2013 total (1.2 million tons) came from Norway (see table 9.1). The quick message is that growth has been very fast in the recent past (see figure 9.1), even more dramatic in Norway than anywhere else (see table 9.1), and that this production is very profitable and of increasing importance for Norwegian gross domestic product (see figure 9.2). The expansion taking place at the industrial site in West Norway in 2011 was part of this boom. Even though this was experienced as significant locally, the numbers in the figures and table show that it was nothing extraordinary in the broader scheme of things. Similar expansions would have been happening in many different places along the Norwegian coast.

But the white paper is not so much about the past as about future growth. Here is a newspaper reporting on its release in 2015: "The stated goal of the Norwegian Authorities . . . is a *fivefold increase in aquaculture production by 2050*. Aquaculture is the 'new oil.' The authorities are seeking to make the conditions that frame this more predictable. This will be achieved by aiming for a 6% growth in salmon and trout biomass every year. In this way, the industry will be able to expand more steadily and predictably. Until now, new licenses have been too unpredictable and contingent" (emphasis added).[6]

So growth is the order of the day. The ministry writes that the government will "facilitate a predictable and environmentally sustainable growth in the salmon and trout aquaculture" (Det Kongelige Nærings og Fiskeridepartement [Ministry of Trade, Industry and Fisheries] 2015, 12). Launching the white paper in March 2015, Norway's center-right prime minister, Erna Solberg, told the press that she "loves" both salmon and salmon farmers. "Salmon," she told the media, "is a fantastic brand for Norway. The salmon is Norway's Ikea."[7] Indeed, as the oil begins to run out, it will become Norway's iconic industry. Just 5 million people live in Norway, but "37 million Norwegian seafood meals are served round the world every day," a figure that will be five times larger by 2050. So the future is rosy, but—yes, there are buts—regulation will also be tighter in the face of challenges, most of which have to do with sustainability. Here is the prime minister's view: "Further growth for the industry, in line with what we have seen in recent years, will be subject to progress in combating lice, escapes and other negative environmental effects."

TABLE 9.1. Global production of farmed Atlantic salmon (in thousands of metric tons)

	2005	2006	2007	2008	2009	2010	2011	2012	2013	2014	2015	2016	2017E[a]
Norway	574	599	723	741	856	945	1,006	1,183	1,144	1,199	1,234	1,171	1,208
Chile	385	369	356	403	239	130	221	364	468	583	598	505	579
United Kingdom	120	127	135	137	144	143	155	159	158	171	166	157	174
Canada	108	115	110	122	122	122	120	137	115	95	135	146	140
Faroe Islands	17	12	19	37	47	42	56	70	73	83	76	77	80
Australia	18	19	25	26	32	33	36	40	39	42	54	51	61
United States	10	10	12	17	16	18	18	20	20	24	20	23	22
Ireland	12	15	15	11	15	18	16	16	11	12	16	16	17
Iceland	7	4	2	1	1	1	1	3	3	4	4	8	12
Others	1	1	2	1	3	4	5	8	11	15	14	12	12
Total	1,252	1,271	1,398	1,496	1,475	1,456	1,634	2,000	2,042	2,228	2,317	2,166	2,305

[a] E indicates estimated figures.

Source: Ministry of Trade, Industry and Fisheries 2015, 25 (updated by the author). Source Kontali Analyse,
Reproduced with permission from the Norwegian Ministry of Trade, Industry and Fisheries.

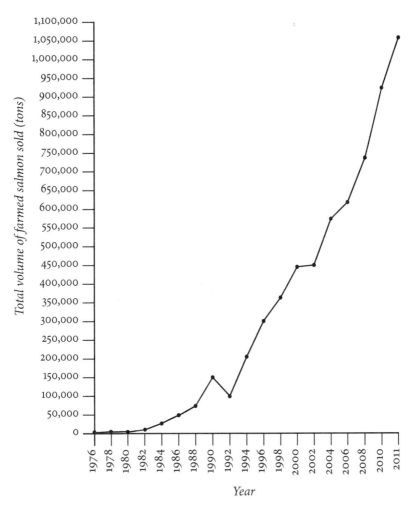

FIGURE 9.1. Farmed salmon production in Norway, 1976–2011, based on sales statistics. Reproduced with permission from Lien 2015, 106.

Growth, yes. An economic future for Norway. But sustainability too. Less recourse to drugs to control sea lice (the prime minister is not alone in worrying about the spread of drug resistance). Fewer escaped salmon. (She does not say this, but many Norwegians, including biologists, worry about the effect of escaped domesticated salmon on the progressively diluted gene pool of their wild cousins; see Lien and Law 2011.) Disease control is important too. So, unsurprisingly, we are learning that in this political and economic world, sustainable practices, if properly understood, properly regulated, properly technologized, and properly managed, will be the patch that recon-

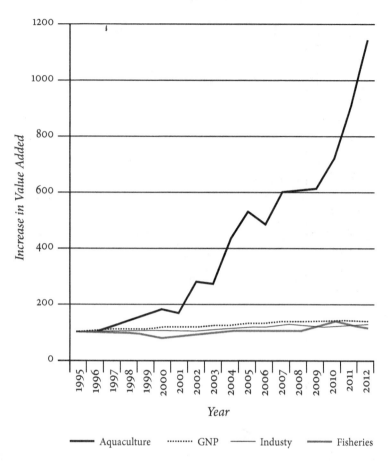

FIGURE 9.2. The development of value creation from aquaculture compared to other industries, fisheries, and gross domestic product (GDP) in Norway (Ministry of Trade, Industry and Fisheries 2015, 23). Source: Nasjonalregnskapet SSB, Reproduced with permission from the Norwegian Ministry of Trade, Industry and Fisheries.

ciles those two great imperatives, economic growth and the limits to growth set by the natural world. Noncoherent (and, for many, contradictory) contexts will thereby be rendered consistent. Such, in large measure, is the point of the white paper. The carrying capacity of the environment does not appear as a manifest absence—ghostlike and uninvited—at this particular policy banquet. Rather, the environment has been issued a formal invitation to sit at the high table in the form of wild Atlantic salmon, sea lice, and the potential for disease. Environment, or "nature," is conjured up as a matter of concern in Norway. But what of the Peruvian anchovies?

To some extent, the pressure on global marine resources in salmon aquaculture is less intense than it was, as a result of a shift toward vegetable sources of protein, such as soy, in feed. Between 2010 and 2013, salmon production in Norway increased by 30 percent, while the total amount of marine ingredients used for salmon feed production fell from 544,000 to 466,000 tons, effectively decreasing dependency on marine protein and marine oils. But the total demand for feed is still significant. In 2012, 1.26 million tons of salmon were produced. In the same year, Norwegian salmon farming consumed 1.63 million tons of feed ingredients, containing close to forty million gigajoules of energy, 580,000 tons of protein, and 530,000 tons of lipids (Ytrestøyl, Aas, and Åsgård 2015, 365).

We will consider these relations, and gaps, toward the end of this chapter, but first let us consider the ceremony. We return, then, to Hordaland, on a day in March 2010 a few years before the publication of the white paper.

Ceremony

It has been a long, hard winter in the fjord country of West Norway, but suddenly the snow is melting fast. Together with Tone, Gro, and Jan, we have spent the morning cleaning, carrying, watching, monitoring, measuring, and feeding—the usual chores that fill the working days. Now we have been called to join the others outside, and there is an air of cheerful anticipation: they are going to move the first fish into the first tank in the huge new building.

Preparations for the transfer have been going on for several days. We've watched two of the giant new tanks being filled with water. Yesterday the maintenance men, Bjørn and Torben, set up a fat translucent pipe that now snakes over the edge of a platform on the existing site and down to the construction site with its new tanks (see figure 9.3). The stairs to climb onto the walkway in the new building aren't built yet, so Jan has used a ladder to climb onto it. We watch as he wrestles with the far end of the pipe so that it is hanging over the water in one of the two tanks that has been filled. There's excitement in the air, and a buzz of conversation on the platform. Knut, the operations manager, and Eirik, the owner, are both there. They're walking around and talking with people in the small throng (see figure 9.4).

The minutes stretch out, but then suddenly we hear a sound. It's the forklift approaching with its orange flashing light. We watch as Torben maneuvers it. Carefully he edges it forward. It is carrying a spherical fiberglass tank, a meter or more in diameter. He lowers this cautiously onto a pile of pallets.

FIGURE 9.3. The new facilities; salmon smolt tanks to the right.
Photograph by John Law.

Once it settles safely, he turns off the engine and gets out of the cab. He pulls at the big pipe and pushes and tugs it to marry it with the outlet at the bottom of the tank he has just delivered. Now everything is ready. As we watch, it becomes clear that Eirik, the owner, is going to pull the lever on the outlet to send the first young salmon washing down the pipe and into the new tank. But before this happens, there is a photo opportunity: Knut takes some photos, and then Gro, one of the workers, grabs the camera from him and takes a whole lot more. Finally, with more photographs, Eirik yanks on the lever. There is a sound of rushing water, and we watch as the first salmon are washed down the translucent pipe.

A few seconds later, there is a cheer from the other half of the crowd. They have chosen to hang over the scaffold safety rail a few meters away and peer over the five-meter drop into the building site. From where they are standing, they can see what those of us gathered round the forklift cannot: the first young salmon are pouring out of the open end of the pipe in a stream of water and dropping into the new tank. The new building, still nothing more than a building site plus tanks, has been inaugurated! Now, for the first time, it houses fish.

FIGURE 9.4. Waiting for the salmon smolt to appear. Photograph by John Law.

It is a big moment. We watch the smolt and see a few starting to swim against the current in their new environment. "Aren't they beautiful!" Knut exclaims as we admire the silvery wiggling salmon as they wash out of the pipe and splash into their new home.

The stream slows to a trickle. The first load of salmon has been delivered. Torben uncouples the pipe from the tank, jumps into the cab of the forklift, and backs it away to go for a second load. And then Knut produces a small box of cigars. These are Cuban; they're from Havana, says Knut, and they are rather good. Knut offers a cigar to Eirik, who accepts it. Then he gestures an offer to everyone else, but it seems that no one else wants to take one yet. Instead, we watch as the two men go through the elaborate process of biting the ends off their cigars and lighting them. As they start to puff, it is as if the ceremony achieves greater significance; suddenly this turns into another photo opportunity, and yet more pictures are taken. There is more chatting, and there is the nice smell of cigars, otherwise smoked only on New Year's Eve or to celebrate the safe arrival of a newborn baby. Knut says to Mari-anne, "You know, you work day after day to achieve something, and then all of a sudden, the day has come!"

Then the packet of cigars is proffered a second time. This time Jan accepts one, and Gro, who went to school with him, takes one as well, and then she shares it with Tone by breaking it in two. Soon a cloud of smoke is hanging above the small throng. Knut repeats what he just said to Marianne, but this time to the entire group. Eirik, the local owner who has made a fortune purchasing and expanding salmon farming facilities in the region, disagrees: "No," he says, "you are never finished. When you are finished, you might as well be dead." He ponders this philosophical point for a short while and then cites a proverb that says that the worst and most despicable (*foraktelige*) position in which anyone can find themselves is to have more money than ideas.[8] The talk continues, with bursts of laughter and friendly gestures.

After a few minutes, Eirik disappears for a moment in the direction of his car and returns with a heavy cardboard box. He puts it down and opens it, murmuring something about having a box of good wine in the trunk of his car. It turns out that he has brought twelve bottles of Marqués de Cáceres, an excellent 2006 Rioja—a bottle for everyone, visitors and fieldworkers included. People happily accept the wine. But then we hear the noise of the forklift as it appears for a second time, Torben still at the wheel. He turns it around again, lowers the tanks, and joins the pipes, and the second load of salmon is ready for delivery. This time it is the turn of the visiting vet to operate the lever—and there is a third photo opportunity, and everyone cheers again. More fish pour down the pipe and into the new tank. More photos are taken as people mill around. Conversations continue amid clouds of cigar smoke. Some work will get done in due course, but, most unusually, the larger part of the afternoon has been given over to the inaugural event.

As we noted at the start of this chapter, ceremonies are special because they are marked and set aside, and the special character of this particular ceremony is marked in a whole range of ways: two working hours that are not spent working, the anticipation, the moments of silence, the cheering, the cigars, the bottles of wine given by the owner to everyone present, the talk about the event over the following days, and then, to be sure, the story just told by the ethnographers. But how is it special? What does it do? And how is it analytically significant?

As we mentioned earlier, the practices that make up a ceremony afford many macro-social contexts, so the issue is always what to bring to presence.[9] Our focus is on growth and on various contexts that this celebration of growth enacts, but then, as we shall argue, autonomy is enacted simultaneously. Let us begin with growth.

Most obviously and straightforwardly, this is a ceremony about growth and expansion. There is the continuous growth of salmon bodies that translates to increasing biomass, which in turn produces profit and economic growth for the company, together with a financial surplus that supports the current industrial expansion.[10] While profitability is central to many of the salmon farming practices, materializing through the balance sheet and massive productions of numbers, questions of finance and investment priorities are not generally topics of discussion among salmon farm workers.[11] The division of labor separates tasks related to "raising salmon" from those related to expanding the firm, so that most employees do not need to take responsibility for the investment decisions and the rate of return required to keep the firm solvent. However, these issues are quite likely among the most critical to the owner and operations manager. We know that together with the finance director they monitor the finances of the company and this particular site week by week. We can also be sure that they are acutely aware of its cash flows, its balance sheets, the ups and downs of pricing in the global salmon markets, the economic implications of disease, and the fact that firms in the industry go bankrupt from time to time. So what does this tell us?

It tells us, first, that one of the contexts for the ceremony is the large-scale and continuing economic expansion by the company. Thus far, the company's investments have usually paid off. The firm's turnover has increased substantially over the last decade, and as global salmon prices have soared in recent years, the company has been profitable and has made large-scale investments. But the new hatchery is just that: new. Viewed from the standpoint of the company, it is a very large-scale investment, and the future balance sheet depends substantially on its success. We do not know what the owner is thinking as he pulls the lever to wash the first salmon into the new facility, but it is difficult to imagine that the firm's balance sheet, the financial risks, and the potential returns are not somewhat on his mind.

Our first suggestion, then, is that the ceremony summons up an absent-present context of economic growth in a world in which there appear to be few intrinsic limits to future profitability. But financial transactions are scarcely self-contained (Callon 1998). They also depend on the industrial future of the firm. And this is a second absence, present as a possibility only, or a risk, related to whether the promises of growth take material form. Will the new tanks be built on time? Will the flows of water and the filters work as they should? Will the ways of extracting the fish that die in the tanks turn out to be workable in an expanding system of production? Will the oxygen system continue to work as it is supposed to? Have the engineering and managerial problems of building the whole installation been solved? Does the firm have the skills and the people it needs to run such a large installation? These are the kinds of questions that have kept the architects, the engineers, the builders, and the managers busy month after month, and that have brought Eirik to the new facility week after week to check on its progress. As soon as we move from the realm of finance to that of industrial engineering and its expansion, there is much that might go wrong practically. Profit is inherently scalable, but given the technical innovations implied, the circumference of a tank is not necessarily scalable in the same way. Perhaps, though, it will be helpful for our purposes to imagine industrial failure in two analytically distinguishable forms.

On the one hand, there is the heterogeneous risk taking—of the managerial and engineering form well described in early actor-network theory.[12] The business of assembling materials, social and physical, is necessarily uncertain. In a sense, this is what engineering and managing are all about. On the other hand, the issue of scalability takes us straight to the heart of uncertainty of a different kind. As Tsing (2012) notes, scalability is a feature of design, and scalable design is notoriously risky. Recall that scalability is about expanding while simultaneously holding relations constant, a "move from small to large without redoing the design" (507). Design that achieves an increasing size usually implies new or shifting relations, and new relations often imply change. Considering the sheer complexity of the heterogeneous relations that literally hold a salmon industrial complex together, the risk of industrial failure is considerable. Considering salmon farmers' reliance on steady deliveries of feed pellets, the fragility of the project is inevitable. Scalable expansion is thoroughly uncertain, and aquaculture is no exception.

As we have seen, the new hatchery is an order of magnitude larger than the existing one. Social and technical upscaling should, or so it is hoped, be possible. The architects, the engineers, and the operations managers are working hard to ensure this happens. The units out of which it is composed— the tanks, the lights, the pipes, and most obviously the salmon, plus the relations among these elements—should in principle all be the same.[13] But, in practice, they are not. Things that work well for a tank with forty thousand salmon may work differently in a tank with sixty thousand—and sometimes for reasons that are hard to identify. This tells us that irreducible indeterminacy is lodged at the core of this expansionary industrial project. We are watching an attempt to grow that may encounter nonscalable limits. The inauguration ceremony celebrates the expansion of the hatchery, if everything goes well. But uncertainty remains. Many things could go wrong, and if they do, the cigar smokers, photographers, and wine recipients of the ceremony will gather in the not-yet-finished buildings to figure out why. But today the smolt have been flushed safely through the translucent tubes, and no one speaks about uncertainties. Nonscalability, then, is a second manifest absence, a second ghost at the seafood banquet, which can be averted only through the skillful handling of relations, material and social.

Reassurance: A Field of Social Equals

This brings us to a third absent-present being that can be summoned to the ceremony. We will tentatively talk of this as the field of social equals, and it is loosely related to what is often referred to in anthropology as community and local belonging. Analytically, we may distinguish between two dimensions performed during the ceremony, hierarchy and egalitarianism. But rather than positing these as existing idioms drawn from some preexisting cultural whole, we would like to draw attention to how the inaugural event became an arena for performing these idioms in a credible manner, in a dynamic situation that is otherwise fragmented, idiosyncratic, and fraught with uncertainty.

For any anthropologist familiar with Nordic ethnography and with the classic work of John A. Barnes (1954), who wrote about nearby Bremnes, the enactment of equality in the event is striking. Barnes came to Bremnes more than sixty years ago, when fishing and small farming had not yet been replaced by North Sea oil engineering and salmon farming as the backbones of local industry. Even so, the resonances between Barnes's ethnography and ours cannot be ignored. Like the structural-functionalists of his era, Barnes's main concern was how natural resources such as land "can pass in orderly fashion from one generation to the next" (1957, 31). His contribution to an ethnography of the Nordic region, however, was not his study of land rights but rather his exploration of social interaction in what appeared to him to be an egalitarian society. Barnes distinguished between three "fields" in what he called the "social system" of Bremnes: (1) a territorially based "social" field of hierarchically arranged administrative units, (2) a hierarchically organized "industrial" field with autonomous units such as fishing vessels and herring-oil factories, and (3) a "social" field without units or boundaries or coordinating organization, composed instead of ties of friendship and acquaintanceship. These are ties that, as he put it, "everyone growing up in Bremnes society partly inherits and largely builds up for himself" (1954, 43). Barnes tells us that this field is highly dynamic: new ties are continuously being formed, and old links broken, and most of the ties are "between persons who accord approximately equal status to one another" (43).[14] This third field has been taken up by other anthropologists doing ethnography in the Nordic region, and in what follows we also draw on those analyses (e.g., Gullestad 1992).[15] It is this third field that concerns us here.

We are particularly intrigued by how egalitarianism is woven into the social fabric of an industrial organization, and how the ceremony simultaneously performs both hierarchy and egalitarianism in the same move. On the one hand, "industrial" hierarchies are being done. The authority of the owner and the local manager is unchallenged and clearly marked. (Who pulls the lever first? Who smokes the first cigars?) But for a visiting British ethnographer, in other respects the scene is remarkable egalitarian. Here are John's field notes:

> To non-Norwegians (or at least UK eyes) in certain respects the event is surprisingly egalitarian. Eirik dresses and carries himself like everyone else in jeans. He isn't immediately recognizable as the owner as he wanders through the small crowd (though it doesn't take long to sort this out). Knut is wearing a checked shirt and dark trousers. Everyone knows that he is the site manager, but he doesn't look different. And since both men are cheerfully chatting with all and sundry, we need to say that the ceremony does hierarchy and community together in a specifically West-coast Norwegian way.[16]

If we follow Barnes, then the celebration is also a specific, egalitarian mode of social interaction, which we may recognize as a successful performance of equality, or the enactment of equals in an otherwise hierarchical industrial setting.

For Barnes, the idiom for the industrial field was hierarchy. But in our salmon ethnography, we note that hierarchy and egalitarianism are often done simultaneously, and the ceremony is no exception. Hence, rather than operating as separate "fields," as suggested by Barnes, work relations and informal social ties do not simply overlap but are also mutually constitutive. So how does this work in practice in the ceremony? Reciprocity is crucial. The wine is a gift, asymmetrical but with the potential for more generalized reciprocity in the long term. The cigars are a form of sharing that says in a slightly quirky and playful way (accompanied by coughs and laughter), "We are all in this together." First, then, and most straightforwardly, equality is being celebrated, but so too is difference. The construction of the new tanks was primarily a project for the owner and the manager (the workers were hardly asked their opinion), but through the ceremony their inauguration becomes a shared event, a form of growth that everyone "owns," albeit in a small and metaphorical manner. For some, it may also have been a reassuring moment, indicating that their employment will be secure for some time to come.

Not only is the owner, then, a clever and successful industrial entrepreneur. He is also skillfully mastering styles of relating to other people that are recognized locally as appropriate expressions of equality (or egalitarianism) as a shared value. As Maja H. Bruun, Gry S. Jakobsen, and Stine Krøijer (2011) note with reference to the experience of being equal in Denmark, egalitarianism is generated, not by equality as such, but by the value-mastering hierarchies that generate such experiences as being equal. With intimate knowledge of the local social norms (he speaks the local dialect and grew up in the region, and he sends his children to the small local school), the owner can respond to any resentment, envy, or uncertainty almost before it emerges by implicitly saying something that loosely translates as "I may be richer than you, I may hold the authority here, but in the end I am actually just like any of you, smoking a cigar and sharing a good moment." If we were to paraphrase Tsing (2013, 21), we might say that the owner is tapping and transforming noncapitalist social relations.

But is this merely a symbolic (and thus hollow, or false) representation of egalitarianism against the foil of capitalist expansion? The answer is no. If we consider, once again, the engineering challenges associated with upscaling, then the mutual dependencies among the participants start to become clear. The owner may have authority and financial power, but if something goes wrong, if salmon get stuck in a damaged pipe, if the oxygen supply fails to do its job, then there is very little he can do. For the new investment to produce the kinds of profits sought, the day-to-day practices of maintaining the tanks and caring for fish are crucial. Hence, the engineering and practical skills of every single person at the banquet are needed. And, what is more, everyone knows this.

Moreover, if he treats his employees as disposable assets and threatens to replace them with cheaper labor sourced elsewhere, they might pack their bags, sell their houses, and move elsewhere. They might follow in the steps of so many others and move with their families to other places where the conditions for farmworkers are more favorable, leaving the owner and *his* family deserted and alienated in their own community. So while it is true that the owner, drawing on a familiar repertoire of egalitarianism, may be said to tap into noncapitalist social relations, it is also true that he crucially depends on these for his own realization of a good life with his family.

We do not want to create an impression of a community devoid of conflict, resentment, or fragmentation. Indeed, it is not all rosy. But reciprocity and a strong sense community in relation to resources that are typically organized as commons have marked these regions for centuries. And perhaps this is why the ceremony did not appear awkward or feigned. While the expansion was clearly the initiative of the owners, its future will be shared by many.

With regard to the industry, the ceremony transforms what up until now has been a gigantic building site into a hatchery by treating it like any other hatchery. It just performs people-and-pipes-and-tanks-and-fish-and-industrial-workers, but on a larger scale. So why go to all the trouble of having a celebration? Why not simply send Torben and Jan to move the first fish while everyone else gets on with their work as usual? Our suggestion is that in this context the reenactment of an egalitarian ethos is particularly powerful. In this hopeful but uncertain moment, when there are, to be sure, no guarantees, another continuity is being summoned into being. If nearly everything fails, it would be the unchanging patterning of relations among equals that would summon the power to fix the broken pipes, or, indeed, if everything goes wrong, to pick up the pieces and start all over again. This is not capitalism as a hit-and-run enterprise. It is old-style capitalism, thoroughly grounded in the social fabric of investors as well as employees, as it is articulated in a very specific place. Our argument is that this is why the people are present. This is why what might have been a purely industrial moment is also an important enactment of community, for the mobilization of community powerfully wards off the uncertainty of seemingly unlimited growth in salmon farming.

But what of the Peruvian anchovies? Through its emphasis on community, reciprocity, and egalitarianism, the ceremony could also be interpreted as a celebration of local autonomy. Establishing a sense of "we are all in this together" also serves to enhance, we suggest, a sense of local empowerment. The implications of exponential aquacultural expansion for marine resources and the availability of feed inputs are literally not present at this banquet. This may be an example of what amounts to a globally significant expansion, but it is thoroughly contained, grounded in local idioms and local egalitarianism. By not noticing these global dependencies, another separation, or detachment, is enacted. The Peruvian anchovies (our shorthand for marine feed resources) are yet another form of manifest absence present at the ceremony. As we shall see, this detachment takes place elsewhere as well. Let us turn to the white paper.

As we saw, in the white paper version of sustainability, the tension between growth and uncertainty was bridged by technocratic and regulatory means. In the future, salmon escapes will be limited, and sea lice and diseases will be controlled. In this way, the future of salmon farming will be sustainable too. The environment summoned by the white paper is a "nature" carefully bounded by the national and judicial territory of the Norwegian nation-state. But deep within the white paper—on pages 59–60—there is another story. This is about feed, and this narrative soon begins to exceed national boundaries. First, it says that the feed producers are required to demonstrate that they are buying fish meal, fish oil, and vegetable raw materials from sustainable sources. Then it tells us that "access to feed and feed ingredients is a global issue" (Ministry of Trade, Industry and Fisheries 2015, 59, our translations). Next, it insists that "there is *no direct correlation between the capacity of Norwegian fish farming and the sustainable global harvesting of feed ingredients*" (59–60). It tells us, for example, that there is little reason to assume that industrial fishing in the Pacific or Brazilian soy harvesting would fall even if production in one or more Norwegian areas were reduced. This is why "*it is not recommendable for the authorities to include feed resources in assessments about changes in production capacity*" (60). The report adds that Norwegian feed producers should be "*aware of their responsibilities and do what they can to produce sustainable feed*" (60). And then there comes this: "There is no doubt that access to feed might limit the growth of aquaculture in Norway and elsewhere in the world" (60).

So, in the depths of the white paper, we finally first learn that growth is sustainable if feed is sustainable. And then we learn that if it turns out that the production of feed is not actually sustainable, salmon production might as well carry on anyway, since there is no direct correlation between the scale of aquaculture activities in Norway and the sustainability of global fisheries. This is because a potential decrease in Norwegian aquaculture would not make much of a difference anyway. In other words, a separation is effectively made between industrial expansion in Norway and the future of global marine resources. The links between these are discursively cut. The ghost of unsustainable marine stewardship is an absence that is briefly made present before disappearing again into a crevice of not knowing. There is no knowing precisely how the correlations among Peruvian fishing, Brazilian soy, and Norwegian salmon production will play out in practice, and in any case, it is the responsibility of the feed producers to source feed sustainably. There is also no mention of the people living elsewhere who might rely on such resources, or on resources that the production of feed effectively replaces. But it is with these uncertainties that the ghost makes its appearance at this policy banquet. This is the moment when the fact that global limits to feed might set limits to fish farming in Norway finally makes its entrance. Yes, it disappears again, but this is a specter that is not banished. There is no more to be said; there are no reassurances; there are no policy measures to monitor this. There is no equivalent of a ceremony that can be summoned up to reconcile growth with unease about growth. Just this: there is no known correlation. And, therefore, there is no need to be accountable. It is as if Norwegian salmon industries can continue to expand, even if global marine resources are unsustainably harvested and oceans depleted, and Brazilian soy fields replace livelihoods based on rain forests—at least for now.

Sustainability and Its Limits

Ceremonies summon up realities, and they summon up uncertainties about those realities. Their patterned actions work to reaffirm those realities and ward off those uncertainties and sometimes, in doing so, they enact new realities. Drawing attention to the ghosts at the banquet, we have sought to highlight the uncertainties that nearly always haunt us when choices are being made. With every moment of enactment, there are also gaps, silences, uncertainties, crevices, even abysses. Our analysis has drawn attention to particular manifest absences: we have brought uncertainty and unscalability to presence, to give it form.

In one way, we should be complimenting the ministry: its honesty lays bare the potential black hole that lies at the heart of growth. Access to feed may diminish. The marine resources may simply be gone one day. If that happens, aquaculture will stop growing. But meanwhile? Meanwhile, growth in the Norwegian salmon industry will continue anyway. Such are the projections of the white paper. Not unlike the inauguration event, a space of relative autonomy is summoned into being. But in contrast to the ceremony at the salmon farm, there is no reciprocity, no reassurance, no field of social equals "all in this together," just a persistent insistence on in- dustrial growth and exponential expansion. Sustainable only within the lim- its of that which can be scientifically known, and relevant only for a nation of imagined equals.

Our ethnographic fieldwork took place primarily within a firm that we call Sjølaks AS, and we thank the firm for this and for additional generous practical support. We are also grateful for the kindness and patience of the employees who participated in our research. The ceremony described in this chapter took place at a firm we call Havlaks, and we are similarly grateful to both this firm and its generous employees, whose names have been anonymized in this chapter. Early versions of the chapter were presented at the workshop Engaging the Material in November 2014 and the Bergen workshop Ontologizing Difference in January 2015. We are grateful to these audiences for their comments, to the editors of this volume, and to Kristin Asdal and Gro Ween, collaborators on the project. The project Newcomers to the Farm was funded by Forskningsrådet, the Norwegian Research Council (project number 183352/S30), with additional research leave and financial support from Lancaster University, the Open University, and the University of Oslo. The chapter was written at the Centre for Advanced Study in Oslo, Norway, which funded and hosted the research project Arctic Domestication in the Era of the Anthropocene during the academic year 2015/2016. We are grateful to all of these bodies.

1. As on every Thursday this year, the owner of the firm is here, overseeing the expansion. There are a few chance visitors from outside—a job applicant, a vet, and two ethnographers. Then there is the operations manager, who runs the site. And, perhaps most important, there are the people who work on the site: the people who look after the young salmon as they hatch out; the men and women who feed and watch the fry; the staff of the small office; the mechanic; and the electrician and the maintenance people.

2. See, for example, Max Gluckman's analysis of the "social situation," famously exemplified in his analysis of the inauguration of a bridge ([1940] 1958); see also Kapferer (2010) and Harvey and Knox (2015), works that explore inaugurations, engineering, and the politics of infrastructural form.

3. We evoke the concepts of ghost and haunting, aware that the latter concept is applied in Jacques Derrida's (1994) discussion of Karl Marx's famous claim in The Communist Manifesto that "a spectre is haunting Europe—the spectre of communism" (Marx and Engels [1948] 1969, 14). Here our aim is slightly different. We wish to draw attention to that which is systematically silenced but also, and necessarily, present, which we call absence-presence (Law 2004, 84).

4. This is an argument that has been made in a range of idioms and a series of different fields. In STS, which is particularly keen on the materialities of assemblage, it is sometimes described as "heterogeneous engineering" (Law 1987).

5. See also Meillassoux (1972) for a similar argument in relation to South African mining.

6. Håkon Okkenhaug, "Vil femdoble oppdrett: Havbruk skal bli den nye oljen. Regjeringen vil gjøre rammene mer forutsigbare," Trønder-Avisa (Trondheim), March 20, 2015, http://www.ta.no/nyheter/article10772058.ece.

7. This and the following citations are from Simon Solheim and Cecilie Roang, "Solberg: Laksen er Norges Ikea," NRK, March 23, 2015, http://www.nrk.no/norge/sol berg_-_-laksen-er-norges-ikea-1.12274859.

8. These were not his exact words, but the sense of what he said is captured by the Norwegian term *forakt* (contempt, scorn).

9. For a methodological discussion of absence and presence, see Law (2004).

10. Though economic growth and industrial expansion are mutually implicated, they are not the same. For relevant distinctions see, for instance, Thévenot (2001).

11. Occasionally such topics emerged during lunch, such as when a man with engineering expertise involved in the current expansion talked about aquaculture investments elsewhere and spoke about how these things are always justified by taking the sum of money and dividing it by the projected number of smolt produced in the future. Since the profit on each fish was substantial owing to high prices on the global market, practically every investment appeared to pay off. Most of the time, however, financial investments were not discussed among the farmworkers.

12. On heterogeneous engineering see Law (1987).

13. Tsing (2012, 508) talks of these as "nonsocial landscape elements," or "nonsoels," by analogy to the term "pixels."

14. For an anthropologist brought up in a more stratified United Kingdom, the Bremnes folk's emphasis on equality was striking: "In Bremnes, as in many other societies, kinsmen, by and large, are approximate social equals. Furthermore, at the present time . . . neighbours are approximately equal in social status. In Norwegian thought, the idea of equality is emphasised so that even between persons of markedly different economic status there is less recognition of social inequality on either side than would, I think, be the case in Britain" (Barnes 1954, 44).

15. Barnes's ideas were later elaborated into the idea of "equality as sameness" by Marianne Gullestad (1992), and subsequently discussed and challenged as a gatekeeping concept of Nordic culture and social norms (Bruun, Jakobsen, and Krøijer 2011; Lien, Lidén, and Vike 2001).

16. Excerpt from John's field notes used in an early version of an article on ceremony as method. Marianne sees this, too, but is perhaps less surprised, and not surprised enough to make this a separate point in her field notes.

REFERENCES

Barnes, John A. 1954. "Class and Committees in a Norwegian Island Parish." *Human Relations* 7, no. 1: 39–58.

Barnes, John A. 1957. "Land Rights and Kinship in Two Bremnes Hamlets." *Journal of the Royal Anthropological Institute* 87, no. 1: 31–56.

Bruun, Maja H., Gry S. Jakobsen, and Stine Krøijer. 2011. "Introduction: The Concern for Sociality—Practicing Equality and Hierarchy in Denmark." *Social Analysis* 55, no. 2: 1–19.

Callon, Michel. 1998. "An Essay on Framing and Overflowing: Economic Externalities Revisited by Sociology." In *The Laws of the Markets*, edited by Michel Callon, 244–269. Oxford: Blackwell; Keele: Sociological Review.

Derrida, Jacques. 1994. *Specters of Marx: The State of the Debt, the Work of the Mourning and the New International*. New York: Routledge.

Gluckman, Max. (1940) 1958. *The Analysis of a Social Situation in Modern Zululand*. Manchester: Manchester University Press.

Gullestad, Marianne. 1992. *The Art of Social Relations: Essays on Culture, Social Action and Everyday Life in Modern Norway*. Oslo: Norwegian University Press.

Harvey, Penny, and Hannah Knox. 2014. "Objects and Materials: An Introduction." In *Objects and Materials: A Routledge Companion*, edited by Penny Harvey, Eleanor Casella, Gillian Evans, Hannah Knox, Christine McLean, Elizabeth B. Silva, Nicholas Thoburn, and Kath Woodward, 1–17. Abingdon, UK: Routledge.

Harvey, Penny, and Hannah Knox. 2015. *Roads: An Anthropology of Infrastructure and Expertise*. Ithaca, NY: Cornell University Press.

Kapferer, Bruce. 2010. "Introduction: In the Event—toward an Anthropology of Generic Moments." *Social Analysis* 54, no. 3: 1–27.

Law, John. 1987. "Technology and Heterogeneous Engineering: The Case of the Portuguese Expansion." In *The Social Construction of Technical Systems: New Directions in the Sociology and History of Technology*, edited by Wiebe E. Bijker, Thomas P. Hughes, and Trevor Pinch, 111–134. Cambridge, MA: MIT Press.

Law, John. 2000. "Transitivities." *Society and Space* 18, no. 2: 133–148.

Law, John. 2004. *After Method: Mess in Social Science Research*. London: Routledge.

Law, John, and Marianne E. Lien. 2013. "Slippery: Field Notes on Empirical Ontology." *Social Studies of Science* 43, no. 3: 363–378.

Law, John, and Marianne E. Lien. 2014. "Animal Architextures." In *Objects and Materials: A Routledge Companion*, edited by Penelope Harvey, Eleanor Casella, Gillian Evans, Hannah Knox, Christine McLean, Elizabeth B. Silva, Nicholas Thoburn, and Kath Woodward, 329–337. Abingdon, UK: Routledge.

Lien, Marianne E. 2015. *Becoming Salmon: Aquaculture and the Domestication of a Fish*. Oakland: University of California Press.

Lien, Marianne E., and John Law. 2011. "'Emergent Aliens': On Salmon, Nature, and Their Enactment." *Ethnos* 76, no. 1: 65–87.

Lien, Marianne E., Hilde Lidén, and Halvard Vike. 2001. *Likhetens paradokser: Antropologiske undersøkelser i det moderne Norge*. Oslo: Universitetsforlaget.

Marx, Karl, and Frederick Engels. (1948) 1969. *Manifesto of the Communist Party*. In *Marx/Engels Selected Works*, vol. 1, 98–137. Moscow: Progress Publishers. https://www.marxists.org/archive/marx/works/download/pdf/Manifesto.pdf.

Meillassoux, Claude. 1972. "From Reproduction to Production: A Marxist Approach to Economic Anthropology." *Economy and Society* 1, no. 1: 93–105.

Ministry of Trade, Industry and Fisheries. 2015. *Forutsigbar og miljømessig bærekraftig vekst i norsk lakse- og ørretoppdrett*. Oslo: Ministry of Trade, Industry and Fisheries. Also available at https://www.regjeringen.no/contentassets/6d27616f18af458aa930f4db9492fbe5/no/pd fs/stm201420150016000dddpdfs.pdf.

Mintz, Sidney Wilfred. 1985. *Sweetness and Power: The Place of Sugar in Modern History*. New York: Viking Penguin.

Thévenot, Laurent. 2001. "Which Road to Follow? The Moral Complexity of an 'Equipped' Humanity." In *Complexities: Social Studies of Knowledge Practices*, edited by John Law and Annemarie Mol, 53–87. Durham, NC: Duke University Press.

Tsing, Anna. 2012. "On Nonscalability: The Living World Is Not Amenable to Precision-Nested Scapes." *Common Knowledge* 18, no. 3: 505–524.

Tsing, Anna. 2013. "Sorting Out Commodities: How Capitalist Value Is Made through Gifts." HAU: *Journal of Ethnographic Theory* 2, no. 1: 21–43.

Ytrestøyl, Trine, Turid Synnøve Aas, and Torbjørn Åsgård. 2015. "Utilisation of Feed Resources in Production of Atlantic Salmon (*Salmo salar*) in Norway." *Aquaculture* 448, no. 1: 365–374.

10. When the Things We Study Respond to Each Other

TOOLS FOR UNPACKING "THE MATERIAL"

———

Anna Tsing

This volume sets out a challenge: to explore those overlapping meanings of "material" that confound distinctions between analysis and the world. Materials are scholarly collections (the material for an analysis) *and* the things around us, whether in a scholarly collection or not. This is an intriguing overlap to explore, particularly as the stakes, of late, have changed. Whereas analysts once agonized over the question, "Are our collections adequate to know the world?," we now ask, "Are they lively enough to participate in the world?" The provocative issue before was representation; now it is animation. Materials as data join materials as things in this provocation.[1]

Yet we are haunted, too, by our predecessors' thoughts on representation. They worried increasingly not just about whether they had appropriate data but also about what they knew from it. The big contributions of the last thirty years have been more concerned about the apparatuses of representation than the representativeness of data. Our ability to ask new questions today depends on the brilliant schemes this period pioneered for us for understanding how the apparatus of data collection becomes knowledge. We learned about colonial discourse and Foucauldian epistemes; we benefited from burgeoning new fields, from feminist science studies to decolonial theory. As inheritors of these schemes, our work on animation foregrounds the apparatus of data collection. Objects, we recognize, emerge through our apparatuses. Thus, we recognize the liveliness of the material through the liveliness of our knowledge apparatuses for engaging with it.

Picking up the challenge of animation, however, poses new dilemmas. Might our attention to the knowledge apparatuses of human analysts sometimes overwhelm our ability to notice the liveliness of the material? Taking animation seriously means allowing material to react to other material, with these materials' own skein of apparatuses, as well as to those apparatuses we throw up as analysts. Yet foregrounding only our own apparatus sometimes blocks attention to that particular form of liveliness. In trying to avoid frameworks in which true things are merely "discovered," we allow ourselves to identify liveliness only in relation to those processes we initiate. If *material* emerges from our *apparatus*, the two would be closely paired in one-to-one relations: our apparatus, our material. We leave aside the material reacting across its varied components; we leave aside nonhuman relational apparatuses. Some of this problem is addressed in the scholarly turn to multiplicity, which shows us multiple knowledge apparatuses acting simultaneously. Yet as long as human knowledge apparatuses continue to make up the frame through which we know multiplicity, nonhuman makings never enter. Identifying human apparatuses as technologies and practices of being, rather than knowledge, might help, but as long as multiple ontologies are human multiplicities of enactment, nonhumans remain passive. Might nonhumans also enact multiplicity?[2]

In this chapter, I worry through this problem by introducing a notion of "assemblage" that has helped me follow the liveliness of the material, in its double sense as data and as world. I use this tool in *The Mushroom at the End of the World: On the Possibility of Life in Capitalist Ruins* (Tsing 2015), where I use the assemblage to illuminate both landscape and political economy. In contrast to purely structural models of capitalism, which tend to be static, assemblage allows attention to history, conjuncture, and what I have called "friction," that is, the unexpected structural effects of historical encounters (Tsing 2005). In this chapter, I extend the landscape discussion to work on assemblage at the border between anthropology and science studies. This allows me to pick one exemplification of the problem of lively material through a focus on multispecies relations. How, I ask, might we learn to notice lively encounters *among nonhuman beings*—rather than just human-nonhuman relations? I mention the political-economy application to make it clear that multispecies relations are not the only topic that matters in addressing animation; the problem of not letting attention to analysts' knowledge practices overcongeal the material is equally important when studying human-centered topics. However, picking a focus helps make the theoretical issues clear. Since the knowledge apparatus is part of the analyst's humanity, can he or she ever move beyond the primary dyad human-to-nonhuman? When in our work are nonhumans allowed to respond to each other, and not just to human analysts? My questions are relational: I do not imagine that material gains vitality all by itself (Bennett 2010). But must all relations, I ask, begin and end with humans?

Anthropos and the Material

The problem of blocking the liveliness of the material is mixed up with the new *anthropos* proposed by critics of human exceptionalism. Bruno Latour (2017) nicely articulates this revision: rather than being a master of nature, the anthropos Latour proposes will be those "earthbound" creatures that accept the limitations of a multispecies earth. Yet consider the implications of an anthropos-material relationship composed of human-nonhuman entanglements. Although one might argue that this frees humans from their burden of mastery, it transfers the burden to the nonhumans, who, forever after, come to life only in the embrace of the human. But why would not the nonhumans be perfectly lively without us? I know the quick answer: at the border between science and technology studies (STS) and anthropology, theorists have worked hard to construct alternatives to those simple positivisms in which things speak for themselves, calling out truths that transcend the research apparatus. I agree with this program. But perhaps it is not enough to posit material that can *only* respond to a human call. Material responds to other material too. Of course, we know such responses through human entanglements; yet to posit that we alone create responsiveness is not enough. Response is not just a function of human dreams and plans.

Consider the major approaches through which theorists have enlivened other beings. Latour is a cofounder of the actor-network theory school, which earned its chops working through problems of the relationship between humans and technology.[3] Technology is a special kind of material: material created to respond to humans and to form prostheses to satisfy our needs and desires. While it is perfectly possible for social theorists to explore the histories of copper ores or electromagnetic fields before and outside their relation to engineers and end users, most theorists of technology are not particularly interested in such histories. They care about what emerges from the relationship between human intentions and the nonhumans that come to serve their purposes. I think this is a fine way to approach technology—

but it is not enough to know "the material" more generally. Certainly, when we get to living beings, other-than-human relationships matter.

The most prominent approach to bringing living beings into the redefinition of the human comes from animal studies, where ethical questions have helped to reframe the relation between humans and nonhumans. If we learn to imagine animals not as a class of deferent or pesky others, but rather as individuals with whom we can develop a relation of mutual response, we might open our social lives beyond the human as we knew it. Deborah Bird Rose (2013), Donna Haraway (2007), Thom van Dooren (2014), and Jacques Derrida (2008) push us in this direction. Through a refocusing of the human self to include animals, we join a multispecies earth. This is helpful, smart, and radical. But it also captures "the material," here the animal, in the embrace of its human companions. We know the animal through its dyadic relations of response with the anthropos, however expanded. Yet one plus one is not enough, even as it is clear that many others make each "one." There is no tool here to follow the responses of the many, each to each other, rather than just to response-seeking humans.

Let me mention one more approach that has achieved prominence in anthropology: the new animism. Theorists such as Eduardo Viveiros de Castro (2015) and Rane Willerslev (2007) have argued for a reopening of the anthropos through attention to non-Western and nonmodern ways of knowing, inhabiting, and making worlds. In the worlds they describe, other beings are animate persons, as lively and as social as humans. This approach is an exciting leap out of customary scholarly categories. Yet the necessities of showing how this leap is done have slanted the analysis toward cosmological abstractions as opposed to practical descriptions of animist beings. Rather than watching the beings interact with each other, most accounts show us how they inform lines of thought that expand human conceptions of ourselves.[4] Analysts' interest remains with cosmologically intentional humans; other beings are extensions of our hopes and dreams. It is difficult to watch all those promisingly animate beings interact with each other.

Each of these approaches is inspiring and necessary for addressing my problem. Taken together, however, they suggest that an irrationally magnified fear of positivism has taken root at the STS-anthropology border, blocking attention to questions concerning the interactions of nonhumans with other nonhumans. Reminding ourselves not to forget the apparatus, we have allowed its singular logic to take up so much space in the analysis that we forget that other dynamics might also be important. Perhaps, too, we have picked models that allow us to obscure this problem. Technology and animals, whether

Western or indigenous, have something in common: they urge us to look close to our self-making dreams. Animals are like us, *persons* indeed, and it is easy to imagine both intimacy and cosmology through them. Perhaps it is time to stray into what Michael Marder (2013) calls "plant-thinking" to draw us into multispecies relations in which consciousness and intention may not be the place to start. Here, more than two can participate in making worlds, and none need be human.

The challenge is to appreciate the dynamism of the other-than-human world without imagining facts that speak for themselves. Necessarily, the analytic apparatus still matters. But rather than limiting oneself to the apparatus of scientists and social analysts, might we also check out the apparatuses of nonhuman others? To explain this point it is useful to adopt the vocabulary of Karen Barad (2007), who writes of the "agential cuts" that shape the world—including what this volume is calling "the material." Since materials emerge from world-making processes, it makes no sense to Barad to see them as results of interactions between already-constituted things. Instead, she argues that materials emerge in "intra-actions," actions internal to the material-making process. Through intra-actions, agential cuts make forms of materiality possible. Her most important example is physicist Niels Bohr's demonstration that light is both a stream of particles and a wave, depending on the apparatus used to study the light, and thus the agential cut. My argument here is that neither apparatuses nor agential cuts need be human. Might not other beings also make agential cuts, in the sense of introducing apparatuses that shape the emergence of matter and the material?

Let me offer a figure. Proteins take on a formal configuration, a "fold," in relation to their intra-actions; when ribosomal protein and RNA bind proteins as functional partners during the formation of the protein building-blocks of cells, they introduce an apparatus that enables particular fold configurations. *Other folds are possible*, but the agential cut of the RNA shapes the potential for further relational action. The fold is formed in intra-action. The material that emerges from the ribosomal activity is in some cases also shaped by intra-actions involving other proteins, "chaperones" of protein folding, with their agential cuts.[5] Of course, we only know this through additional apparatuses involving laboratory science, but that hardly erases the intra-actions of RNA, ribosomes, and proteins. Imagine the choreography of protein synthesis and you'll see: agential cuts are more than human.

How might an anthropologist go about noticing interactions and intra-actions among varied nonhumans—without falling back into the assumption that truth congeals naturally around things?[6] Ontological approaches to animacy can help us here. Enactments of being need not distinguish humans and nonhumans. We just need to get used to the fact that nonhumans, like humans, frame ways of being through their practices. We might call each of these frames an apparatus. They interact in what Viveiros de Castro (2004) calls "equivocations," that is, moments in which incommensurable frames occupy the same event; equivocations happen all the time, among nonhumans with each other as well in human-nonhuman interactions.

To develop this argument in the next sections, I suggest several courses. First, I address a common objection. Second, I offer practical materials, that is, the material as it might emerge in anthropological and STS practices. Third, I show how these engage each other in a revitalized concept of the assemblage. Assemblages are a means to notice constitutive intra-actions within the material. Finally, I offer a few examples from recent collaborative fieldwork in central Jutland.

Humans Are Human?

Before going further, let me address the most common riposte I hear to suggestions that social analysts might study relational dynamics among nonhumans. "How would we even know about such interactions," my interlocutors ask, "except through our human ways of knowing?" The thought here is correct. As I am a human, everything I do and imagine must be human—including my grasp of interspecies interactions. But consider the narrowing of the scope of analysis here: everything humans know and do is human. This tautology is hardly sufficient for understanding anything. It defines "human" as a limit, not an open-ended quest; it denies the transformative power of training, intimacy, experience, or prosthetics. It makes learning a joke, since we have established our encapsulation before asking a question.

Consider the ordinary procedures of humanist anthropology. When I did ethnographic research in the Meratus Mountains of Kalimantan, Indonesia, I worked hard to develop a working knowledge of Meratus Dayak language, history, and culture (see Tsing 1995). This did not transform me into a Meratus person, but it did allow me to attune myself to what was going on enough to get some significant glimpses of local dynamics. The same procedure is possible with nonhumans. I train myself; I hang out with my subjects; I do not refuse the help of prosthetics such as microscopes. My goal is to learn practices of attunement through which I can sense local dynamics. As in ethnographic research, I expect to be wrong a lot of the time, especially at first; I start again and practice until I sense that my hesitant attunements are working.

This is a practice of honing agilities. Haraway's (2007) discussion of agility training with her dog, Cayenne, is just right for thinking through this problem. "Agility" is a game in which the woman guides the dog through obstacles. Haraway is in training in this process as well as Cayenne. Only when the woman learns to attune herself to the dog can she offer signals Cayenne can understand. Here I extend the term "agility" to refer to historically shifting talents, across species. In this sense, every living being has agilities, whether human or not, and we all are engaged in practices of interspecies attunements, although not necessarily with humans. As we train, we transform, becoming something not outside our species, but still more than a static species enclosure. We attune to new relations and apparatuses with which we had not been familiar before; we continue to impose our own, but we aim to keep them open enough to work well with those of others. So, yes, human is human, and, no, this does not mean we must simply gaze at our navels.

Sometimes, in seeking those fragile attunements, it is important to contrast human ways of being with others. Many lichens grow slowly and age not at all; I age quickly in comparison (Pringle 2017). Such contrasts can be helpful. But to use contrasts as an excuse for not getting to know the other seems to me as bad as excluding immigrants because they haven't yet trained themselves in your country's lifeways.

Just which kinds of training are most relevant to appreciating interspecies dynamics? Leaving this question open is important to me. One might want to develop vernacular agilities of many kinds—from indigenous cosmology to criminal arts—as well as fluency in various elite discourses and official sciences. It is in layering these forms of training that social analysts might ask about interspecies dynamics without taking for granted scientific authority. Furthermore, there is something about the challenge of our time—the possible destruction of planetary livability—that might require uncomfortable juxtapositions of ghosts and geology, science and science fiction, the mundane and the monstrous. Varied genre experiments seem in order (see Tsing et al. 2017 for more on this). This chapter's step-by-step exposition—somewhere between a handyperson's guide and a travel memoir—is just one of varied semivernacular modes of telling more-than-human sociality.

Material Practices

Three interventions, all arrived at collaboratively, have guided my thinking about how to get into the material without so shadowing it with my own body that its internal dynamics disappear. The first is direct observation. Anthropologists and STS scholars are not afraid of direct observation of human beings. When we learn from participant observation, we do not accuse ourselves of positivism. We imagine that we can make the fieldwork situation part of our analysis.

The same should be true for direct observation of nonhumans. It is fascinating to me that so many STS scholars refuse to learn anything *themselves* about the research objects of the scientists they study. They talk to the scientists, and they follow their knowledge work—but they erect a wall against the nonhuman objects of the study, except as the scientists relate them. The same is true in one wing of the anthropology of the environment: anthropologists report what other people (e.g., residents, conservationists) say about the environment, but they refuse to get to know anything about the natural world themselves. It's as if touching a nonhuman so contaminates the analyst with positivist truth claims that it has become taboo to even look. This is silly.

It takes great machines and laboratories to attend to some parts of the nonhuman world, but there are plenty of other things that can be studied using methods that are not so different from what anthropologists use in fieldwork. The work of field biology, for example, is quite similar to ethnography: it involves watching and describing the social relations the analyst finds. In my study of matsutake mushrooms, I tracked commercial and ecological relations through related techniques (Tsing 2015). I talked to people; I looked at forests and camps and supply lines; I put together histories from their human and nonhuman traces. Elsewhere, I have described some of the ways of looking at the landscape that, it seems to me, contribute to a more-than-human anthropology (Tsing 2012). None of the methods I describe for nonhumans (e.g., looking at form, watching social gatherings) deviate radically from those well known to ethnographers. And while they expand the discussions we might have about knowledge practices, they do not force my hand in the direction of positivism.

I had help learning to imagine direct observation as a tool for noticing multispecies dynamics, and my debts to Andrew Mathews (e.g., 2017) and Zachary Caple (e.g., 2017) are particularly strong. Mathews showed me how to read the social history of forests through form. Caple has pioneered ways to combine natural history and ethnographic technique, making such a combination seem possible. My collaboration with these scholars gives me the confidence to break the taboo: we can appreciate the liveliness of the material in part by getting to know it better through fieldwork.

My second methodological intervention also derives from collaboration, in this case with Elaine Gan. It is to attune oneself to *time* as a way of identifying both human and nonhuman responsiveness. Gan and I have developed a concept of "coordination" to watch the intra-actions of the material (Gan and Tsing n.d.). "Coordinations," as we use the term, are non-centralized temporal responses across difference. They allow us to watch action and emergence without requiring intentional communication or mutual legibility among participants. World making can proceed with or without planning, and privileging intentionality as the basis of responsiveness too often brings us back to human lifeworlds. Coordination, in contrast, allows us to acknowledge the incommensurable ontics of various beings at the same time as we watch the becomings they sponsor in their encounters. As Gan explains elsewhere:

> Temporality [is] a series of coordinations across incommensurabilities or qualitatively different ontologies. Using Deleuze and Guattari's concept of a manifold or an assemblage of rhizomatic becomings . . . , coordinations arise out of multiple trajectories that may be considered as sequences and thresholds for intimacy and immensity, continuity and change. Coordinations are not coincidental occurrences, or things that just happen to occur simultaneously. Coordinations emerge from sequences that sediment, recur, endure, echo, extinguish, and lie dormant. From these variations, and intersections between variations, a specific attunement unfolds and recurs. Matter and milieux become and remember through a manifold of temporalities, or a coordination across historically constituted differences that conjugate and concrete. (N.d., 2–3)

Our case takes us to Japanese peasant forests, where humans, pines, oaks, and matsutake mushrooms coordinate in making a space that is livable for all of these. Farmers cut oaks for firewood and charcoal; oaks sprout from their stumps, becoming stable features of the architecture of the forest. The open forest of coppiced oaks makes way for pine, which without human disturbance would not enter these forests. Pine, in turn, grows with matsutake mushrooms, which feed from the roots while supplementing the trees with nutrients. Humans appreciate the fungal reproductive bodies as a gourmet food. These coordinations make a forest. Furthermore, we show how they are part of contingent histories, both human and not human. These coordinations are shaped by industrialization, war, and urbanization, on the one hand, and introduced species, climate change, and disease, on the other. Humans are part of the story, but humans do not make the story. To work with coordinations as a guide allows multiple protagonists to emerge in the heart of the material.

My third methodological intervention, already suggested in the matsutake-forest case, is to ground research and analysis in a landscape.[7] A landscape is the sediment of human and nonhuman activities, biotic and abiotic, both meaningful and constructed without intent. Landscapes are active lifeworlds, held by material traces and legacies, yet open to emerging forms and possibilities. I follow ecologists in making difference a key property of my "landscapes": a landscape can be at any scale, but it always involves a diversity of patches. A patchwork of farms and forests is a landscape, but so too is a leaf on which insects and fungi have created microecologies. Thinking with landscapes opens analysis to a constrained multiplicity. The material expands to include the relationships that make places and niches. But it need not open so far as to require everything to enter the analysis. This is key to the challenge of rethinking the material for nonhuman-to-nonhuman analysis.

Consider again why the material so often seems just one thing in its relation to the anthropos. An abstract relation involves two: here, the analyst and the material. The dyadic distinction between anthropos and material is confirmed *merely by abstraction*. In contrast, if we reintroduce the landscape of the material, everything changes. A relation grounded on a landscape is suddenly crowded by other relations, which demand to be told. The material becomes multiple, and its components are engaged in their own constitutive interrelations. The converse is equally important. It is difficult to abstract all the relationships that form a landscape. More and more crowd in, and the mathematics of responsiveness becomes increasingly arcane. A landscape is easier to handle in its concreteness—not as a set of dyads in a vacuum but within the geographic and historical contours that give it a particular composition and character. This is its strength as an analytic tool.

My alertness to landscape owes much to conversations with Heather Swanson, who showed me that water as well as land grounds the analysis of more-than-human sociality (e.g., Swanson 2014). Swanson's study of salmon required attention to two radically different waterscapes: the river in which salmon are born and to which they return to spawn, and the open sea where they spend most of their adult lives. By taking each of these waterscapes seriously—as well as the land around the water—she shows multiple inter-locutors for salmon, including both humans and nonhumans of varied sorts. Rather than abstracting human-salmon relations, she grounds them in the worlds salmon make. The material emerges from these land- and water-scapes rather than performing atop them.

Assemblages: Unpacking the Material

These three methods come together in enabling a concept of the assem-blage. The assemblage is a tool for exploring the constitutive dynamics of landscapes. My assemblages are coordinations across varied ways of being—human and not human, living and not living, and in and outside of En-lightenment practices. Through investigating landscape-based gatherings of coordinations, fieldwork might loosen the falsely imagined unity of the material in its relation to the apparatus of analytic investigation.

My use of the term "assemblage" draws from both ecology and social theory. Ecologists speak of "species assemblages," characteristic gatherings of species. The term moves beyond the fixed and bounded connotations of ecological "community." "Assemblage" keeps open questions of how the varied species in a species assemblage influence each other. Some species are predators or prey; others compete with each other; still others help each other out in mutualistic relations. Furthermore, species come and go. As-semblages are open-ended gatherings. They allow us to ask about commu-nal effects without assuming them. They show us potential histories in the making.

Neither species nor organisms, however, are the best units for the as-semblages I propose. Even where living beings are key elements of the as-semblage, I want to see identities coalesce *in the assemblage*, and so I cannot write their contours into preexisting units. Instead, I watch gatherings of "ways of being." Species identification can be a good clue to the ways of being of living things, but it is only one clue. We know this well for humans. Farmers and scientists "do" landscapes differently, despite belonging to a single species, because of their ways of being, which are shaped by hab-its and legacies we gloss as "culture" and "history." Habits and legacies are equally relevant to the lives of other species. An organism in one environ-ment may be a peaceable companion to its neighbors; out of that setting, it may become a virulent destroyer. Species identifications are not enough to know such ways of being, which draw me into environmental histories and microecologies.

The concept of ways of being also brings me into social theory. I'm interested in assemblages as sets of coordinations across difference, that is, across situations in which one partner in a coordination may operate quite differently than another, and without mutual legibility. Following Helen Verran, it may be useful to call such strategies of existence "ontics." Verran contrasts everyday ways of being, ontics, with philosophies of being, "ontologies."[8] Ontics under the abstracting gaze of reflection become ontology; ontologically interesting practices in life, in contrast, are ontics. For Verran, both terms refer to human apparatuses. There is no reason I can think of, however, not to extend ontics to nonhumans. (Ontology may be more difficult: do nonhumans have their own philosophies?) Assemblages, then, group discrepant ontics, human and not human. They allow us to ask about response and interaction without ontological unity. And thus, too, they sponsor inquiries into forms of ontological multiplicity in which humans are not the only ones with apparatuses of agential cuts.

Other social theorists use the term "assemblage" differently. The two most common usages of which I am aware are to mean discursive formations (Ong and Collier 2005) or to mean actor-networks (Latour 2007). Each of these uses has quite different goals and promises than the one I promote here. And while I suppose it is an act of great hubris to try to get a word to mean what you as opposed to others want, the term is not so set in stone yet that it seems to me unmovable, nor is it a keystone in either of the frameworks I just mentioned. Furthermore, the fact that "assemblage" is used as the English translation of philosopher Gilles Deleuze's *agencement* (Phillips 2006) only helps me—by providing a wide field of interpretation in which the main constraint is allegiance to undoing constraint.

One way of specifying my variant is to add the qualifier "polyphonic." Here's how I explained that qualifier in my recent book:

Polyphony is music in which autonomous melodies intertwine. In Western music, the madrigal and the fugue are examples of polyphony. These forms seem archaic and strange to many modern listeners because they were superseded by music in which a unified rhythm and melody holds the composition together. In the classical music that displaced baroque, unity was the goal; this was "progress" in just the meaning I have been discussing: a unified coordination of time. In twentieth-century rock-and-roll, this unity takes the form of a strong beat, suggestive of the listener's heart; we are used to hearing music with a single perspective. When I first learned polyphony, it was a revelation in listening; I was forced to pick out separate, simultaneous melodies *and* to listen for the moments of harmony and dissonance they created together. This kind of noticing is just what is needed to appreciate the multiple temporal rhythms and trajectories of the assemblage.

For those not musically inclined, it may be useful to imagine the polyphonic assemblage in relation to agriculture. Since the time of the plantation, commercial agriculture has aimed to segregate a single crop and work toward its simultaneous ripening for a coordinated harvest. But other kinds of farming have multiple rhythms. In the shifting cultivation I studied in Indonesian Borneo, many crops grew together in the same field, and they had quite different schedules. Rice, bananas, taro, sweet potatoes, sugarcane, palms, and fruit trees mingled; farmers needed to attend to the varied schedules of maturation of each of these crops. These rhythms were their relation to human harvests; if we add other relations, for example, to pollinators or other plants, rhythms multiply. The polyphonic assemblage is the gathering of these rhythms, as they result from world-making projects, human and not human. (Tsing 2015, 23–24)

To work with assemblages, then, requires habits of noticing. These are key to a richer engagement with the material in which materials interact with each other as well as with us. The best way to show you what I mean is to move into some small examples.

Multispecies Assemblages in the Ruins of Industrial Mining

In my current work with the Aarhus University Research on the Anthropocene (AURA) working group, we have convened a team of researchers to take a look at landscapes both shaped by and exceeding the design of human activities. Our current site is an abandoned mining area in central Jutland, Denmark (Tsing and Bubandt 2018; Tsing 2017). During and after World War II, brown coal was dug from beneath the ground and sold for industrial energy. Mining ceased in the 1970s, leaving the area full of lakes—that is, , holes where brown coal was removed—and sand dunes, the piled overburden. The area was difficult for living things because mining had unearthed layers of pyrite-rich clay, which oxidized to sulfuric acid. Furthermore, the sand piles were unstable, and underground slides made it too dangerous for human development. Trees were planted in some places; however, compared to most of Denmark, a low bar for landscape management was envisaged. In this promisingly "wild" terrain, members of our research group have asked about how materials interact with each other.

For my own part in the research, I have made fungi a guide to assemblages emerging from the acid sands. This has been made possible by the generous assistance of mycologists Henning Knudsen and Mikako Sasa, who have guided me. I have worked with a small team including Elaine Gan, Thiago Cardoso, Pierre du Plessis, and Nathalia Brichet. We are a fragment of a larger group of researchers who often circulate across projects.[9] This wealth of researchers, with our varied disciplinary skills and commitments, does not make things easy. This is not normal science. We work around and against each other. Are sporadic and anecdotal observations significant? To what extent should our apparatus of research and analysis be essential to our deliberations? Our research is a negotiation of such questions, and thus of our relation with the material.

Two research problems have emerged for me. First, what grows up in these ruins? Almost everything alive and bigger than a microbe was wiped out; plants and animals had to start all over. Second, I am interested in the constant (if irregular) more-than-human disturbance that shapes the place. Our site is a place to study "bare-ground ecohistories," that is, histories in which humans and nonhumans have each worked to remake a radically altered landscape anew.[10] Both humans and nonhumans are historical actors; neither succeed as intentional designers, planning neatly managed landscapes. Human disturbances include the unintended results of activities (e.g., mining) in which landscape consequences are given hardly a thought. In this, humans are rather similar to other aggressive species on the landscape. On the postmining Brown Coal Beds, weedy lodgepole pines and overcrowded red deer have each had major landscape effects. Each of these—humans, lodgepoles, and red deer—might be said to be churning the landscape, rather than limiting their disturbances to just one instance. The assemblages I trace are the result of this multispecies churning, with its multiple agential cuts.

Let me take you to a few small examples of the coordinations through which assemblages form in this place. First, bare-ground ecohistories: trees are able to establish themselves on the overburden sand dunes because of the help of ectomycorrhizal fungi, that is, fungi that gather nutrients hidden within the comparatively barren sand and make them accessible to the roots of trees (Gan and Tsing 2018). This is particularly noteworthy for exotic species, such as lodgepole pine, brought to Denmark without their favorite fun-

FIGURE 10.1. *Paxillus* mushrooms in the sand piles. Photograph by
Elaine Gan, used by permission.

gal companions. Lodgepole is a North American species, but it grows fast
and furiously in the Brown Coal Beds. This is because it has been successful
in working with open-minded local fungi, that is, ones that are not too picky
about their tree hosts. In figure 10.1 we see lodgepole (in the background),
whose roots encroach on bare sand through the help of *Paxillus involutus*,
perhaps the most ubiquitous ectomycorrhizal fungus in Denmark.

What kind of anthropology is this to notice pines and fungi, working together? In the terms I have set out here, mycorrhizas form an apparatus for
coordination. Pines and fungi have quite different ways of being; that they
form joint structures is an instance of the productiveness of the assemblage.
There is certainly communication between root and fungus, but not mutual
intelligibility. The analysis here might take up the problem of divergent ontics joined in the coordinations of the assemblage. Of course, my noticing is
not irrelevant to the analysis. But its goal is to articulate with the apparatuses
within the material, rather than to assume that only the interface between
my apparatus and the material, imagined as a homogeneous thing, matters.
Apparatus is a practice-based concept; it does not depend on cognitive intention. Mycorrhiza is an apparatus in the same way that fieldwork is. Both
matter.

Assemblages modify landscapes, in part through their interaction with
other assemblages. In figure 10.2 the foregrounded mushrooms are coconut-
scented *Lactarius*, a fungus that grows mainly with the roots of birch. If you

FIGURE 10.2. *Lactarius* growing with birch under a lodgepole canopy.
Photograph by Anna Tsing.

follow the photograph back, toward the center you can see the light blush
of leaves of the little birch tree to whose roots the mushrooms are attached.

The exciting thing about finding this arrangement, for me, involved the
fact that this small birch tree was growing in the middle of a well-developed
lodgepole pine forest—a place that is far too shady for the happy establish-

ment of birch. But with the help of the fungus, the birch is hanging on. The birch survives because of the fungus; the assemblage is the starting unit for collaborative survival—and thus world making. The landscape is an assemblage of assemblages—here lodgepoles and birches, each with nurturing fungi, each working to establish ways of being through available coordinations. Through such apparatuses, materials respond to materials, and worlds are made.

Each set of organisms adds its own agilities—its apparatuses for world making. Each works with and against the others. Human tree planters brought the first lodgepoles, which took off beyond their wildest dreams. The new forests sprang up just as another ecological history was unfolding in Jutland: the return of the red deer. Red deer occupied Jutland after the last retreat of the glaciers, but they were increasingly reduced by hunting and landscape change; some three hundred years ago, free-roaming red deer were killed off to protect farms. In the last twenty-five years, as farms have been abandoned, red deer have wandered back. The Søby Brown Coal Beds have been a refuge for them because human presence is limited by the instability of the sand. Furthermore, as soon as they made their presence known, hunters began buying up the land and encouraging reproduction by providing extra food. Red deer populations exploded. Every evening, the deer come out to eat grass or farmers' crops. During the day, the deer are crowded in the comparatively nontasty forests. As one hunter explained, the deer bite the trees' bark not because they like it but because "they are bored."

Deer-damaged trees die, sometimes allowing other species to succeed them. Fungi take part. Damaged trees are quickly infected by parasitic and decomposing fungi, which are often responsible for the final blow. Here too is coordination and landscape making, although in unpredictable fits and starts. Assemblages emerge from all the practice-based apparatuses of coordination on the scene: red deer boredom, tree vulnerability, fungal appetites, and the availability of successor trees waiting in the undergrowth. Figure 10.3 shows a deer-damaged willow (see the bite mark at the lower end). It is infected with *Crepidotus* (the hanging white caps), which consumes the dead and dying wood.

This scene of multispecies coordinations was not designed by the deer, nor does it add up to a self-regulating ecological system. It is part of the ecological history of this place, with its crowded deer populations. It is a disturbance caused by deer churning. In the same way, humans have not designed this landscape, but human churning—including feeding the deer, which gives rise to crowding—is key. Churning, whether of humans, deer, or trees,

FIGURE 10.3. *Crepidotus* growing on deer bites on willow. Photograph by Elaine Gan, used by permission.

makes landscapes historical rather than static. And the way to appreciate this history is through noticing the apparatuses of the nonhumans as well as the humans. Our apparatuses succeed to the extent they expand to coordinate with those of others.

Material responds to material, not just to us.

Cultural anthropologists who never read scientific journals may make the mistake of seeing the preceding section as a form of natural science. In fact, however, the natural history description I just gave is not intelligible as scholarship in the natural sciences, just as it equally falls outside of most definitions of the humanities. Yet there is something to be said for occupying the productive seams between varied intellectual trajectories. By "seam," I am thinking of the visible line in a stream where two or more currents of water hit each other without fully merging. This is a place where fish make use of quiet pockets formed within the turbulence to lie in wait for the foods drawn by each current. Seams of this sort do not cordon off fixed fields; they open possibilities for what Marilyn Strathern calls "awkward relations" (1987) and "partial connections" (1991). Here it is possible to both hold apart conventions and, simultaneously, imagine what might happen if they mixed and melded.

The seam I try to work in the previous section is that between observation and history. Observation is a perfectly respectable concept in the natural sciences, but to make it part of scholarship, it ordinarily must be pulled into some kind of systems thinking in which ahistorical natural laws can be seen in action. As one ecologist explained to me, she loves fieldwork for its natural history observations, but when it comes time to publish an article, she must turn to "theory," which, for her, refers to systems modeling in which observations can be removed from their moments of contingent connection to speak to general, mechanical principles that sustain the world. While in the nineteenth century natural history in itself seemed a contribution to science, by the early twentieth century biologists had found a way to remove history from their analyses, thus establishing laws. History is a chain of unrepeatable events and connections; by removing history, the life scientists imagined they might find something more solid and stable. Meanwhile, the humanities have become the home for the unrepeatable, the qualitative, and the anecdotal—that is, the historical. Yet by focusing on those abilities imagined as separating humans from other living beings, such as language, cognition, and reflection, the humanities have had less interest in observation, especially when it comes to nonhumans. It is this divergence that creates a productive seam across history and observation.

Anthropological fieldwork has been one site for negotiating this seam, at least when it comes to observing human practices. During fieldwork, anthropologists are alert for what people do as well as what they say. Even before the recent anthropological interest in nonhumans, the discipline encouraged attention to practices and the differences they make in shaping societies over time. This chapter has suggested that we extend this courtesy to nonhumans. By following nonhuman practices and agilities, we might extend our already developed questions of how practice-based apparatuses of knowledge and being make a difference. Toward that goal, this chapter has focused on methods. By careful attention to landscapes as sites of co-ordinations, it becomes possible to construct a new kind of ecological history in which nonhumans as well as humans build worlds. One key to this is to see that nonhumans, like humans, create worlds through apparatuses, including those historically changing talents I call "agilities." In learning to appreciate more-than-human agilities, with their potential for intra-active agential cuts, we have a chance to see what happens when the things we study respond to each other.

The result, I am arguing, may not be an easy revision of disciplinary practice but rather a negotiation of awkward relations. Still, it is here that we learn to occupy the "slow science" of reflection and reworking that Isabelle Stengers has taught us to appreciate: "to accept what is messy not as a defect but as what we have to learn to live and think in and with" (2018, 120).

NOTES

1. I am grateful to Knut Nustad for soliciting this chapter, and to the participants of the Engaging the Material workshop for their comments. Animation provocation: In addition to the more-than-human scholarship discussed here, I am thinking of Ingoldian phenomenology, "new materialism," the ontological turn, and various other attempts to bring *things* to the center of social inquiry. (See, for example, Ingold 2013; Bennett 2010; Henare, Holbraad, and Wastell 2006.)

2. For multiple ontologies, see Mol 2002; Lien 2015. Sebastion Abrahamsson, Filipo Bertoni, and Annemarie Mol's (2015) consideration of *relational materialism* is helpful for the issues I explore here; my addition is to include relations that are not initiated by humans.

3. Latour (2007) offers a methodological introduction.

4. I find exceptions to this generalization in the writings of Richard Nelson (1983) and Eduardo Kohn (2013), who offer closely observed histories of the animate beings of indigenous worlds.

5. This discussion of protein synthesis derives from personal conversations with biologist Bente Vestergaard, who also generously made suggestions about this paragraph.

6. In this chapter, I move in and out of Baradian intra-action—depending on the historical action I highlight. I need interaction (which begins with congealed products of intra-action) as well as intra-action to show materials responding to each other.

7. "Landscape" is a term that must be redefined and reclaimed in order to be useful here. After cultural geographers turned against landscape as an exemplification of Western objectification, as in European "landscape painting," anthropologists stopped doing anything of much interest with the term. My attempts to reclaim the term begin with Kenneth Olwig's (1996) discussion of the Nordic genealogy of landscape as a moot, a gathering to discuss *things* of importance. My landscapes are heterogeneous sites of assemblage, in which assemblage is a moot of human and nonhuman ways of being. Many things of importance coalesce, whether intentionally or not. This approach allows dialogue with ecologists' "landscape," a heterogeneous ecological matrix. "History" is another term I redefine and reclaim. My histories are more-than-human tracks and traces and stories about them. Progress-oriented teleology is only one kind of history, and hardly the most important one for learning about landscapes.

8. I understood the contrast most clearly from Verran's presentation at a University of California, Davis, Sawyer Seminar (Verran 2013), but see also Verran (2001).

9. Our team includes Nils Bubandt, Rachel Cypher, Maria Dahm, Natalie Forssman, Peter Funch, Frida Hastrup, Colin Hoag, Mathilde Højrup, Thomas Kristensen, Katy Overstreet, Pil Pedersen, Meredith Root-Bernstein, Jens-Christian Svenning, Heather Swanson, Line Thorsen, and Stine Vestbo.

10. In choosing the term "bare-ground ecohistories," I wrestle with a conversation ecologists have started on "novel ecosystems" (Hobbs, Higgs, and Harris 2009). The latter term is used against ecological restoration, since advocates refuse to discriminate against any kind of disturbance; this seems irresponsible. The term's intellectual problems are equally pressing. What is novel, and what is not? When can we assume the stable and self-regulating features of a system? In contrast, the term "bare-ground ecohistory" admits to anthropogenic alternation but does not assume that self-regulating sustainability will follow.

REFERENCES

Abrahamsson, Sebastion, Filipo Bertoni, and Annemarie Mol. 2015. "Living with Omega-3: New Materialism and Enduring Concerns." *Environment and Planning D: Space and Society* 33, no. 1: 4–19.

Barad, Karen. 2007. *Meeting the Universe Half Way: Quantum Physics and the Entanglement of Matter and Meaning.* Durham, NC: Duke University Press.

Bennett, Jane. 2010. *Vibrant Matter: A Political Ecology of Things.* Durham, NC: Duke University Press.

Caple, Zachary. 2017. "Holocene in Fragments: Stories of Florida's Water, Land, and Phosphate Fertilizer Industry." PhD diss., University of California, Santa Cruz.

Derrida, Jacques. 2008. *The Animal That Therefore I Am.* Bronx, NY: Fordham University Press.

Gan, Elaine. N.d. "An Inquiry into Miracles: Timing IR36 and the Green Revolution." Unpublished manuscript.

Gan, Elaine, and Anna Tsing. N.d. "How Things Hold: A Diagram of Coordinations in a Satoyama Forest." Unpublished manuscript.

Gan, Elaine, and Anna Tsing. 2018. "Using Natural History in the Study of Industrial Ruins." *Journal of Ethnobiology* 38, no. 1: 39–54.

Haraway, Donna. 2007. *When Species Meet*. Minneapolis: University of Minnesota Press.

Henare, Amiria, Martin Holbraad, and Sari Wastell, eds. 2006. *Thinking through Things*. London: Routledge.

Hobbs, Richard, Eric Higgs, and James Harris. 2009. "Novel Ecosystems: Implications for Conservation and Restoration." *Trends in Ecology and Evolution* 24, no. 11: 599–605.

Ingold, Tim. 2013. *Making: Anthropology, Archaeology, Art and Architecture*. London: Routledge.

Kohn, Eduardo. 2013. *How Forests Think: Toward an Anthropology beyond the Human*. Berkeley: University of California Press.

Latour, Bruno. 2007. *Reassembling the Social: An Introduction to Actor-Network Theory*. Oxford: Oxford University Press.

Latour, Bruno. 2017. *Facing Gaia: Eight Lectures on the New Climatic Regime*. London: Polity.

Lien, Marianne. 2015. *Becoming Salmon: Aquaculture and the Domestication of a Fish*. Berkeley: University of California Press.

Marder, Michael. 2013. *Plant-Thinking: A Philosophy of Vegetal Life*. New York: Columbia University Press.

Mathews, Andrew. 2017. "Ghostly Forms and Forest Histories." In *Arts of Living on a Damaged Planet: Ghosts and Monsters of the Anthropocene*, edited by Anna Tsing, Heather Swanson, Elaine Gan, and Nils Bubandt, 145–156. Minneapolis: University of Minnesota Press.

Mol, Annemarie. 2002. *The Body Multiple*. Durham, NC: Duke University Press.

Nelson, Richard. 1983. *Make Prayers to the Raven: A Koyukon View of the Northern Forest*. Chicago: University of Chicago Press.

Olwig, Kenneth. 1996. "Recovering the Substantive Nature of Landscape." *Annals of the Association of American Geographers* 86, no. 4: 630–653.

Ong, Aihwa, and Stephen Collier, eds. 2005. *Global Assemblages*. Hoboken, NJ: Wiley-Blackwell.

Phillips, John. 2006. "Agencement/Assemblage." *Theory, Culture, and Society* 23, nos. 2–3: 108–109.

Pringle, Anne. 2017. "Establishing New Worlds: The Lichens of Petersham." In *Arts of Living on a Damaged Planet: Ghosts and Monsters of the Anthropocene*, edited by Anna Tsing, Heather Swanson, Elaine Gan, and Nils Bubandt, 157–168. Minneapolis: University of Minnesota Press.

Rose, Deborah Bird. 2013. *Wild Dog Dreaming: Love and Extinction*. Charlottesville: University of Virginia Press.

Stengers, Isabelle. 2018. *Another Science Is Possible: A Manifesto for Slow Science*. Hoboken, NJ: Wiley.

Strathern, Marilyn. 1987. "An Awkward Relation: The Case of Feminism and Anthropology." *Signs* 12, no. 2: 276–292.

Strathern, Marilyn. 1991. *Partial Connections*. Savage, MD: Rowman and Littlefield.

Swanson, Heather. 2014. "Landscapes, by Comparison: Practices of Enacting Salmon in Hokkaido, Japan." In *AURA's Openings*, 22–42. More-Than-Human Working Papers 1. Aarhus, Denmark: Department of Culture and Society, Aarhus University.

Tsing, Anna. 1995. *In the Realm of the Diamond Queen: Marginality in an Out-of-the-Way Place*. Princeton, NJ: Princeton University Press.

Tsing, Anna. 2005. *Friction: An Ethnography of Global Connection*. Princeton, NJ: Princeton University Press.

Tsing, Anna. 2012. "More Than Human Sociality: A Call for Critical Description." In *Anthropology and Nature*, edited by Kirsten Hastrup, 27–42. New York: Routledge.

Tsing, Anna. 2015. *The Mushroom at the End of the World: On the Possibility of Life in Capitalist Ruins*. Princeton, NJ: Princeton University Press.

Tsing, Anna. 2017. "The Buck, the Bull, and the Dream of the Stag: Some Unexpected Weeds of the Anthropocene." *Suomen Antropologi* 42, no. 1: 3–21.

Tsing, Anna, and Nils Bubandt, eds. 2018. "Feral Dynamics of Post-industrial Ruin." Special section, *Journal of Ethnobiology* 38, no. 1.

Tsing, Anna, Heather Swanson, Elaine Gan, and Nils Bubandt, eds. 2017. *Arts of Living on a Damaged Planet: Ghosts and Monsters of the Anthropocene*. Minneapolis: University of Minnesota Press.

van Dooren, Thom. 2014. *Flight Ways*. New York: Columbia University Press.

Verran, Helen. 2001. *Science and an African Logic*. Chicago: University of Chicago Press.

Verran, Helen. 2013. "Carrying the Dead along with Us: What Is a Postcolonial Archive?" Paper presented at University of California, Davis, April.

Viveiros de Castro, Eduardo. 2004. "Perspectival Anthropology and the Method of Controlled Equivocation." *Tipiti: Journal of the Society for the Anthropology of Lowland South America* 2, no. 1: 3–22.

Viveiros de Castro, Eduardo. 2015. *The Relative Native: Essays on Indigenous Conceptual Worlds*. Chicago: Hau Books.

Willerslev, Rane. 2007. *Soul Hunters: Hunting, Animism, and Personhood among the Siberian Yukaghirs*. Berkeley: University of California Press.

CONTRIBUTORS

MARISOL DE LA CADENA is a professor of anthropology at the University of California, Davis. Her research interests include the study of politics, multispecies (or multientities), indigeneity, and history. She is author of *Earth Beings: Ecologies of Practice across Andean Worlds* (2015) and *Indigenous Mestizos: The Politics of Race and Culture in Cuzco, Peru, 1919–1991* (2000), both published by Duke University Press.

RUNE FLIKKE is an associate professor in anthropology at the University of Oslo. He has extensive research experience with African Independent Churches in Durban, South Africa, and concluded a four-year research project on vaccination in Malawi. He is the author of a series of articles covering issues of health, healing, and weather and atmosphere and is currently writing on issues of nature conservation, alien species, and conceptions of changing landscapes in South Africa.

PENNY HARVEY is a professor of social anthropology at the University of Manchester. She has done fieldwork in Peru, Spain, and the United Kingdom and has published on technology, infrastructure, expertise, materiality, and the modern state. Recent publications include *Roads: An Anthropology of Infrastructure and Expertise* (coauthored with Hannah Knox, 2015) and *Infrastructures and Social Complexity* (coedited with Casper Bruun Jensen and Atsuro Morita, 2016).

INGJERD HOËM is a professor of social anthropology at the University of Oslo. For twenty years, she has carried out ethnographic research in the Pacific, especially in Tokelau. Her research focuses on the politics of communication. She is the author of *Languages of Governance in Conflict: Negotiating Democracy in Tokelau* (2015) and *Theater and Political Process: Staging Identities in Tokelau and New Zealand* (2004).

CHRISTIAN KROHN-HANSEN is a professor of anthropology at the University of Oslo. He has done fieldwork in the Dominican Republic and the United States, and his research interests are centered on the study of power and violence, political and economic life, and history. His publications include *Making New York Dominican: Small Business, Politics, and Everyday Life* (2013) and *Political Authoritarianism in the Dominican Republic* (2009).

JOHN LAW is a professor emeritus at the Open University, United Kingdom, and a leading scholar of science and technology studies and actor-network theory. He collaborates with a number of scholars on topics related to power, politics and framing, and practices of knowledge. He is coeditor of *Complexities: Social Studies of Knowledge Practices* (with Annemarie Mol; Duke University Press, 2002) and author of *Aircraft Stories: Decentering the Object in Technoscience* (Duke University Press, 2002).

MARIANNE ELISABETH LIEN is a professor of social anthropology at the University of Oslo. She has done research in Norway and Australia on topics including food production and consumption, nature, and domestication practices. Her most recent book is *Becoming Salmon: Aquaculture and the Domestication of a Fish* (2015), and she coedited *Domestication Gone Wild: Politics and Practices of Multispecies Relations* (Duke University Press, 2018), together with Heather Swanson and Gro Ween.

KEIR MARTIN is an associate professor in social anthropology at the University of Oslo. He completed his PhD in 2006 after two years of fieldwork in East New Britain Province, Papua New Guinea, working among the Matupi community in the aftermath of the volcanic eruptions of 1994. He is the author of a monograph, *The Death of the Big Men and the Rise of the Big Shots* (2013), and a number of published articles covering issues of contested transactions, social movements, land tenure, tourism, and possessive individualism.

MARIT MELHUUS is a professor of social anthropology at the University of Oslo. She has conducted research in Argentina, Mexico, and Norway, focusing on economics, gender, morality, and biotechnologies. She is the author of *Problems of Conception: Issues of Law, Biotechnology, Individuals and Kinship* (2012) and has coedited *Machos, Mistresses, Madonnas: Contesting the Power of Latin American Gender Imagery* (1996) and *Holding Worlds Together: Ethnographies of Knowing and Belonging* (2007).

KNUT G. NUSTAD is a professor and head of the Department of Social Anthropology at the University of Oslo. He works with political and environmental anthropology and theory, broadly defined, for the most part with a focus on South Africa. Nustad has conducted research on informal political processes in urban settlements, development policy, and state formation, as well as land reform, conservation, and protected areas. He was educated at the University of Oslo (BA) and Cambridge University (MPhil and PhD). His latest book is *Creating Africas: Struggles over Nature, Conservation and Land* (2015).

ANNA TSING is a professor of anthropology at the University of California, Santa Cruz, and holds a Niels Bohr Professorship at Aarhus University, where she codirects Aarhus University Research on the Anthropocene with Nils Bubandt. Her publications include *Friction: An Ethnography of Global Connection* (2005), based on fieldwork in Indonesia, and *The Mushroom at the End of the World: On the Possibility of Life in Capitalist Ruins* (2015).

INDEX

abalozi (head of the diviner), 190
Abercrombie, Thomas, 158n2
absences, 21, 197–199, 200, 203–204, 209–210, 211, 215, 217n3
actor-network theory, 19, 24n9, 223, 232
Acuña, Máxima, 56n21; agrammaticality of, 48–50; alliance with her lawyer against the corporation, 50, 54, 56n23, 57; critics of, 48, 56n16; as environmentalist, 47–49, 52; legal counsel for, 50, 54, 56n23; practices her refusal to leave, 49–50; refusal to sell land to mining corporations, 47–49
adaptation instead of relocation, 89, 95, 97
adoption, 129, 130–131, 137
Adorno, Theodor, 167
affective, the, 10–12, 14, 24n9, 62, 66, 68, 76
African Independent Churches. *See* Zulu Zionists
agential cuts, 225, 232, 234, 240
aggregates, 17, 150, 152, 153, 154
agilities, 227, 240
agrammaticality, 48–50
AID (artificial insemination with donor sperm), 128–130
air: aerial threads as defiling (*imimoya emibi*), 187; birds belonging to, 189; dependency, 179, 185; disease associated with, 21–22, 181–182; miasma, 21, 179–184; nature of, 184, 185–186; politics of, 21–22, 180; pollution, 43, 187–188; sanitation of, 43, 180, 181, 183
Allen, Catherine, 154

alliances, 11, 44–45, 47–50, 52–55, 52*fig*, 56nn22, 23, 57
amalathi (ritual), 189
animacy, 144, 222, 225–226
animals, 24n9; birds, 56n17, 188–190; in Hluhluwe-Umfolozi Park, 173; human self including, 224; hunting, 18, 168, 171, 237; the material and, 224; red deer, 234, 237–238; threats to wild animals, 168–169. *See also* salmon farms
animism, 17, 144, 224
anonymity, 107–110, 113, 116–117, 124–125, 129–130, 133–135, 138
Anthropocene, 1, 2, 6, 40
Anthropo-not-seen, 2, 11, 35, 40, 41, 45, 48–50, 51. *See also* Acuña, Máxima; Awajan Wampis; Mapuches; Runakuna (people)
anthropos, 3, 40–42, 81, 173, 223–224, 230
apartheid in South Africa, 186
apparatuses, 225, 232, 234–235
aquaculture. *See* salmon farms
architecture, 147, 181–182
Arendt, Hannah, 21
Artificial Procreation Act (Norway, 1987), 128, 130
Assai Consult, 115
assemblages: actor-network theory, 19, 24n9, 223, 232; agential cuts, 225, 232, 234, 240; agriculture as polyphonic assemblages, 232–233; community, 199, 212–214, 231; co-ordinations in formation of, 232, 234–235,

Caple, Zachary, 228–229
ceremony: as atypical event, 197–198; economic growth reflected in, 209–210; egalitarianism performed in, 211–214; as enactment of community, 199, 213–214; gaps exposed by, 197–198; ghosts in, 21, 199, 203, 204, 209–210, 215; hierarchy performed by, 212; manifest absences at, 197–198, 209–211; as moments of condensation, 197, 199; photographs of/photo opportunities, 206, 208; reenactment of egalitarian ethos, 214; social interaction in, 211–212; transfer of salmon to tanks, 205–207, 206*fig*, 207*fig*. *See also* rituals
Chadwick, Edwin, 180–181, 182
Chakrabarty, Dipesh, 1, 4
Chapigny, Robert, 185
Chaum, David, 108–109, 111
children: adoption of, 129, 130–131, 137; AID and identity of, 129; identity of, 129–133, 137, 140n18; knowledge of biogenetic origins, 16, 124, 127–132, 133–134, 136, 138; *morstilhøright* (mother-belonging), 132–133; paternity established, 140n18
Children's Act (Norway), 127
China: concrete and urbanization in, 151, 158n6
chlorine gas attacks during World War I, 179, 184
cholera, 21, 180, 181
Christ figures, 154
Christianity, 41, 92
Chuquicamata copper mine (Chile), 55n7
cigars, 207–208, 212
Clark, Nigel, 157
climate, 10, 12, 85–86, 89–90, 92–93, 95–97, 180, 184–186
clubes (voluntary associations), 65, 70–71, 74
coal mining, 7, 44, 90, 97, 233–234, 235, 237
cognitive sciences, 24n9
Comaroff, Jean, 76–77
Comaroff, John, 76–77
commensuration: and refusal to leave, 12, 47–51, 89, 96–97
Commission of Inquiry into the Alleged Threat to Animal and Plant Life in St Lucia (Kriel Commission), 169–170
communication, 38–39, 84, 114, 144

compartir (sharing resources), 66, 67
comradeship, 11, 65–66, 71, 74, 211–212
concrete: aggregates mixed with, 17, 56n23, 150, 152, 153, 154; cement, 151; characteristics of, 17, 145, 149–151, 154; composition of, 17, 150, 151, 152, 153, 154; history of, 150–153; human interventions in, 17, 150, 152, 153, 154, 155; mixing of, 152–153; in Peru, 16–17, 149–150, 152; seismic disturbances, 154–155; steel, 150, 151; uses of, 151, 152, 155–156, 157, 158n6; vitality of, 17, 57, 144, 151, 152; work as, 61
conservationism: EIA (environmental impact assessment), 162–166; negation of preindustrial presence in the landscape, 17–18, 166–167, 170–171; public protests, 169–170; retrospective relationship between people and environment, 166–169; sense of place, 162–163; wilderness in, 163, 164–166, 165–166, 168, 172–174
Conway, Edmund, 104
coordinations, 83, 229–230, 232, 234–235, 237
credit cards, 105, 107–108, 118n3
Crepidotus, 237, 238*fig*
cross-border surrogacy, 137
crowding, 83, 94, 95, 183–184, 237
currency: changing value of, 113; circulation of, 16, 107–108, 113–114, 115–116, 117; credit cards, 105, 107–108, 118n3; *kula* valuables (Trobriands), 113, 119n17; regulation of, 107, 109, 110–112, 116–117; social embedding of, 107; as utopian, 105–106, 107–108
Cusco (Peru), 149, 154
Cuzco, 46

dams, 44, 169–170
Dark Wallet, 110
Dean, Carolyn, 148–149
"The Declaration of Bitcoin Independence" (Touriansk), 111–112
deer herds, 83, 234, 237–238
de la Cadena, Marisol, 2, 10–11, 145
Deleuze, Gilles, 20, 48, 229, 232
Derrida, Jacques, 217n3, 224
Descartes, René, 184
detachment, 16, 198
Difference Engine (Babbage), 155
Dion, Leon, 114, 115
dirt, 181, 183

Index   251

235, 237; oil extraction, 7, 35–36, 42, 45–46; opposition to, 35–36, 38–39, 43–44, 50, 54, 56n23, 57; shale gas, 55n8; water contamination, 43, 46. *See also* mining headings

factory work, 63, 65
Faiva, Paula, 95
Fakafotu (god of storms and hurricanes), 92, 97
Fakaofo (Tokelau), 85, 86*fig*, 92
Falé (island in Fakaofo), 94
fale pisikoa (Peace Corps houses), 87
family formation. *See* assisted conception; fatherhood; motherhood
fatherhood: AID (artificial insemination with donor sperm), 128–130; as biological, 129; child's citizenship, 137; cross-border surrogacy, 137; establishment of, 127, 128, 129, 140n18; infertility, 129; insemination child's impact on, 129; *pater* v. *genitor* distinction, 134; uncertainty of, 127. *See also* sperm donation
fatumanava (hearts), 93
Fehérváry, Krisztina, 158n5
Ferguson, James, 118
filiation, 127–129, 134–135, 138, 140n19
filth accumulation, 182
financial transactions/investments: anonymity in, 16, 107, 108–109, 110, 113, 116–117; and economic growth, 12, 86–87, 91*fig*, 200–205; exploitation in, 35–36, 43–44, 47–49, 167, 170; risk in, 209–210; security of, 15, 109, 110–112; state regulation of, 107, 109, 110–112, 116–117; trust in, 15–16, 109; verification of, 108–109. *See also* currency; salmon farms; tabu currency
fishing, 87, 92, 169
flexibility (use of term), 98n2
Flikke, Rune, 21–22, 92, 93, 186
fold formation, 225
food supply: health risks in, 87–88, 94; hepatitis infection, 87, 88, 94; after hurricanes, 89; imports, 88, 94, 200, 204, 214; migration caused by shortages, 89; tulaga (concept), 96
force migrations, 36, 167, 170
forests: access to natural resources, 171; expansion of, 173–174; forced outmigration, 170, 173; human-environment relations in, 170–174, 229–230; introduction of nonnative

species, 172, 234–235, 236; red deer populations in, 234, 237–238
Forty, Adrian, 150, 151
Foucault, Michel, 41, 111, 181, 184x
fracking, 42, 43, 55n8
freshwater lens, threat to, 87, 88
friction, 222
friendship, 11, 65–66, 71, 74
fungi, 234–236, 237

Gan, Elaine, 229
García, Alan, 36
gender, 3, 16, 93, 124, 137–138
genetic material, 111–112, 115, 118, 137, 140n17, 144, 225
geographies of sacrifice, 43–44
geological imaginaries, 154, 156–157
geopolitics, 150, 151, 158n6, 432
ghosts, 21, 197–199, 200, 203–204, 209–211, 215, 217n3
Gibson, James J., 185
gift-exchange networks, 3, 112–113
global capitalism, 59–61, 66–69, 77n3, 87–89, 94, 200, 204, 214–216
global warming, 23n3, 90
Gluckman, Max, 197, 217n2
gold standard, 103–104
Gordillo, Gastón, 147, 166, 167, 172
Graeber, David, 76
grafting techniques, Inka, 16–17, 148–149, 155
Great Cattle Killing (1856–1857), 182
Greater St Lucia Wetland Park, 161
"great unwashed" (Bulwer-Lytton), 181, 183
Greene, Shane, 37
Gregory, Christopher, 104, 112, 113, 119n7
Gro (fishery worker), 205, 206, 208
Grusin, Richard, 24n9
guardians of the lagoons, 46–51, 56n23.
    See also Acuña, Máxima
Guatteri, Félix, 229
Gudynas, Eduardo, 43
Gullestad, Marianne, 218n15
Guyer, Jane, 105

Haraway, Donna, 45, 144, 224, 227
Hardt, Michael, 68, 69
Hart, Keith, 105–106, 107, 108, 116, 119n7
Harvey, David, 67

labor: affective components of, 68, 76; division of, 205–208; mobilizations of, 61–63, 148, 212; monitoring of, in open cities, 182; mutual dependencies, 213–214; slave labor, 8–9, 42, 198; working conditions, 65, 67–68

la compañía (the company), 71

Lactarius mushrooms, 236–237, 236*fig*

La Curva del Diablo (Devil's Curve), 35, 44

lagoons, 46–47, 49, 52, 52*fig*

lalolagi ("the world"), 85, 86*fig*

Lambek, Michael, 125

land: appropriation through pollution, 43–44; being together with, 11, 48–49; deer herds, 83, 234, 237–238; ecological amputations, 43–44; guardians of, 47–49, 170–171; identification with, 36–37, 47–49, 88–89, 148; *not only* (use of term), 11, 49–50, 51, 56n12; as source of productive capacity, 148; state interventions in, 7–8, 36–37, 168–170

landscape, 12, 86*fig*; assemblages, 222, 235–236; components of, 230–231; contestations, 161–162; crowding, 83, 94, 95, 183–184, 237; expansion of social network of coordination and deterioration of, 95; geological imaginaries in, 154, 156–157; human involvement with, 167–168, 170–173, 234, 241n10; in modernist understanding of nature, 184; mushrooms in, 60, 228–230, 234–236, 234–237, 235*fig*, 236*fig*, 237; negation of preindustrial human presence in, 17–18, 166–167, 170–171; people removed to make place for, 167–168; social distinctions, 88–89, 95; social science model of, 164–165; species identification, 231; use of term, 241n7

Latin American Development Bank, 43

Latour, Bruno, 2, 3, 23n4, 55n6, 223

Law, John, 21, 212

Lazar, Sian, 69

legislation: as acts of stabilization, 125, 139n4; assisted conception, 125, 127–129, 130, 133–135, 138, 140nn18, 19; controlled movement of populations, 183–184; donor disclosure legislation, 133–134, 135; imagination in codification of, 125

Leni (Awajun Wampis leader), 37

libertarianism, 110–112

lichens, 227

Lien, Marianne Elizabeth, 21

liveliness, 126, 145–146, 222–223, 224

livery-cab companies. *See* bases

livery-cab drivers: children's education, 72; *clubes* (voluntary associations), 65, 70–71, 74; Dominican identity of, 65, 66–67; friendships of, 11, 65–66, 71, 74; *independientes* (independent contractors), 66–68; pastimes of, 66, 71; political involvement, 66, 72, 74; territory for, 11–12, 64, 67; work ethic of, 66–68; working conditions, 11, 65, 67–68, 70

lodgepole pines, 234–235, 236

Macfarlane, Robert, 3

Machiavelli, Niccolò di Bernando dei, 62

malnutrition, 88, 94

Manchester school, 5, 197

manipulation, 48, 56n16, 109, 130

Manuin Valera, Santiago, 36, 38, 40

maopoopo (harmonious whole), 93

Mapuches, 46

Marder, Michael, 225

margins (use of term), 98n2

marriage, 124–125, 127–130, 134–135, 138, 140n19

Martin, Keir, 8, 15, 141n23

Marx, Karl, 62, 217n3

masculinity: comradeship, 11, 65–66, 71, 74; feeling of belonging, 66, 71; *hombre independiente*, 66–68; money power of Big Shots, 114, 116; myths of, 67; pastimes and, 66, 71; personal dignity, 67; political involvement, 66, 72, 74; sharing resources (*compartir*), 66, 67; in social spaces, 11

matagia (inspiration), 93

material flows, 158n3

material/materialism: access to, 7–9, 168–169; agential cuts, 225, 232, 234, 240; animism, 17, 144, 224; anthropos, 3, 40–42, 81–82, 223–224, 230; apparatuses, 225, 232, 234–235; arising from creative action, 76; coordinations, 83, 229–230, 232, 237; dynamic energy of, 158n3; genetic material, 111–112, 115, 118, 137, 140n17, 144, 225; Ingold on, 145–146; liveliness, 126, 145–146, 222–223, 224; material determinism, 76; new materialism, 24n9; other-than-human, 2–3, 15, 17, 19, 24n10, 144–147, 158n2, 225; relational materiality, 55n17; soft matter, 146, 150–151,

material/materialism (continued)
155–156; spatial orientation, 88; STS (science and technology studies), 197–199, 217n4, 223–224, 228; in Tokelau, 88–89; vital materialism, 146–147. *See also* assemblages; bitcoin; currency; stone and stone structures; tabu currency

maternity: AID (artificial insemination with donor sperm), 128–130; biogenetic connectedness, 124, 129–132, 133–134, 136, 138; and biological identity of the child, 131, 140n12; certainty of, 127, 140n19; *mater semper certa est* rule, 127, 138; *morstilhøright* (mother-belonging), 132–133; wombs, 124, 126, 131, 137

mater semper certa est rule, 127, 138
Mathews, Andrew, 228–229
Matikotop Enterprises, 115
matsutake mushrooms, 228–230
Maurer, Bill, 111
Mauss, Marcel, 71–72
Mazzarella, William, 10
media, 24n9, 45, 163
megalithic stone slabs, 92
Melhuus, Marit, 15
Meratus Mountains (Kalimantan, Indonesia), 226–227
Mhlongo, Sazi, 187–188
miasma: air quality and, 179, 183; fevers caused by, 180–181; Galenic medicine, 184; populations associated with, 21, 181, 183; stenches as indication of, 182, 183
migrations, 63, 67, 89, 95, 97, 167, 170, 173
Miller, Daniel, 105, 107
miniatures, construction of, 154, 156
mining: carrying capacity of abandoned mine area, 84–85; coal mining, 7, 44, 90, 97, 233–234, 235, 237; copper mining, 55n7; EIA (environmental impact assessment), 162–166; environmental impact of, 43–44; fracking, 42, 43, 55n8; pollution, 43–44; silver extraction, 42–43; strip-mining, 17, 162
mining corporations: compensation offered by, 145; legal action against, 50, 54, 56n23, 65–66; resistance to, 44, 47–49, 51–52; violence against land owners, 46–48, 50
Mintz, Sidney, 7–8
Mitchell, Timothy, 7

moneymaking, 61–62, 104–106
Moore, Aelia, 2
moral values, 14, 92–93, 124
more-than-human sociality, 230–231
morstilhøright (mother-belonging), 132–133
motherhood: AID (artificial insemination with donor sperm), 128–130; biogenetic connectedness, 124, 129–132, 133–134, 136, 138; and biological identity of the child, 131, 140n12; certainty of, 127, 140n19; *mater semper certa est* rule, 127, 138; *morstilhøright* (mother-belonging), 132–133; wombs, 124, 126, 131, 137
mountains, 154, 158n2, 190, 226–227
Mukerji, Chandra, 150
multispecies coordination, 222, 234–238
mushrooms, 60, 228–230, 234–237, 235*fig*, 236*fig*
muthi (herbal healing remedies), 188
mutual dependencies, 213–214
mycorrhizal fungi, 234–235

Nakamoto, Satoshi, 106
Natal Parks Board, 164
National Cultural Commission, 115
nature: agrarian capitalism, 7–8, 168–169; as constructed, 165–171; as cultural category, 18, 172; establishment of reserves, 168–170; human interference in, 46, 165, 168–175; hurricanes, 88, 89, 90, 93, 94; intrinsic value of, 163–164; lagoon water, 46–47; trees, 172, 182–183, 191, 234–237; weather, 88–90, 92, 93, 96, 97, 185; wilderness, 163, 164–166, 168–170, 172–174. *See also* animals; assisted conception; egg donation; environmentalists/environmentalism; forests; sperm donation
Negri, Antonio, 68, 69
neoliberalism, 6, 69, 72, 77n2
networks: actor-network theory, 19, 24n9, 223, 232; kinship, 13, 82, 96, 123, 125–126, 135, 218n14; of obligation, 114; and a place to stand (*tulaga*), 12, 13, 95, 96; socios, 64, 65, 70, 71, 73
New York City For-Hire Base Group, 74–75
New York State Federation of Taxi Drivers, 72
New Zealand, 13, 89, 90, 95, 96
nibbling (Dean), 149
Nietzsche, Friedrich, 185

nonhumans: agential cuts as, 225, 232, 234, 240; apparatuses of, 225, 232; bare-ground ecohistories, 234; ghosts, 21, 197–199, 200, 203–204, 209–211, 215, 217n3; liveliness of, 126, 145–146, 222–223, 224; mushrooms, 60, 228–230, 234–237, 235*fig*, 236*fig*; observation of, 197–199, 217n4, 223–224, 226, 228; other-than-human, 2–3, 15, 17, 19, 24n10, 144–147, 158n2, 225; relational capacities of, 14, 22; spirit, 125, 162–164, 186–187, 189–191; as world building, 234–236, 237, 240. *See also* animals; forests; nature; vitality

Norway. *See* assisted conception; salmon farms
Norwegian Biotechnology Act, 122, 123, 124
Norwegian Biotechnology Advisory Board, 136
not only (use of term), 11, 49–50, 51, 56n12
novel ecosystems, 241n10
Nukunonu (Tokelau), 85, 87–88, 91*fig*, 92
Nustad, Knut G., 15, 17, 93, 94

occult economies, 76–77
oceans, 88, 230–231
odors, 188
oil extraction, 7, 35–36, 42, 44–45, 45–46
Olwig, Kenneth, 241n7
one-world world, 56n22, 165
ontological turn, 1, 18, 19–20
ontology: as composition, 19–20; difference, 18, 146–147; dualist ontology, 164, 165, 173–174; human apparatuses, 232; indigenous conflict as ontological, 37; object-oriented ontologies, 14; ontics, 232, 235; surface-before-medium ontology, 184–185; written culture, 24n11
open cities, 182
order of nature, 132–133
other-than-human, 2–3, 15, 17, 19, 24n10, 144–147, 158n2, 225
outhouses, 87–88, 91*fig*
owner of fishery: behavior at ceremony, 206, 207, 208, 210; dependence on employees, 213–214; egalitarianism communicated by, 213–214; employee relations, 213–214; as entrepreneur, 213; transformation of non-capitalist social relations by, 213–214

Pacific Warriors, 90, 97
Panic of 1893, 103

Papua New Guinea. *See* kina (PNG currency); tabu currency
Paraná Chaco, 55n8
parentage/parenthood, 16, 124, 127, 135
Parry, Jonathan, 104–105
Parsons, Talcott, 61
partial connections (Strathern), 239
pater est rule, 127–129, 134–135, 138, 140nn18, 19
paternity, 124; AID (artificial insemination with donor sperm), 128–130; biogenetic connectedness, 124, 129–132, 133–134, 136, 138; cross-border surrogacy, 137; establishment of, 127, 128, 129, 140n18; identity of, 133–134; infertility, 129; insemination child's impact on, 129; *pater est* rule, 127–129, 134–135, 138, 140n19, 140n18, 19; *pater v. genitor* distinction, 134; sperm donation, 131–132; uncertainty of, 127
Paxillus mushrooms, 234–235, 235*fig*
Peace Corps, 87
peasant forests in Japan, 229–230
Pedersen, Morten Axel, 19–20
Peirce, Charles, 158n2
Perminow, Arne, 96
perspectivism, 18, 38, 82–83, 88
Peru: anchovy exports, 200, 204, 214; concrete in, 16–17, 149–150, 152; extractivism, 11, 46; indigenous confrontations with government, 35–37, 44; road construction projects in, 152–153, 157; Señor de Qoyllor Rit'it shrine, 154
plantations, 8, 9, 89, 198
plant thinking (Marder), 225
Player, Ian, 166, 168
PNG kina, 113–114, 115
pokono (fathoms of tabu), 113, 119n18
politics: activism, 35–36, 39, 47–51, 90, 97; alliances, 44–45, 47–50, 52–55, 52*fig*, 56n23; disagreement, 11, 35–36, 37–42, 47–50; engagement with, 20–21; of extirpation, 41, 45; geopolitics, 150, 151, 158n6, 432; government interventions, 35–36, 39, 44–45, 116–117, 168–169; leadership, 72, 74–75, 85, 92–93, 114, 115; libertarianism, 110–112; livery-cab industry, 72, 74–75; neoliberalism, 6, 69, 72, 77n2; regulation of currency, 107, 109, 110–112, 116–117. *See also* assisted conception

politics as usual (liberal modern politics), 11

pollution, 8–9, 43–44, 187–188

polyphonic assemblages, 232–233

Portland cement, 150, 151

positivist methods, 22, 224, 228

Pottage, Alain, 139n3

presidente del departamento de disciplina, 69–70

Produktivkräfte (Marx), 62

public health policy, 181–183

racial segregation, 92, 183–184

Raffles, Hugh, 144–145

railway construction, 42

Rancière, Jacques, 11, 37–39

reciprocity, systems of, 66, 113–116, 211–214

red deer, 234, 237–238

refusal to leave, 12, 47–51, 89, 96–97

register of sperm donors, 133

Reinert, Hugo, 158n4

relationality, 13–14, 55n17

relocation of populations, 86, 89, 95, 97, 145, 183–184

Renata Bessi, 55n8

representationism, 165

reproductive technologies: anonymity, 129, 130, 133–135, 138; children's knowledge of biological origins, 16, 127–132, 133–134, 136, 138; commodification of substances, 136–137; gender inequality in, 124, 136, 137–138; IVF (in-vitro fertilization), 128, 130; legislation, 125, 127–129, 130, 133–135, 138; as meddling with nature, 123–124; social imagination in, 125; third-party gamete donation, 124, 126, 130, 135. *See also* egg donation; eggs; fatherhood; motherhood; sperm; sperm donation

research methods, 5, 22, 197–199, 217n4, 223–224, 226–228

respiratory problems, 186

rheology, 146, 158n3

Richards Bay Minerals company, 162

risk, 67, 198, 209–211

rituals: *abalozi* (head of the diviner), 190; *amalathi* (ritual), 189; as assemblages, 197; ceremonies, 197; of healing, in Zulu Zionist congregations, 186–188; *imphepho* (incense) in, 188–189; sacrificial offerings, 148;

shamans in, 18, 19, 155–156; spaces for, 154, 190–191; wind in, 186–187

rivers, 37, 230–231

RNA, 225

road construction, 152, 155

rocks, 43, 148–149, 153–154

Roe, John, 182

Roe-Chadwick scheme, 182

Romanticism, 17, 169, 174

Rose, Deborah Bird, 224

rubble, 147, 167

ruins, 147, 170–174, 234

Runakuna (people), 46, 56n13

sacrificial offerings, 148

Sahlins, Marshall: causality and material environment, 93; material environmental factors in Tokelau, 95; material perspectives of, 82, 83; on political leadership, 85; political organization and material environmental factors, 83; on population relocations, 96; on production and political organization, 85; Tokelau landscape in model of, 93–94

Sallnow, Michael, 158n8

salmon farms: absent-present context of economic growth, 209–210; in Bremnes, Norway, 211; commodification of labor forces, 198; disease control in, 199, 203, 204, 215; division of labor, 205–208; global dependencies, 200, 204, 214–215; growth of, 200–203, 202, 203*fig*; mutual dependencies, 213–214; risk-taking, 209–210; scalable expansion, 198, 210; transfer of salmon to tanks, 205–207, 206*fig*, 207*fig*

same-sex couples: as parents, 16, 127

Samoa, 88–89, 90

sand, instability of, 234–235, 237

Sandemose, Aksel, 140n11

sanitation, 181–183

Santiago Navarro, 55n8

scalability, 198, 199, 210–211, 216

Schaffer, Simon, 156

sea lice, control of, 199, 203, 204, 215

seam (term), 239–240

Seaman (livery base), 73–74

security, 108–109

semiosis, 19, 24n10, 144, 158n2

tabu currency (continued)
16, 113–114, 115; customary value of, 116, 117; free market in tabu shells, 114; interchangeability with state currency, 113–114; PNG kina, 113–114, 115; reciprocal obligations, 16, 114–115; Tolai tabu, 113

Taussig, Michael, 8–9

taxi industry. *See* bases; livery-cab drivers

temporality, 5, 18, 229

territory, 35–38, 40, 43–44, 148

Thandi (informant), 186–187

Themba (prophet and founder of Zionist congregation), 186, 188, 189

third-party gamete donation, 124, 126, 130, 135

Tiv, 105, 118

ToAtun (grassroots villager), 116, 117

Tokelau: access to overseas goods, 88–89, 96; climate of, 85–86, 90; financial investment in, 86–87, 96; food supply in, 86, 87–89, 94; hierarchy, markings of, 88–90; housing construction, 91*fig*, 92, 96; hurricanes in, 89, 90; land reclamation, 88–89; landscape of, 85, 86*fig*; lifestyles, 86, 88–89, 92, 96; material culture in, 13, 85–86, 87–89, 96; New Zealand relations with, 13, 89, 90, 95, 96; social networks, 12–13, 86, 95, 96; technology in, 82, 92, 95, 96, 97; water resources, 85, 87, 88–89

Tone (fishery worker), 205, 208

Torben (fishery worker), 205–206, 208, 214

Tourianski, Julia, 111–112, 113

tourism, 18, 167, 169

ToVue, Ronald, 115

tracks (*umkhondo*), 187

Traditional Healers Association, 187–188

transfer of salmon to tanks, 205–207, 206*fig*, 207*fig*

trees, 172, 182–183, 191, 234–237

Tsing, Anna: analysis of scalability, 5–6, 198, 210; apparatus, 224; on capitalism, 63, 213; causality and material environment, 93; on coordination, 95; on crowding, 94, 95; on cultural diversity, 69; on landscape, 12, 93–94; material perspectives of, 82–83; mobilization of labor, 61; modern analytical mode of attention, 56n13; mushrooms, 60, 228–230, 234–237, 235*fig*, 236*fig*; politics of knowledge, 22; on practices of attunement,

226–227; on supply chains, 59–60. *See also* landscape

Tui Tokelau (high god of the heavens), 92

tulaga (concept), 12, 13, 95, 96

Turpo, Mariano, 49

Uber, 77n5

Ultra-Sanitarians, 180

umkhondo (tracks), 187

umkuhlane (common cold), 187

umoya, 186, 187, 189, 190

umsamo (storage room for ritual artifacts), 190

UN Convention on the Rights of the Child (1989), 133

UNESCO, 161, 162

Vaca Muerta (Argentina), 45–46

van Dooren, Thom, 224

Van Wyk, G. F., 173

Verran, Helen, 232

vision, 19, 40, 184

vitality: of concrete, 17, 144, 151, 152; of DNA molecule, 111–112, 115, 118, 137, 140n17, 144; grafting, 16–17, 148–149, 155; and the human-nonhuman connection, 146; materiality, 16–17, 144, 145–147, 222–223; of stone, 144, 154

Viveiros de Castro, Eduardo, 11, 18–19, 37, 39, 224, 226

voluntary associations, Dominican, 11–12, 79

von Clausewitz, Carl, 41

Wagner, Roy, 24n11

war, 9, 35, 41, 44, 46–51, 55n6, 179, 184

waste disposal, 12, 43, 46, 87–89, 94, 169, 182

water, 94; and the analysis of more-than-human sociality, 230–231; cement's exposure to, 152; collection and storage, 92; contamination of, 43, 46, 47–49, 87, 88; dams, 44, 169–170; estuaries, 169; indigenous peoples as, 46–47; materiality of, 158n3; oceans, 88, 230–231; salmon, 230–231

way of the hand that lets go, the, 96

ways of being (concept), 232, 234, 237

Wayúu, 44

weather, 88–90, 92, 93, 96, 97, 185

Weber, Max, 61

Weston, Kath, 10